LINCOLN CHRISTIAN UNIVERSITY

English
Learners,
Academic
Literacy,
and Thinking

English Learners, Academic Literacy, and Thinking

LEARNING IN THE CHALLENGE ZONE

PAULINE GIBBONS

FOREWORD BY JIM CUMMINS

HEINEMANN
PORTSMOUTH, NH

Heinemann
361 Hanover Street
Portsmouth, NH 03801–3912
www.heinemann.com

Offices and agents throughout the world

© 2009 by Pauline Gibbons

All rights reserved. No part of this book may be reproduced in any form or by any electronic or mechanical means, including information storage and retrieval systems, without permission in writing from the publisher, except by a reviewer, who may quote brief passages in a review.

"Dedicated to Teachers" is a trademark of Greenwood Publishing Group, Inc.

The author and publisher wish to thank those who have generously given permission to reprint borrowed material:

Adaptation of "Jane Goodall Reflects on Working Toward Peace" by Jane Goodall, Ph.D., DBE, from the Santa Clara University website *Architects of Peace*. Reprinted by permission of the Jane Goodall Institute. For more information about Dr. Goodall and the Institute, please visit www.janegoodall.org and www.rootsandshoots.org.

Library of Congress Cataloging-in-Publication Data
Gibbons, Pauline.
   English learners, academic literacy, and thinking : learning in the challenge zone / Pauline Gibbons.
       p. cm.
   Includes bibliographical references and index.
   ISBN-13: 978-0-325-01203-2
   ISBN-10: 0-325-01203-2
   1. English language—Study and teaching (Middle school).   2. Language arts (Middle school).   I. Title.

LB1631.G43 2009
428.0071′2—dc22   2009002239

Editor: Kate Montgomery
Production management: Sarah Weaver
Production coordinator: Vicki Kasabian
Cover design: Jenny Jensen Greenleaf
Typesetter: House of Equations, Inc.
Manufacturing: Louise Richardson

Printed in the United States of America on acid-free paper
13   12   11   10   ML   2   3   4   5

This book is dedicated to my sister, Jean Ann Lines,
a great teacher who was committed to social justice in schools,
and who saw the best in all her students.

127032

191032.

Contents

·····················

Foreword by Jim Cummins   *ix*

Acknowledgments   *xiii*

1   English Learners, Academic Literacy, and Thinking:
Defining the Issues   1

2   Intellectual Work in Practice: A View from the Classroom   19

3   Literacy in the Curriculum: Challenges for EL Learners   43

4   Engaging with Academic Literacy: Examples of Classroom Activities   58

5   Building Bridges to Text: Supporting Academic Reading   80

6   Scaffolding EL Learners to Be Successful Writers   106

7   Planning Talk for Learning and Literacy   130

8   Planning for a High-Challenge, High-Support Classroom:
Setting Up EL Learners for Success   152

Appendix 1: Summary of Teaching and Learning Activities   *169*

Appendix 2: Types of Connectives (Signaling Words)   *172*

Appendix 3: Typical Features of Some Written School-Related Genres   *173*

References   *179*

Index   *185*

Foreword

·····················

As I read through Pauline Gibbons' inspirational book, a number of ideas jumped off the pages. These ideas express insights about teaching English learners (EL) with striking clarity and force. For example, Gibbons emphasizes the centrality of planning for *intellectual quality* in designing curriculum and instruction for EL students. Drawing on the research of Newmann and Associates (1996), she highlights the finding that "students from all backgrounds are more engaged when classroom work is cognitively challenging than when it consists solely of conventional low-level work" (p. 1). Intellectually challenging curricula, according to this research, also raise the achievement of all students and reduce equity gaps associated with income and ethnicity. Unfortunately, as she points out, many programs for EL students "have traditionally been more defined by low-level drill and practice activities and a focus on basic grammatical forms excised from authentic contexts of language use" (p. 2)

Gibbons introduces the notion of *learning in the challenge zone* to highlight the centrality of curriculum and instruction that simultaneously provide "*high challenge* (tasks we cannot do unaided) accompanied by *high support* (the scaffolding that enables us to complete these tasks successfully" (p. 16). The book provides a wealth of classroom examples of what learning in the challenge zone looks like in practice and how teachers can engage even beginner EL students in rigorous and intellectually challenging subject-based tasks.

A related and central theme of the book is the need for all teachers to develop students' knowledge of the academic, subject-related literacy of their own curriculum area. The book offers a clear explanation of the challenges that academic literacy may pose for EL students, and suggests numerous literacy-based activities that can be used across all curriculum areas.

Linked to these ideas is the concept of *rich tasks*. These are tasks that focus on central ideas of a topic or issue and require students to demonstrate deep knowledge of the field, rather than simply knowledge of isolated facts. One example, presented in Chapter 2, involves students presenting their learning about Antarctica in the format of a popular television current events show where they take on adultlike roles as presenters, directors, studio managers, scriptwriters, interviewers, and members of an "expert panel." Gibbons points out that in the process of presenting the program, "students need to manipulate the information and ideas that they have previously developed, and combine facts and ideas in order to synthesize, generalize, explain, and interpret"

(p. 22). She points out that "if you watch students involved in such tasks, what strikes you most is the enthusiasm and excitement with which the tasks are tackled, perhaps because they are engaged in tasks over which they have some ownership and invest-ment" (pp. 34–35). Rich tasks also result in an end product (e.g., text and visuals, per-formance, multimedia) that has relevance beyond the classroom and is presented to an audience broader than the teacher. In our research, we have used the term *identity texts* to refer to these end products. Students invest their identities in creating the product or performance, and once produced and shared it holds a mirror up to students in which their identities are reflected back in a positive light (Cummins, Brown, and Sayers 2007).

These ideas about learning challenge the more typical assumption that EL students need to acquire a considerable amount of English before they can engage in this kind of intellectually challenging curriculum. How can EL students generate new knowl-edge, create literature and art, and act on social realities before they have acquired English? Answers to these questions are woven into the fabric of this book. Gibbons' central point is that EL students will acquire the kind of academic English they need to succeed in school only in the process of engaging in activities that simultaneously challenge and support them, and which foster the development of what Patrick Manyak (2004) has termed *identities of competence*. Furthermore, these high-challenge, high-support tasks must be implemented in subject areas across the entire curriculum if optimal development of students' academic literacy is to occur.

Although many of these ideas may seem radical when applied to beginner EL stu-dents in the regular subject-matter classroom, the pedagogical principles advocated by Gibbons are, in fact, in the mainstream of cognitive science research. We are simply talking about *apprenticeship learning* involving collaboration between experts (teachers) and novices (students). This collaboration builds on students' prior knowledge and stretches their expertise within the challenge zone (or in Vygotskian terms, the zone of proximal development). School learning is linked to the real world thereby enabling students to demonstrate their deep understanding of a topic. A central aspect of this approach to learning involves positioning students as the people they might become. The instructional focus is on their "*potential* achievement through explicit support rather than on their current levels of achievement in English and so allows for teach-ing to be at an appropriate cognitive level" (p. 39). Gibbons points out that when EL students are treated as the people they might become, they are given a new identity— they are defined by their current and future accomplishments rather than by their pres-ent limitations in English.

This book is full of insights such as these, and related classroom applications, that illustrate how feasible it is to engage EL students in rigorous and challenging tasks that position them as intelligent, imaginative, and linguistically talented. In the United States context, the book is particularly timely in view of the increase in high-stakes standardized testing that has been ushered in by the No Child Left Behind Act. Historically, education in the United States and in many other countries has been characterized by a pedagogical divide whereby low-income students typically receive instruction based on drill and practice while more affluent students are much more likely to be encouraged to use the full range of their cognitive abilities. However, the increase in standardized testing mandated by the No Child Left Behind Act has dramatically increased the pedagogical divide in the United States as a result of the punitive sanctions imposed on schools that fail to demonstrate "adequate yearly progress" (Cummins 2007).

Thus, the principles highlighted by Pauline Gibbons are diametrically opposed to the pedagogical realities experienced by a large number of EL and low-income students within the context of the initial phase (2002–2009) of the No Child Left Behind legislation. Because EL students were expected to achieve grade expectations on standardized tests after a year of exposure to English (despite the fact that extensive research shows that a minimum of five years is typically required for students to catch up academically), teachers in many states spent an inordinate amount of time on test preparation. Instruction during this period drew primarily on drill and practice activities, mandated scripts allowed minimal time for instructional conversations, and superficial facts and skills substituted for inquiry and deep understanding.

This instructional approach has been a dismal failure for both EL students and low-income students generally. For example, the *Reading First Impact Study*, published in November 2008 by the U.S. Department of Education, reported that "Reading First did not produce a statistically significant impact on student reading comprehension test scores in grades one, two, or three" (2008, xv). The lack of improvement in reading comprehension among low-income students, despite the $6 billion allocated to the Reading First initiative, can be attributed largely to the drill and practice pedagogical prescriptions that were virtually mandated by Reading First (Cummins, Brown, and Sayers 2007).

In a rational universe, the upcoming reauthorization of No Child Left Behind would acknowledge the failure of previous policies and pedagogical prescriptions and strive for educational equity among low-income students on the basis of the scientific knowledge base regarding effective instruction. As outlined clearly in this book, this knowledge base highlights the importance of

- positioning students as competent rather than deficient;
- supporting them in completing cognitively challenging tasks and projects; and
- encouraging them to invest their identities in learning as a means of developing academic expertise.

As I write this in January 2009, newly inaugurated President Obama's two children have begun to attend the Sidwell Friends School in Washington, DC. This is the same school that Chelsea Clinton attended in the 1990s during President Clinton's term in office. Perhaps the education deemed appropriate for the children of presidents might have some relevance to the development of educational policies for the masses. The website of the Friends School expresses succinctly its educational philosophy, and not surprisingly, it is entirely consistent with what we know about learning and also the pedagogical principles outlined in this book. The Middle School educational philosophy is expressed as follows:

> The rigorous curriculum focuses on basic skills, a disciplined manner of inquiry, individual creativity, and good study habits. Students are encouraged to cooperate rather than to compete and to share their special gifts and talents. (www.sidwell.edu/lower_school/academics.asp)

The School also emphasizes the "frequent discussions of issues of equality, peace, and social justice in our classrooms" (www.sidwell.edu/middle_school/lifeinms.asp).

This emphasis on inquiry, creativity, cooperation, and identification of student talents, together with a focus on equality, peace, and social justice are totally absent from the No Child Left Behind pedagogical prescriptions. Let us hope that leaders within the new administration will extend their understanding of educational quality (as applied to their own children) to all children as they rethink and reauthorize the No Child Left Behind legislation. However, regardless of whether policy makers acknowledge the right of *all* children to an education characterized by intellectual quality, educators retain considerable degrees of freedom in the pedagogical choices they make. For educators individually and collectively who aspire to implement a curriculum based on intellectual quality, and who recognize the importance of infusing the teaching of academic literacy across the curriculum, Pauline Gibbons' book provides inspiration and guidance. The wealth of classroom examples based on actual practice convincingly refutes the argument, reflected in much current practice, that EL and low-income students are incapable of benefiting from an intellectually challenging inquiry-based curriculum. The Obama mantra, "Yes We Can," is implicit in every page of this wonderful book.

Jim Cummins
Toronto

References

Cummins, J. 2007. "Pedagogies for the Poor? Re-aligning Reading Instruction for Low-Income Students with Scientifically Based Reading Research." *Educational Researcher* 36: 564–72.

Cummins, J., K. Brown, and D. Sayers. 2007. *Literacy, Technology, and Diversity: Teaching for Success in Changing Times*. Boston: Allyn & Bacon.

Manyak, P. C. 2004. "'What Did She Say?' Translation in a Primary-Grade English Immersion Class." *Multicultural Perspectives* 6 (1): 12–18.

Newmann, F., and Associates. 1996. *Authentic Achievement: Restructuring Schools for Intellectual Quality*. San Francisco: Jossey Bass.

U. S. Department of Education. 2008. *Reading First Impact Study. Final Report*. Washington, DC: Institute for Educational Sciences.

Acknowledgments

····································

I would like to acknowledge, first and foremost, the many hundreds of teachers I have had the privilege of working with. Thank you for your generosity in sharing your classrooms with me, and for being willing to put into practice many of the activities in this book. Thank you especially to the teachers whose voices and insights are reflected in some of the quotations, and for your commitment and interest in helping find new ways of thinking about teaching English language learners. Your classrooms have been an inspiration! Thank you also to the EL students in these classrooms. Your insights about your own learning, and what helps you to learn, never cease to amaze me. May you become the people you have the potential to be!

My thanks to Jim Cummins for writing the foreword. Thank you for your gracious words about the book.

Thank you also to my son Mark, whose cartoons illustrate some important messages and brighten up the pages of this book, and to my friend and colleague Laurie Brady, for reading and commenting on early drafts.

Finally, thank you to my wonderful supportive editor, Kate Montgomery, especially for your understanding and thoughtfulness during difficult times, and to all the production team at Heinemann. I have appreciated your collaborative approach and your care in producing this book.

To all these people, thank you for helping to bring this book to fruition.

1 English Learners, Academic Literacy, and Thinking

Defining the Issues

The integration of language and content should relate language learning, content learning, and the development of thinking, and should aim to find systematic connections among them.
—Bernard Mohan, "LEP Students and the Integration of Language and Content"

What This Book Is About: Raising Expectations

The title of the book draws together a number of related dimensions critical to the education of English language learners (henceforth EL learners or ELLs) in the years spanning upper elementary, middle, and early secondary school. The book aims to raise expectations about what is possible for these learners. It is primarily concerned with the notion of literacy engagement and development in an intellectually challenging curriculum where *thinking* is valued: that is, a curriculum where all students, including EL learners, are afforded the opportunities to think creatively, transform information, engage in inquiry-oriented activity, and construct their own understandings through participating in substantive conversations and, critically, are given the scaffolding and support to be successful.

Much previous research has suggested the significance of such high-challenge classrooms for successful educational outcomes for all learners. Newmann et al. (1996) have presented three significant findings in relation to raising levels of academic achievement and intellectual quality: first, that students from all backgrounds are more engaged when classroom work is cognitively challenging than when it consists solely of conventional low-level work; second, that all students, regardless of social or ethnic background, achieve at higher levels when they participate in an intellectually challenging curriculum; and third, that equity gaps diminish as a result of engagement in such curricula. Yet the development of curriculum distinguished by intellectual quality and the development of higher-order thinking has in reality rarely been a major focus of program planning for EL learners. Rather, many programs have traditionally been more defined by low-level drill-and-practice activities and a focus on basic grammatical forms excised from authentic contexts of language use. As one group of writers has put it, "ELLs' lack of oral language proficiency has often hindered their opportunity to receive cognitively stimulating and content-level appropriate instruction in school" (Carrasquillo et al. 2004, 30).

This book offers suggestions about planning for "intellectual quality" in a curriculum that at the same time is *also* concerned with integrating second language learning with the development of subject content. For EL learners, this high-challenge classroom must be one where they are given the kinds of scaffolding and linguistic support that will enable them to engage in learning and be successful learners, in terms of both their English language development and the development of their subject knowledge. A major premise of the book is that this dual notion of "high challenge" and "high support" (Mariani 1997) is critical for EL learners: while teachers make what Newmann et al. (1996) refer to as "relentless demands for students' best efforts" (214), students are set up for success through a range of explicit instructional supports. As later chapters will suggest, these supports are embodied in the way that teaching and learning activities are planned and in the nature of classroom interactions. You will find more about what constructs a high-challenge, high-support classroom later in this chapter.

The development of intellectually challenging programs requires us all, as educators, to monitor our own assumptions of students and perhaps to challenge and rethink our own expectations of what learners are able to achieve. While the book is about ways of providing students with intellectual challenge, it also takes the view that this can only occur when teachers also challenge their own expectations of what students are capable of. As Cummins (2000) has pointed out, the way in which teachers talk with and about students grows out of how they construct their students as learners and how they see their own identities as educators.

Educators have long been aware that low expectations by teachers are a self-fulfilling prophecy: the less that is expected of students, the less they will achieve (see, for example, the seminal work by Rosenthal and Jacobsen 1968). Studies of streaming and tracking (Gamoran et al. 1995; Mehan 1992; Oakes 1985) show that one of the main reasons some students do not achieve high academic performance is that schools do not require them to perform work of high intellectual quality. Conversely, high expectations by teachers correlate with higher achievements by students (Darling-Hammond and Schon 1996; Carrasquillo and London 1993; Brophy and Good 1986). Carasquillo and Rodríguez (2002) illustrate how these high expectations seem to be a characteristic of exemplary teachers. Freeman and Freeman (1998) describe a teacher who worked with a student who had been previously deemed as having a learning disability and who had a reputation for being disruptive in class but who eventually achieved "beyond her wildest dreams." They comment that "the most important lesson we can learn as teachers is that our students have unlimited potential" (256).

And so this book also challenges teachers to reflect on their own expectations of students and on the kind of learning environment they create in their classrooms. But effective teaching requires more than using the ideas and resources found in a book, and more than a set of one-size-fits-all teaching "gimmicks." Through the ways they design and implement the teaching and learning activities of their classroom, and in the classroom environment they create, teachers are critical in making good ideas context responsive—that is, making them relevant to their own unique situations and to the needs of their students. For this reason the list of questions at the end of each chapter is intended to make the ideas in the book relevant to your own context, by identifying ways in which your particular students may be supported in developing the language and thinking skills associated with intellectually challenging work. If you are using this book with other teachers, then the questions should stimulate some useful conversations.

This chapter introduces the key ideas suggested in the title of the book: literacy in the middle years of schooling and the implications for EL learners, and the notion of "intellectual quality" and an intellectually challenging curriculum. It also introduces the sociocultural approach to learning that underpins the ideas in the book. At the end of this chapter you will find a brief summary of what each chapter contains.

Literacy in the "Middle Years"

There is a large amount of research that shows how access to high educational outcomes in secondary school is primarily dependent on the socioeconomic background of students, their ethnicity, and their gender. Parents in middle-class families are likely to have themselves completed secondary school or tertiary education and to be employed in jobs that require considerable reading and writing. Children from these families, regardless of their ethnic background, are likely to come to school with an orientation to language use that mirrors that of the school. They come to school with a ready-made orientation to the kind of language that serves as a bridge into the reading and writing of secondary school, and so they are more likely to succeed when faced with the challenges of increased literacy in high school. However, children who come from lower socioeconomic backgrounds, or children who come to school speaking another language or a nonstandard dialect of English, are less likely to be familiar with the language and literacy of school. To have real equality in life choices, these children need to be able to control the academic language of school as well as the language or dialects of their families and communities. In reality, the economic roles that students go on to occupy depend largely on how successfully they engage with the reading and writing demands of secondary education. No matter what educational philosophy dominates, schools remain a successful device for providing a stratified workforce, where students whose families are more oriented to reading and writing are more likely to succeed at school and to go on to professional positions. Yet it is probably fair to say that literacy across the curriculum is rarely taught explicitly in secondary schools, the assumption perhaps being that students will have already learned literacy skills at their elementary school. This book aims to help teachers in the middle years to address this gap.

As students progress through school, there are a number of periods of transition when the literacy demands placed on students increase and where gaps in literacy in the second language may constitute a major barrier to further engagement and success in learning. Three such critical periods are:

- The transition from early to late elementary: by around the second or third year of school there is an increase in literacy-related tasks and some use of "academic" and subject-related English.
- The transition from upper elementary to middle school: in the middle grades (that is, around grades 5–8) there is an (often rapid) increase in subject-specific literacy and academic language, as literacy becomes a primary mode for learning new knowledge.
- The transition from upper middle school to the final years of high school: at this time students need to control high levels of discipline-related language and increasingly abstract concepts in all subjects.

The second of these periods is the focus of this book. At this time in their school life, in the "middle years" between the upper levels of elementary school and the lower levels of secondary school, all students are faced with the study of what are often new subjects and are learning to think, read, and write in subject-specific ways. Students must also learn to access, critique, and synthesize increasing amounts of information from both traditional and electronic sources. In terms of reading, there is a shift from "learning to read" to "reading to learn." Without an adequate control of the language of instruction in this increasingly language-dense environment, some EL learners may hit a language wall: the abstraction of the language and its subject-specific nature create a barrier that denies students' access to full understanding of the subject-related concepts, and ways of learning and thinking, on which learning in the final years of schooling is founded. In the United States, partly as a result of the adequate yearly progress (AYP) expectations of No Child Left Behind (U.S. Department of Education 2001), external pressure to support EL learners' academic progress has also increased (Crawford 2004). Research suggests that instruction that is focused simultaneously on language, literacy, and content development is critical in addressing these students' needs (Meltzer and Hamman 2005; Berman et al. 2000; Carrasquillo and Rodríguez 2002).

What Is "Academic Literacy"?

In this book, discussion about literacy and language refers to EL learners' development of English. While mention is made of mother tongue use in a number of the activities described throughout the book, it is outside the scope and focus of this book to discuss bilingual approaches to learning in detail. However, this omission is not intended to detract from the value of these approaches for learning and participation. This book should be read in that light, and readers will find many possibilities for mother tongue use in the overall pedagogical approach suggested.

Academic literacy is about far more than reading comprehension and decoding, because the language associated with academic learning traditionally "codes" knowledge in ways that are different from everyday ways of expressing what we know. This new coding is linguistically unfamiliar to many students, not only ELLs. A young child, for example, will talk about a refrigerator magnet as "sticking to" a refrigerator but note that it doesn't stick to a wooden table. Coded more scientifically, we may express this context-specific way of knowing as a generalization: *magnets attract certain kinds of metal* or *some metal is attracted by a magnet*. Increasing the degree of abstraction, the fridge experience could then be recoded as: *magnetic attraction only occurs between ferrous metals*. The disciplinary language of science also makes it possible to express more complex concepts such as a *magnetic force field*. As Martin (1990) points out in relation to science discourse, "it codes an alternative perspective on reality to commonsense [knowledge], a perspective accumulated over centuries of scientific enquiry" (86).

Similarly, the development of literacy within *any* subject in the school curriculum involves learning to control new language. Here is a further example of how language changes according to context. At the time of writing this we have had some extremely heavy rain over a period of several days. I commented to a friend that the rain had washed away most of the soil in a section of my garden. Of course this is a perfectly appropriate piece of language in the context in which I used it, but if I wanted to think and talk about the "big ideas" around soil erosion, the notion of rain washing away soil would not get me very far! For example, I would need to know and understand the verb *erode* rather than *wash away* and be able to nominalize it (turn it into a noun) in order to talk about the concept of *erosion*.

So it is important to recognize that the kinds of technical language we find in academic contexts is not simply "jargon," although it is often dismissed as this. Rather, using the appropriate terminology is integral to the concepts being learned: understanding the term *photosynthesis* is not separate from biology content knowledge. But neither is it simply a question of learning new vocabulary, although this is certainly a significant part of subject-related literacy. Disciplinary literacy also means being able to express more concisely and precisely the complex ideas and concepts that are embedded in the content of a subject and that are essential for learning in that subject.

To illustrate this further, consider this sentence and imagine how you would explain it to a young child:

The extended drought caused the crops to fail, resulting in a widespread famine and many deaths, especially among the children and the elderly.

You would need to say something like this:

There was no rain for a very long time. The farmers had planted crops like maize and wheat and corn, but because it didn't rain, all the crops died. Because there were no crops there was nothing for the people to eat, and they became very hungry. Because they didn't have enough to eat, many of them died, especially the children and old people.

You can see that although the two texts have similar meanings, it takes more than double the words to express them in the second text—sixty-four compared with twenty-three in text 1. This is because there is much assumed knowledge in the first text that is made explicit in the second. A further difference is in the grammar of the two texts; for example, causality is expressed by *because* in the second and by *caused* and *resulting in* in the first. But more importantly, the language of the second text provides no way of talking about the broader concepts—the big ideas—of *drought* and *famine*, and no way of *relating* these two concepts in order, for example, to talk about *the causes of famine*, or to talk about *drought-related famine* in a new and different context.

In addition to the more obvious specialist vocabulary and grammatical patterns that are evident in the examples above, academic literacy also needs to take account of the different kinds of genres or text types and generic structures particular to specific subjects. A written discussion is constructed differently in science or social studies or English: each discipline has its own conventions and patterns of thinking that make it distinct from others. Or, to put it another way, it "packages" knowledge differently. As Mary Schleppegrell (2002) has suggested:

> The language of each discipline has evolved in ways that enable the construal of the kinds of meanings that the discipline *requires*. . . . [B]y analyzing the ways of using language that are *valued in different disciplines*, we can illuminate the key issues that face teacher and students in gaining disciplinary knowledge. (120, italics added)

Thus different disciplines require very different literacy skills, including the reading of different types of texts and the use of different text structures, different presentation formats, different ways of organizing language, and different standards of evidence (Meltzer and Hamann 2005). These differences extend into spoken language too: how teachers talk about science is different from how they talk about English or mathematics, and how we write poetry is different from how we write history or science or mathematics. Content standards now widely used in U.S. schools, and syllabus statements in Australia and the U.K., in fact require that students know how to think, read, write, and talk like a historian or a scientist or a mathematician. Being subject literate means understanding how the "big ideas" of the discipline are organized and evaluated and is thus clearly related to being able to think and reason in subject-specific ways: think, for example, of the differences between carrying out an inquiry in science or in history or in social studies. Using critical thinking as an example, Langer (1992) suggests subject-specific differences in how this skill is used:

> Although critical thinking behaviors such as questioning and analyzing are involved in science and in English classes, the reasons for involving them, the ends to which they are put, and the ways they are engaged in, differ in marked and identifiable ways. For example, in biology and physics classes, questions seem to be asked primarily for

clarification of the unknown (for explication), while in English, questions are often asked to explore possible interpretations (for investigation). (2, cited in Meltzer and Hamann 2005)

Since so much academic language is subject related, it is really more accurate to talk about *academic literacies* rather than *academic literacy*. Developing the spoken and written literacy of a particular subject is not only a key to performing well on standardized tests in content area learning; it is also, as later chapters make clear, the key to being an effective learner in intellectually challenging work.

Of course there are some similarities across the academic language of different subjects. In general all academic language tends to be more "written like," less personal, more abstract, more explicit, more lexically dense, and more structured than the face-to-face everyday language with which students are familiar. Some literacy teaching strategies are generic in that they can be applied across the curriculum, and this book contains many examples of these generic strategies. But this should not mask the fact that much literacy teaching—the teaching of vocabulary development, for example, or the teaching of specific text types—is only meaningful and relevant when it is taught within the context of a particular subject. You will find more about these issues in Chapters 3 and 4, together with a range of examples of teaching strategies that focus on literacy.

Implications for Teaching Subject Literacy

One of the implications for discussing literacy in this way is that it is about much more than reading and writing. In order to read and write effectively students need also to be able to use what Chang and Wells (1988) refer to as "literate talk." In their talk they need to make their reasoning explicit, use language precisely, question and critique others' ideas, and be prepared to rethink their own ideas. While not all classroom talk needs to be of this type, later chapters will show how being able to use language in these ways has positive benefits for the development of reading, writing, and thinking. Conversely, the development of reading and writing likewise supports the development of oral language. Most definitions of literacy now include attributes such as critical thinking and the ability to use language appropriately in a range of contexts. The definition used for the International Year of Literacy in Australia (which drew on the definition developed by the United Nations), for example, stated that literacy involves the integration of listening, speaking, reading, writing, and critical thinking and includes the cultural knowledge that enables a speaker, writer, or reader to recognize and use language appropriate to different social situations. It also suggests that the aim of literacy teaching is to develop an active literacy that allows people to use language to enhance their capacity to think, create, and question and that helps them to participate more effectively in society.

Clearly a major implication of recognizing that literacy is subject related is that in order to support students in their development of academic literacy, subject teachers must themselves understand the language demands of their own subject and be able to explicitly teach subject literacy to students. Without this explicit and planned teaching of literacy, the development of EL learners' academic literacy skills is unlikely to occur in a mainstream class; it cannot be assumed that they will simply "pick up" what they need to know. Unfortunately, as EL specialists are aware, many subject or content teachers are reluctant to devote time to students' literacy development, seeing it instead as the domain of the English teachers (Langer and Applebee 1988). This book takes the stance that in English-medium education, all teachers are teachers of English, and so the book is intended not only for EL specialists but also for content teachers who have EL learners in their classes. (It is worth remembering that making mainstream classrooms responsive to EL learners by incorporating academic language and literacy learning is an adaptation that will benefit *all* learners.)

The Learners

Who Are "EL" Learners?

There is a wide variety of terms for the group of learners that are the focus of this book. In North America, Australia, and the U.K. they are described variously as limited English proficient (LEP); language minority; English as a second language (ESL); English as a new language (ENL); non-English-speaking background (NESB); bilingual; language background other than English (LBOTE); and English as an additional language (EAL). Students who are described in any of these ways are a very diverse group. Some may be highly literate in their mother tongue, others may have little or no literacy in any language. Some may have come from war-torn countries as refugees, others may come from families who have chosen to immigrate to improve their lives economically or to offer their children more life choices. Some may be fluent in the conversational aspects of English, others may have some English literacy but little experience in using spoken English. Some may be newly arrived in the country, others may be second-generation migrants who have not had an opportunity to develop the more complex aspects of literacy. Some may come from families who have had experience of tertiary education, others may be the first in their family to attend high school, or school of any kind. And within these diverse groups there will be diversity too in their social and economic situations and in their expectations of schools.

In this book I have used the term *EL learners* or *ELLs* because this term focuses on what all the students in an otherwise very diverse linguistic, cultural, and socioeconomic group have in common (Freeman and Freeman 1998). For the purposes of this book I also borrow from the inclusive description by Meltzer and Hamman (2005), who describe them as "students who come to school with a first language other than English and whose opportunities to fully develop English literacy to grade level have not yet been fully realized" (4). Finally, the use of this term more clearly distinguishes the learners from the learning program itself.

But while there is a range of terms in use, most writers in the area agree that un-mediated instruction for EL learners is not equitable: indeed treating all students equally, and thus ignoring differing starting points, is virtually guaranteed to produce unequal outcomes at the end of schooling. Among the potentially most educationally disadvantaged students are those for whom English is not their first language but who, having been born in the host country, have not developed literacy skills or high-level language skills in their first language either (Harklau et al. 1999). Other EL learners may end up spending a lot of their school life in lower-track/lower-stream classrooms, and even those who do receive some English language support may have been exited from EL or bilingual programs at a point when they are still not as proficient in aca-demic language as English native speakers at the same grade level. And increasingly, students entering the work force require higher levels of literacy than ever before, well-developed communication skills, and the ability to solve problems, think creatively, and make informed decisions. Measured in terms of factors such as secondary school completion rates, participation in advanced classes, and postsecondary pursuits, it has been suggested that the million-plus young ELLs in the United States are less success-ful than their native-English-speaking peers (Abedi 2005). Similarly in the U.K. and Australia, certain groups of learners traditionally fare less well in the school system.

EL Learners in Content Classrooms

Content or subject teachers should not be the only educators of EL learners, and systematic bilingual and specific second language teaching should also be part of a school's overall response to EL learners. Separate or some kind of "sheltered" instruc-tion may also be the best option for more recently arrived EL learners (see, for exam-ple, Carrasquillo and Rodríguez 2002). But as a result of the impacts of policies that pressure schools to "mainstream" EL learners, ELLs often end up in unsupported, English-only content classes, or conversely, in withdrawal or segregated classes where they have little access to authentic meaning-based interactions. In Australia, North America, and the U.K., the majority of second language learners will, in reality, spend most of their time in the mainstream classroom, and may or may not receive extra sup-port from specialist EL teachers after the initial stages of learning English. Rarely is sufficient specialist support available beyond this, and so for most of the time subject and mainstream teachers carry the dual responsibility of content and language teach-ing, including, as discussed above, supporting their students in developing specific sub-ject literacy. It is to these teachers, as well as to specialist EL teachers, that this book is addressed.

Content classrooms, however, are not intrinsically inappropriate for ELLs—indeed, this book rests on the premise that content classrooms have the *potential* to be the best contexts for developing a second language in school. What makes mainstream contexts inappropriate is that most curricula fail to take the needs of EL learners into account, particularly their language and literacy needs. But when subject teachers are aware of the place of language in learning, recognize the demands placed on students who are

9

negotiating complex levels of academic language, and are able to draw on suitable strategies that will support the development of academic language and the forms of literacy that are intrinsic to a particular subject, there are convincing arguments for integrating EL learners as far as possible within the context of mainstream teaching. Here are some of these arguments:

- We know that using a new language to learn about other things is an effective way of developing a second language (see, for example, Mohan et al. 2001). The subjects of the curriculum provide authentic contexts for meaningful language use and authentic purposes for using written and spoken language. A program that integrates subject content and language takes a functional approach to language teaching and learning, in that it focuses on the subject-specific language needed for learning rather than aspects of language taught in isolation and taken out of a meaningful context.

- We know, as much research has made clear, that the development of academic language takes far longer than the development of the typically informal language of everyday contexts, and despite an often rapid growth in their conversational fluency it may take around five years for EL learners to develop the more academic and subject-related registers of school (Cummins 2000; McKay et al. 1997; Collier and Thomas 1997; Collier 1995). We need to remember that this time lag is also a function of the fact that EL learners are in reality "catching up" in English with a moving target: English native speakers are also continuing to develop their academic language skills, especially in the middle years of school. Concurrent teaching and learning of both subject content and language responds to this time lag and allows EL learners to go on learning subject content as they develop their English.

- Nonintegrated approaches—that is, instruction in language alone—cannot usually address the subject-specific nature of academic language, because language-only classrooms are isolated from the very contexts that provide meaningful situations for subject-specific language use. Neither can we expect English language specialist teachers to have the specialist disciplinary knowledge of the various curriculum subjects. In language-only classes, there may be little relationship between the language being presented in the class and the language required for participation in mainstream contexts. As suggested earlier, there remains a place for specialist EL classes and for sheltered learning of various types at some times, especially for recently arrived students (see Echevarria and Graves 1998). But for most of their school lives, mainstream classes remain the major context in which students will have regular access to learning subject-specific academic language in a meaningful and immediately relevant context.

- Language and content cannot be separated: concepts and knowledge on the one hand, and subject-specific language, literacy, and vocabulary on the other, are interdependent. (Think, for example, of the examples given earlier referring to *drought, erosion,* and *magnetic attraction,* and of how the language constructs the concept.) In an integrated program, language learning and subject learning can therefore be mutually supportive of each other and provide for the natural "recycling" of language and concepts so important for EL learners. For example, language-based tasks in a curriculum area can recycle concepts and knowledge through a focus on relevant academic language and genres; and developing subject knowledge and concepts in activity-based group work is facilitated through interaction, as students ask questions, clarify what they have said for others, or solve problems collaboratively. And in these kinds of learning processes abstract subject concepts themselves are more easily clarified and understood, and new language is most meaningfully developed.

• Integrating language and content also allows for EL support to be offered in an ongoing way through school. Support for EL learners is usually offered when a student first enters school, when the need for language support is most evident, but is then gradually withdrawn as a student moves through school. The assumption here is that the critical factor for deciding on whether support is needed is the length of time a learner has spent in school. While this is certainly a factor, it is also important to ensure adequate support at the critical periods identified earlier, even for EL learners who appear to be "fluent" in spoken English. Thus it may be that a more appropriate way to conceive of EL support is to tie it more closely to the critical points of schooling identified earlier. And since the need for English language support extends far beyond the initial years of an EL learner's commencement of school, an integrated program at a whole-school level allows for more extensive and long-term support, especially at critical times.

Below is one woman's story of her experiences as a young elementary English language learner in Australia. Julia is now a successful teacher, but her words are a strong plea for the kinds of integration that this book argues for:

I remember when I first arrived in Australia I would go for special English classes. We used to have the classes after recess in this demountable [portable classroom] that was next to the bathrooms. I used to wait in the bathrooms until the bell went and then once I knew that everyone was in class I would dart into the special English room. I remember understanding everything in my special English class but once I got back to my normal class I didn't know what was happening. It seemed like they were two

"I don't think the two teachers ever really spoke to each other."

11

different worlds. I don't think the two teachers ever really spoke to each other, and I think that my classroom teacher thought it was the job of the ESL teacher to do English with me. I remember her saying things like: "You should have done this with Mrs P."

I don't remember what I learned but I do remember how I felt: I was constantly embarrassed and I would try and draw as little attention to myself as possible, and sometimes just sit and pretend to be doing what the other children were doing. What I learned from my own experiences as an ESL learner is that classroom teachers need to teach English for ESL learners through regular classroom subjects, and not see language learning for ESL students as something separate.

Some Current Perspectives on "Intellectual Quality"

Recently in the United States, the U.K., and Australia there has been, in various forms, ongoing work in school reform (for example, see Walqui 1999 and Newmann and Wehlage 1995), all of which is underpinned by the recognition that for *all* students the content and quality of the curriculum must be of high quality and designed to develop higher-order thinking skills. As discussed briefly at the beginning of this chapter, Newmann et al. (1996) have concluded that raising levels of academic achievement leads to all students achieving at higher levels and to equity gaps being diminished. Similar arguments have been put forward by August and Hakuta (1997), and Walqui (1999). Referring to the dual impact of increasing school diversity in the United States and the calls for reform that have as their goal the attainment of higher standards for all students, Walqui (1999), citing August, Hakuta, and Pompa (1994), argues: "Language-minority students must be provided with an equal opportunity to learn the same challenging content and high-level skills that school reform movements advocate for all students" (6).

However, deciding on criteria for establishing such a curriculum involves revisiting a number of old controversies. These include the extent of teacher control versus student control over learning activities; the extent to which learning should be connected to students' lives; the extent to which all students should learn the same things; and the degree of emphasis given to the mastery of discrete facts, definitions, and skills versus problem solving and thinking that require integration and depth of understanding (Calderon 1999). This book presents the view that, far from ignoring the skills and knowledge of the traditional curriculum and the language and literacy learning essential for EL learners, an intellectually challenging and real-life-oriented curriculum presents many *more* opportunities for language learning (and for explicit teaching) precisely because such skills and knowledge are presented within meaningful contexts, are used in the service of broader educational goals and integrated authentic tasks, and involve students in language-based collaborative work.

A number of researchers and educators have identified criteria for classrooms where such authentic intellectual work occurs. Newmann et al. (1996) have identified three criteria that together constitute their definition for high-quality intellectual accomplishment: the construction of knowledge, disciplined inquiry, and the value of learning beyond school. These three criteria are reflected throughout much of this book and are briefly discussed below:

- *Construction of knowledge.* Student achievement must be *based* on a foundation of prior knowledge; that is, the kind of knowledge that others have produced. But mere reproduction of knowledge does not in itself constitute intellectual quality. The conventional curriculum typically asks students to reproduce definitions or texts that others have produced. A more intellectually challenging curriculum would require students not only to be familiar with such traditional knowledge but would, for example, require students to summarize and synthesize information from a range of sources and then use it in a new context or in a different mode to construct something original.
- *Disciplined inquiry.* This consists of three features:
  1. The use of a prior knowledge base; that is, the traditional knowledge of the field.
  2. The development of in-depth understanding rather than a superficial awareness of often unrelated items of knowledge.
  3. The expression of one's ideas and findings through elaborated and extended communication—for example, through extended dialogues, expositions, narratives, explanations, and increasingly, a range of electronic forms. This is in contrast to much traditional pedagogy, which asks students to display only a superficial awareness of a large number of topics and often requires only brief one-word or one-sentence answers.
- *Value beyond school.* Increasingly, in a number of countries, standards documents, curriculum frameworks, and syllabuses are challenging educators to make school learning both relevant to and related to the real world.

Most traditional school achievement criteria document the individual competence of the learner through various forms of decontextualized demonstration such as examinations, quizzes, or exercises. In contrast, adult achievements in the real world—for example, the writing of a letter to a newspaper or the design of a house or the discovery of new ways to treat serious illnesses—have impact on others and an authentic purpose that goes far beyond the demonstration of their personal competence. In authentic work in school, students also make connections between what they are learning and the real world, and their achievements actually influence others. A recent example of this comes from New Zealand. As a science project, two secondary-age students analyzed a well-known blackcurrant drink made by an international company that promoted the product as a healthy drink for children, claiming it contained high levels of Vitamin C. The students showed conclusively that this was not the case, leading to the company having to change its advertising and being fined.

In Australia similar frameworks for thinking about intellectual quality have also been developed. Drawing on the work of Newmann, the *Queensland School Reform Longitudinal Study* (2001) includes the following indicators for intellectual quality:

- *Higher-order thinking.* Higher-order thinking requires students to manipulate information and ideas in ways that transform their meaning—for example, when students combine facts and ideas in order to synthesize, generalize, explain, hypothesize, or develop a conclusion or interpretation. Higher-order thinking is concerned with students' constructing knowledge, not simply reproducing it.
- *Deep knowledge and deep understanding.* Knowledge is said to be "deep" when students are able to name, define, explain, and make use of the crucial "big ideas" or central concepts of a topic or of the discipline. Deep knowledge therefore involves more than knowledge of isolated "facts," and would be evident, for example, when students construct and sustain a coherent line of argument, when they are able to make use of key ideas and concepts in a new context, or when they are able to relate ideas across disciplinary areas. Deep understanding involves students in publicly demonstrating this deep knowledge.
- *Substantive conversation.* In classes where there is substantive conversation there is considerable extended teacher-student and student-student interaction around the "big ideas" of the topic and, in this extended talk, evidence of deep knowledge and understanding. Such conversations are very different in form and content from traditional classroom talk. In substantive conversation students have the opportunity to offer extended responses both to the teacher and to other students and to initiate ideas and questions for discussion. Features of substantive conversation include intellectual substance, equality of dialogue involving the sharing of ideas, coherent exploration of content where students build on one another's ideas, and sustained interactions.

An Approach to Teaching and Learning: High-Challenge and High-Support Classrooms

Many teaching approaches are now based broadly on the work of Vygotsky (1978, 1986), who offers a very different view of teaching and learning from two other major approaches still in evidence in school. The latter can broadly be described as teacher-dominated "transmission" approaches (where teachers are seen to transmit skills and knowledge into the "empty minds" of their students) and "progressive" approaches (where learners are seen to construct their own knowledge and where the role of the teacher is to "facilitate" this learning through the stage management of appropriate learning experiences).

Both of these approaches can be critiqued from the standpoint of EL learners. Transmission-based approaches work against the central principles of language development, namely that using the language in interaction with others is an essential process for both first and second language learning (see Chapter 7). Transmission-based approaches, coupled with low expectations of what students are capable, unfortunately often dominate the teaching of English language learners and other students seen as "disadvantaged," and many compensatory programs focus heavily on low-level literacy and numeracy skills that offer no intellectual richness or opportunities for high-level literacy development. Although progressive pedagogy offers a welcome focus on the learner and on learner-centered activity, it too has been critiqued in the past because of its lack of explicit teaching, especially in relation to language. While these common ideologies appear to be very different, they are alike in that they both view learning as essentially an individualistic activity and the learner as independent of others and self-contained.

In contrast, a Vygotskian view of learning sees it as essentially a collaborative activity, occurring within a particular sociocultural setting. An individual's intellectual and linguistic development is seen, to a significant extent, as the product of his or her education, not a prerequisite for it to occur. Thus, for example, while we are all biologically programmed to learn language, how well we learn it and the purposes for which we are able to use it successfully are a matter of the social contexts and situations we participate in. As Wells (2007) has suggested, "who we become depends on the company we keep and on what we do and say together" (100).

This sociocultural approach to learning recognizes that with assistance, learners can reach beyond what they can reach unaided, participate in new situations, and take on new roles. People learning to drive, for example, are initially very reliant on their instructor for support, but as they gain in skills and confidence the instructor's support gradually diminishes until they are able to drive alone. This assisted performance is encapsulated in Vygotsky's notion of the zone of proximal development, or ZPD, which describes the "gap" between what learners can do alone and what they can do with help from someone more skilled. This situated help is often known as "scaffolding" (Gibbons 2002).

Scaffolding, in the way it is used here, has three major characteristics:

- It is *temporary* help that assists a learner to move toward new concepts, levels of understanding, and new language.
- It enables a learner to know *how to do something* (not just what to do), so that they will be better able to complete similar tasks alone.
- It is *future oriented:* in Vygotsky's words, what a learner can do with support today, he or she will be able to do alone tomorrow.

Scaffolding is therefore teacher support in action, and is at the core of learning and teaching for autonomy (Mariani 1997).

Vygotsky also drew a clear relationship between the dialogues we participate in as children (and as adults) and the development of thinking, arguing that the development of cognition is also the result of participation with others in goal-oriented activities. Most people, for example, can remember situations where they have been helped to find solutions or understand difficult concepts by talking with others. We learn and develop new ideas through this collaborative talk. Vygotsky argues that this external dialogue with others is gradually internalized and becomes "inner speech," creating our personal resources for thinking. It follows, then, that the conversations learners have at school impact on how well they develop the kind of high-quality thinking described earlier.

Implicit in these ideas is the idea of *high challenge* (tasks we cannot do unaided) accompanied by *high support* (the scaffolding that enables us to complete these tasks successfully). One notion of what constitutes a high-challenge, high-support classroom has been developed by Mariani (1997), who suggests that the quality and quantity of the challenge and support we provide, and the way the dimensions of challenge and support intersect, construct four kinds of classroom environments. These are summarized in Figure 1.1.

From the perspective of the learner, a high-challenge classroom with low levels of support creates frustration and anxiety and may lead to learners giving up and ulti-

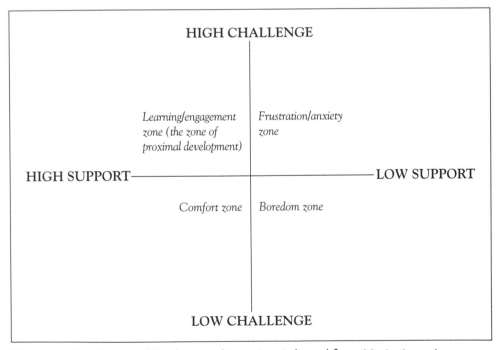

Figure 1.1. Four Zones of Teaching and Learning (adapted from Mariani 1997)

mately opting out of school. Low challenge and low support is likely to lead to boredom, with similar resistance to school. Low challenge and high support allows learners to work in their "comfort zone," but not a lot of learning will take place, and neither will learners develop autonomy and independence in their learning. In the fourth quadrant, the combination of high challenge and high support allows learners to be stretched to reach their potential and to successfully engage with new learning: here they learn in their zone of proximal development. This central idea of "learning in the challenge zone" is the backdrop against which the remainder of the book should be read.

Subsequent Chapters

The themes introduced in this chapter are taken up again in subsequent chapters. While these major themes recur throughout the book, each chapter focuses on a more detailed exemplification of key issues:

- Chapter 2 takes up in more detail the ideas about intellectual quality presented earlier. It describes some classrooms and programs where this approach has been put into practice with EL learners and identifies seven key intellectual practices.
- Chapter 3 focuses on literacy across the curriculum. It describes some of the differences between everyday spoken language and academic language and highlights some of the specific linguistic issues in academic language that can create barriers to comprehension for EL learners.
- Chapter 4 describes a range of teaching and learning activities that teachers can use across the curriculum to support learners in the development of literacy and academic language.
- Chapter 5 focuses on reading. It describes a range of reading activities by which teachers can support learners in accessing the meaning of complex written texts and becoming more autonomous readers.
- Chapter 6 describes a teaching and learning process whereby teachers can support learners' writing development across the curriculum using a range of genres or text types.
- Chapter 7 looks at the role of spoken language in the development of academic language and literacy. It describes how talk between teacher and learners, and between learners, can create "learning-rich" contexts for language development and subject learning.
- Chapter 8 focuses on key issues of planning and programming. It discusses two kinds of scaffolding, and a process for planning an integrated unit, and includes a framework of questions for reflecting on the integration of language and content.

Summary

This chapter foreshadows the major purposes and themes of the book:

- The notion of academic literacy and the barriers to learning it may create.
- The significance of language and literacy development in the middle years for EL learners.
- The importance of an intellectually challenging classroom for all learners, together with high levels of language and literacy support that will enable learners to engage in learning in such classrooms.
- Some criteria for describing intellectually challenging work.
- A pedagogical approach incorporating high challenge and high support.

To Think About . . .

1. How are students in your school supported in their development of subject-specific literacy? Could they be better supported?
2. There are many ways to think about "intellectual quality." What does the term mean to you? Is there anything you would add to the descriptions of intellectual quality given in this chapter?
3. If you are a classroom teacher, think of one teaching and learning task you have recently given to your students that fits your definition of intellectual quality. What were students required to do? What support was given to EL learners to help them complete this task?

Suggestions for Further Reading

Mariani, L. 1997. "Teacher Support and Teacher Challenge in Promoting Learner Autonomy." *Perspectives: A Journal of TESOL Italy* 23 (2).

Carrasquillo, A., S. Kucer, and R. Abrams. 2004. "English Language Learners in United States' Schools." Chapter 1 in *Beyond the Beginnings: Literacy Interventions for Upper Elementary English Language Learners*. Clevedon, UK: Multilingual Matters.

Meltzer J., and E. Hamann. 2005. "Research-Based Adolescent Literacy Teaching Strategies That Vary by Content Area." Part 4 of "Meeting the Literacy Development Needs of Adolescent English Language Learners Through Content-Area Learning." Northeast and Islands Regional Educational Laboratory, The Education Alliance at Brown University.

Walqui, A. 2007. "Scaffolding Instruction for English Language Learners: A Conceptual Framework." In *Bilingual Education: An Introductory Reader*, edited by O. Garcia and C. Baker. Clevedon, UK: Multilingual Matters.

2 | Intellectual Work in Practice
A View from the Classroom

Well, I think the idea of "intellectual challenge" does have a lot of different dimensions because it can mean many different things. One of the ways I think about it is for students to be able to make their own meaning out of material and to construct something new out of it instead of just reproducing it . . . transferring it into a new situation or using it to do something else . . . and to consider new possibilities, to open up the way they think about things.

—Grade 7 history teacher

What Counts as Intellectual Quality?

Deciding what counts as intellectually challenging learning, or, to put it another way, to decide on the criteria for "intellectual quality," is a complex task. Chapter 1 introduced some key notions associated with the idea of intellectual quality, drawn from a number of current sources. These include students' construction of knowledge and their participation in disciplined inquiry, higher-order thinking, deep knowledge and understanding, and substantive conversations. What is important to the teacher whose comment begins this chapter is that her students do more than simply reproduce what they learn. She suggests that they should also analyze and synthesize information and apply it to new contexts, a process sometimes referred to as "construction of knowledge." Bruce King and Schroeder (2001) describe the differences between construction of knowledge (which they also refer to as *authentic work*) and reproduction of knowledge:

> In the conventional curriculum, students identify the knowledge that others have produced (e.g., by recognizing the difference between verbs and nouns, labeling parts of a plant, or matching historical events to their dates). In authentic work, however, students go beyond memorizing and repeating facts, information, definitions, or

formulas to produce new knowledge or meaning. This kind of work involves higher-order thinking in which students analyze, interpret, or evaluate information in a novel way. The mere reproduction of knowledge does not constitute academic achievement. (3)

One group of teachers on being asked what students would be doing in an intellectually challenging classroom likewise spoke of the importance of learners' being involved in activities that require higher-order thinking. They mentioned a range of processes that this might involve: asking questions; solving problems; drawing reasoned conclusions; using sustained subject-related talk; explaining concepts and ideas; thinking critically and creatively; designing and planning; self-assessing; justifying opinions; transferring knowledge across discipline areas; interpreting information for use in different contexts and for different purposes; learning how to learn; taking on adultlike roles in carrying out tasks; developing subject-specific academic language; linking concrete knowledge with scientific knowledge; questioning everyday experiences; and making links between abstract concepts.

In summary, then, we can think of an intellectually challenging curriculum as one where learners are afforded the opportunities to:

- engage in higher-order thinking and in disciplined and inquiry-oriented activity;.
- construct their own understandings through participation in substantive conversations with others;
- transform and apply their learning in new contexts; and
- take on new roles and relate school learning to real-world contexts.

This chapter offers a view from the classroom, and illustrates what these broad notions "look like" in the ongoing tasks and talk of day-to-day classroom life. In most of these classrooms there were high numbers of EL learners. The chapter goes on to discuss the implications for pedagogy and introduces the notion of apprenticeship learning, and the potential that this offers for EL learners' language development.

Before reading the next section, think for a moment about the kind of practices you would expect to see in an intellectually challenging classroom. How would the ideas about the construction of knowledge and authentic work be reflected in practice? What would you expect learners to be doing, and what kinds of roles would they be taking on?

Seven Intellectual Practices

This section gives examples of some key intellectual activities that represent how the broad ideas above can be put into practice in classrooms with large numbers of EL learners.[1] They include classes with newly arrived migrants and refugee students, and students who, although they have mastered basic conversational English and are well able to talk about familiar everyday topics, are yet to develop the more formal and academic English associated with subject learning and literacy. (See Chapter 3 for a detailed discussion of academic language.) Because the focus is on what actually happens in the classrooms, the term *intellectual practices* is used to refer to the recurrent and regular practices in which students are engaged. Seven such practices are described below. They are not of course intended to present a full picture of everything that occurs in a high-challenge classroom! Hopefully, though, they will offer a springboard that will help you, as you reflect on your own teaching context, to take on and adapt those practices that seem relevant, and add additional practices. (The practices are numbered for ease of reference, not to signify any order of priority.)

Intellectual Practice 1:
Students engage with the key ideas and concepts of the discipline in ways that reflect how "experts" in the field think and reason

Engagement with key discipline-related ideas and concepts involves students in pursuing a coherent line of reasoning through activities that require them to "mirror" the ways of thinking and meaning of scientists, historians, or mathematicians; that is, to use content and processes that are central to the particular discipline. This requires students to have some "deep knowledge" of the field, rather than simply a knowledge of isolated facts. Of course we should not discount the importance of students' being familiar with traditional items of knowledge (indeed such knowledge is critical to thinking creatively and innovatively within the discipline). But it is the use to which such knowledge is put that is significant in students' developing an in-depth understanding and knowledge of the field.

Example: Grade 7 History
Students are studying Ancient Egypt. As part of their research they take on the role of archaeologists in examining re-creations of artifacts and tomb paintings that are on display throughout the school. The students are given the task of explaining the significance of these works in terms of what they *signify* about the way Egyptians lived. That is, the students need to produce responses that go beyond literal understanding and reproduction of knowledge about artifacts and tomb paintings. They need to interpret what they are observing in terms of what can be learned from it, a process that mirrors the work of archaeologists and historians, and to do this against the background of what they have already learned about the topic. This kind of activity is in sharp contrast to one, for example, which requires students simply to label the artifacts or to answer comprehension questions based on a reading about the Egyptians.

Intellectual Practice 2:
Students transform what they have learned into a different form for use in a new context or for a different audience

Information-transfer exercises have long been common practice in language class-rooms and are excellent ways to focus on language learning as well as content. These exercises require students to transfer information from one form to another—for ex-ample, to represent the information contained in a text as a graph. Here, however, the notion of transfer is much broader and refers to students' reconstructing knowledge for new contexts, different purposes, and/or other audiences or into another medium or artifact. The transformation usually involves a reconstruction of considerable amounts of learning.

Example A: Grade 5 Social Studies
The class has studied Antarctica for some weeks: its physical features, its history, en-vironmental issues, and related political issues. This leads to a class presentation to other classes about what they have learned. The children present their learning in the format of a popular morning TV current events show with which they are all familiar. The process of preparing for this involves students' taking on adultlike roles as pre-senters, directors, studio managers, scriptwriters, and interviewers. Groups of students work on different parts of the show, which includes a commercial for Tourism Australia, a weather report, a debate about environmental issues by "experts," news, and inter-views. In the process of presenting the program, students need to manipulate the in-formation and ideas that they have previously developed and combine facts and ideas in order to synthesize, generalize, explain, and interpret. As they transform what they have learned about the disciplinary "content" into a TV show, the students need to ex-plore the differences between formal written language and the more informal spoken language of the show. One student (who in the show represents Tourism Australia and presents an advertisement for tourism in Antarctica), comments: "We learned all the different qualities about Antarctica, why people go there to visit. And so we had to learn a lot about Antarctica and then we put it into our lines."

Example B: Grade 6 Social Studies
Year 6 students have been working on a unit about their local community. They have carried out considerable research on issues such as house prices, recreational facilities, and local shopping outlets. The school has a number of newly arrived migrant and refugee students, and the students use the knowledge they have acquired to create an information booklet about the area for the parents of these children. This requires con-siderable transformation of the information gained from the research of the area, in-cluding how to present the final substantial product as a very professional-looking booklet, which they desktop publish. The booklet is not only tangible evidence of their learning but also serves a valuable and real-life purpose in orientating newly arrived families in the area.

Example C: Grade 7 History

The transformation of students' learning in this class results in the production of a physical artifact. Based on considerable research about the shapes, patterns, and colors of early Egyptian jewelry, students produce their own pieces of jewelry and also make a museum card for each piece. One student explains that this activity, including the making of the museum card, required a detailed knowledge of the topic:

> And it was actually really fun because we got to do all this stuff about jewelry and you got to make your own jewelry and that was, you know, you were learning a lot about Egyptian jewelry but you were also doing it . . . and you got to make a museum card for it and . . . to make the museum card you had to really know about it.

Intellectual Practice 3:
Students make links between concrete knowledge and abstract theoretical knowledge

This refers to the relationship between everyday knowledge and concepts and between discipline-related concepts and literacy. Chapter 1 gave an example of this, comparing a child's concrete and everyday experience of magnetism (*the magnet sticks to the fridge*) to the same phenomenon as expressed more abstractly within a scientific framework (*magnets are attracted to ferrous metals*). Being able to use the appropriate language to express the scientific concept is of course of central importance, and this is discussed in detail in Chapter 3. Learning to control this academic language (or *register* as Chapter 3 describes it) is one of the most demanding challenges for EL learners.

At the same time, we do not want students to "parrot" academic language without understanding it, any more than we want them to be constrained by having access only to everyday ways of using language. This ability for students to understand and talk about the connections *between* concrete and theoretical knowledge—to be able to express ideas in both concrete and abstract ways and recognize the relationship between them—is perhaps one of the most important characteristics of "deep knowledge" of a subject.

Example A: Grade 7 Integrated Music and English Unit

All the students in the class have arrived in Australia within the last year and attend a special Intensive English Center that caters to secondary-age students who are newly arrived from a non-English-speaking country. Most students remain in these centers for about a year before moving on to regular secondary schools, and receive intensive English support in the context of secondary subjects taught by teachers trained in both their subject specialty and as EL teachers.

The students are about to leave the center to go to local high schools and are working on the theme of "belonging" in an integrated music and English unit. Clearly, questions around conformity, identity, and belonging are particularly relevant to the personal experience of students who have recently moved to a new country, and who have had to deal with personal and emotional loss in leaving their home country, and the need to participate and develop a sense of belonging in a new culture and language.

Based on a range of songs that the students have studied, the music teacher develops with the students a response to the question *do you have to conform or compromise to belong?* Students have opportunities to share ideas initially in same-language groups using their mother tongue before sharing these "rehearsed" ideas in mixed groups through the medium of English. Until the notions of *conform* and *compromise* have been explored further, the teacher initially rewords the question more concretely as *talk about how you have had to change in order to fit in with your friends*. Drawing on the students' personal experiences, the teacher guides the students to express these personal experiences in more abstract ways, introducing to them the more abstract terms *conformity* and *compromise*.

In their English class the same students have studied a version of Shakespeare's *The Taming of the Shrew* and have used this study to continue their exploration of the themes of belonging and conformity. As part of the unit, the students are asked to think about their own experiences of leaving their country and settling in a new one. Among many activities, they complete, in groups, the four sentence beginnings below. Some of the responses of the students have been added in parentheses:

When I left my country I left . . . (*my friends, dreams, my grandma, my home, war*).
When I came to Australia I found . . . (*sunshine, friends, fun, feel free*).
When I came to this school I found . . . (*help, friends, new ideas, lovely teachers*).
As I leave this school I feel . . . (*sad, missing my friends, scared, grateful*).

The teacher works with each group individually to recode some of these responses into more abstract terms such as *friendship, sadness, joy, freedom,* and *harmony.*

In these classes, then, the students have developed abstract ideas couched in more abstract terms on the basis of their personal and concrete experiences, initially expressed in their mother tongue. Moving from concrete to abstract has involved students in shifting between "everyday" and more academic English, and between their first and second languages. Much of this new learning is then transformed (see intellectual practice 2) and used in a new context: at the end of the unit students present a concert based on the notion of "belonging" to the whole school. This includes stories and songs performed in English and in the students' first languages.

Given the relatively low levels of English competence, the teachers have not compromised on intellectual demand. They have high expectations of what their students can achieve, while using the students' personal resources of language and experience to develop sophisticated and generalizable abstractions and concepts.

Example B: Grade 10 U.S. History

This example is drawn from a paper (McConachie et al. 2006) referenced at the end of this chapter in the further reading list. The writers describe a tenth-grade history class studying a unit on immigration, which includes as one of the overarching questions,

What are some of the forces pushing people away from their homelands and pulling people to immigrate to the United States? Since more than half of the students are first- or second-generation immigrants, the teacher taps into what the students bring to the topic from their personal lives. The class generates a number of "pushes," such as war and poor living conditions, and "pulls," such as job opportunities or freedom. These concrete understandings are then built on by the teacher as the class studies the conditions and historical context of the homelands of particular groups of immigrants. In the second part of the unit, students analyze the public debate over immigration and the responses to it by the United States in different eras. Each of these examples shows how teachers have built on their students' concrete experiences, and used these to develop abstract and theoretical concepts.

Intellectual Practice 4:
Students engage in substantive conversation

Substantive conversation involves extended talk around the substantive ideas ("big ideas") inherent in a topic and focuses on creating understandings of subject matter. As well as building on what students already know, the process of taking part in substantive conversations leads to an increased understanding of subject content, since it creates space for students to explore new ideas, clarify their understandings, initiate questions, and make their reasoning visible to peers. Such conversations promote shared understandings. Unlike traditional classroom talk where the teacher controls all the talk (which is often aimed, through teacher questions, at testing what students know), substantive conversation is more reciprocal and extended, with students taking a much more central and significant role in directing its flow and content.

This kind of talk not only is important for helping students develop understandings of subject content but also has particular significance for second language learning: Merrill Swain (2000) has shown how extended talk is not simply an indication of what has already been learned, but since it involves learners in ongoing interaction, also itself provides an enabling context for new language learning. She comments that knowledge-building dialogue "is where language use and language learning can occur" (97). So for EL learners in particular, substantive conversation provides important contexts for both content learning and language development.

Substantive conversations can occur both between teacher and student in whole-class work, and between students in pair and group work. Typically, substantive conversations have a number of characteristics that set them apart from the traditional short teacher-student exchanges whereby teachers ask low-level recall questions and evaluate students' responses:

- Substantive conversations are sustained, showing the continuation of a thought or idea.
- Students have opportunities to initiate topics or raise questions.
- Students make extended contributions to conversations.

- Students give opinions and views, making their reasons for these views explicit, and build on one another's suggestions; when there is disagreement or argument, groups remain socially cohesive.
- There is intellectual substance as students draw on a knowledge base of the subject—for example, their talk includes some subject-specific language and ideas central to the discipline.
- Students are treated as worthy conversational partners by one another and by teachers, and ideas are taken seriously.
- When the teacher is part of the conversation, there are generally equal contributions to the talk by teachers and students.
- The teacher takes up opportunities to clarify and extend conceptual thinking and models subject specific language.
- The teacher avoids, as far as possible, asking simple display questions,[2] instead asking questions that probe or extend students' thinking or reasoning.

You will find more about substantive conversations and classroom talk in Chapter 7.

Example A: Grade 7 Science

In a unit of work on energy and forces, students are required to carry out scientific investigations, using an appropriate experimental design, to test the validity of common myths such as *toast always lands with the buttered side down*; *heavy objects fall faster than light objects*; *the heavier a pendulum the faster it swings*; and *objects float in water because they are lighter than water*.

In previous lessons students have developed some familiarity with the processes of scientific investigation. Having chosen the myth they want to work with, each group of four is given a single copy of what the teachers call a "thinking sheet." This is a series of questions intended to remind students of the process they should be following and structure their thinking in ways relevant to the scientific task they will later carry out. Giving one copy per group is significant, because it encourages students to talk together to decide on the answers to the questions. The questions include:

Do we agree with the myth? Why? Why not?
How might we test this (give three suggestions and choose one).
What are the two variables?
What steps will we need to follow?

And after the experiment has been carried out:

Do we need to make any changes to our experiment? Why?
What have we learned about designing experiments?
What question have we helped to answer?
What is the scientific fact that explains our results?

Using the "thinking sheet," the students engage in substantive disciplinary-related talk, in particular around key concepts such as *dependent, independent, and controlled variables*. The thinking sheet plays an important role in allowing students to "talk their way in" to understanding complex concepts, encourages them to make their ideas explicit, provides a context in which to apply what they have learned, and requires the use of subject-specific language.

Example B: Grade 7 Math

McConachie et al. (2006) offer an example of the significance of substantive conversation (although they do not use this term) for developing students' understandings of a math problem. The problem is based on a short narrative about a student who purchases an item using a 20-percent-off coupon and then uses a second coupon for 10 percent off to reduce the price still further. The task is for the students to decide whether the bill would be for the same amount if the whole 30 percent had been taken off at once, and to explain and justify their answer. Most of the students believe that the first scenario would be the better deal. Though they are right in their answer, their explanation for their decision—that it is because there are two subtractions rather than one—is not. Students are shown how to make sense of the problem by doing a calculation for each of the scenarios. Having solved both calculations correctly, the students begin to talk about an explanation for the answer. Satisfied that the students are beginning to understand, the teacher then asks them to "talk as a team" in preparation for presenting a written explanation to the class.

As in the previous classroom example, students are scaffolded in their thinking and are then given time to talk through that thinking. It is only by making time for such substantive conversations that teachers can find out how students are reasoning and thinking, whether that thinking is correct, and how to respond to incorrect assumptions.

Intellectual Practice 5:
Students make connections between the spoken and written language of the subject and other discipline-related ways of making meaning

Language is the primary system for making meaning in school, but in addition, different subjects make use of alternative ways of representing information, such as diagrams, graphs, tables, maps, or flowcharts. Other systems for making meaning include mathematical or chemical symbols and musical notation. Students who are engaged in disciplinary learning need to learn to "read" these visual representations just as they learn other forms of literacy. They also need to be able to interpret and explain them through language.

While presenting meanings in nonlinguistic ways is an intellectually challenging activity, it may, conversely, also be a supportive one for EL learners, because it provides them with an alternative source of meaning that may be more accessible than language alone. Mathematical symbols, for example, may be quite comprehensible to an EL learner who is already familiar with them, and serve as a bridge to the related spoken or written language. Using alternative representations of meanings alongside language may help make complex language and abstract concepts more comprehensible to EL learners, such as the use of the calculation to help students understand a problem in intellectual practice 4.

Example: Grade 5 Mathematics/Information Technology (IT)

In an integrated mathematics and IT class, groups of students explore a number of myths—such as *your arm span is the same as your height*; *taller people have bigger feet*; *drinking a liter of water makes you heavier*—to decide on their validity and develop their own strategies for testing them. A major focus for the class is on how their findings are to be represented. The teacher models the use of different types of graphs (bar graph, pie graph, line graph, and sector graph), and the students work in groups to present and explain their findings to their peers using Power Point presentations.

For many of the students, designing the graphs in a Power Point program requires the development of new IT skills. As is often the case, IT skills vary considerably throughout the class, and the teacher encourages peer tutoring and works with less confident students herself. Since the students' presentations are to be accompanied by their own explanations of how the graphs should be read, some time is also spent on students' planning what they will say in these presentations and the best way to explain what their graphs represent. In this example, the use of an alternative system for presenting information works in tandem with the use of language.

Intellectual Practice 6:
Students take a critical stance toward knowledge and information

Taking a critical stance toward knowledge and "accepted wisdom" requires students to recognize that it can be questioned. Traditional views of knowledge in schools see it as a given body of facts, "a body of truth to be acquired by students" (*Queensland School Reform Longitudinal Study* 2001). In reality this view of knowledge is inconsistent with the reality of much authentic disciplinary work, which acknowledges that knowledge is not static: indeed, it is changing at a pace previously unknown in the history of humanity.

In the classroom, this "problematization" of knowledge means that students are encouraged to take a critical approach to reading a text, identify bias, critique different views, pursue a novel line of inquiry, offer an alternative solution to a problem, or change their own thinking as a result of new learning. As the earlier examples have suggested, much of the work in an intellectually challenging program involves students in collaborative problem solving and so in dealing with alternate views.

Example: Grade 7 History

Students have been asked to decide whether or not a particular Chinese emperor was a just and fair ruler. Although they have been given access to a lot of historical material, it is left to the students to decide on how they should interpret these sources. Their history teacher comments on her approach to the teaching of history, emphasizing she wants students to learn to draw conclusions and to question sources:

> They had a whole lot of material about a Chinese emperor, and then they had to test a hypothesis, was he a fair and just ruler? So instead of just learning that he did all these things, they had to use the material to deduce something. . . . I think the concept that there are really no right answers is the important one. . . . I try always to raise questions rather than [provide] answers. I spend a lot of time in class talking about what the questions are, asking what are different ways you could look at this?

Students comment that they find this process difficult but have enjoyed the challenge. Their comments suggest their developing understanding that written history reflects the biases, ideologies, and assumptions of the writer:

> *I actually decided he was good . . . all the evidence against him was kind of biased.*
> *But you can't really say, because it's so long ago and like all stuff's been written about him.*
> *'Cause it's one of the . . . you know there isn't a real answer, you can't get it right or wrong, it's just how you do it. . . . That's what's kind of scary about it.*

Intellectual Practice 7:
Students use metalanguage in the context of learning about other things

Language plays a central role in any intellectual activity, and using it effectively in reading, writing, and speaking is central to learning and to demonstrating learning. But as well as learning how to *use* language, students also need to develop a language to talk *about* language—that is, to develop *metalanguage*. What this means in reality is that students are able to talk about language for the purposes of developing their language use, such as to develop more effective writing skills, develop an explicit awareness of how to read more effectively, or understand how different ways of expressing an idea may be more or less effective depending on context. For example, there may be explicit talk about the structure of a science report in the context of writing up an experiment, so that students are learning about language in the context of using it. In this process the teacher talks about language, for example, drawing students' attention to the function and form of the passive voice in this context, and how to express cause and effect. Running through all the other intellectual practices that have been described is the practice of talking and reflecting on language itself.

Example: Grade 8 Social Studies

Students have been discussing the logging of old-growth forests and have researched arguments from both the supporters (the loggers) and opponents of logging. At the end of the unit of work they present their ideas in the form of a written discussion.[3] The purpose of a discussion is to persuade the reader to take a particular point of view. Discussions present arguments and counterarguments around a particular issue and usually offer a conclusion or recommendations favoring one side.

In this classroom the teaching of content went hand in hand with the teaching of the language and literacy that were integral to the task the students were engaged in. The teacher had modeled a number of examples of this genre and previously discussed with students the social purpose, structure, and language associated with a discussion. To provide further scaffolding and to help students become more autonomous, the teacher now provides each student with a language criteria sheet (see Figure 2.1) for a written discussion, to which students can refer as they are writing and also use as a self-editing tool once they have completed their writing. The criteria sheet summarizes some of the key language that makes for an effective piece of writing in this genre and is an example of the teaching of metalanguage (language about language). The teacher has focused particularly on the overall structure of the genre and on some typical conjunctions that signal the structure.

- Does my discussion have an appropriate title?
- Have I included all the parts of a discussion?
  - identification and introduction to the issue
  - arguments for and supporting points
  - arguments against and supporting points
  - conclusion (my view)
- Have I introduced the "arguments for" with appropriate conjunctions (e.g., *first, second, in addition, besides, moreover*)?
- Have I used an appropriate conjunction to signal where the counter-arguments begin (e.g., *however, on the other hand, nevertheless, conversely*)?
- Have I linked related arguments appropriately (e.g., *similarly, likewise, equally*)?
- Have I introduced the conclusion appropriately (e.g., *therefore, finally, in summary, in conclusion*)?
- Does my conclusion make clear what side I favor?
- Have I introduced examples appropriately (e.g., *for example, to illustrate, in other words*)?
- Have I used correct technical vocabulary?
- Have I checked the punctuation and spelling?

Figure 2.1. Criteria Sheet for Editing Your Work

Developing Intellectual Practices in the Classroom

The kinds of practices described above do not of course exist in isolation from one another. As you were reading you will probably have noticed that several of the examples could be seen as representing more than one of the practices: the graphing activity, for example, could also be viewed as an example of learning being transformed. And in many of the classroom examples it is possible to see almost every practice occurring at some stage. It is important, then, to see these practices not in isolation from one another but as a cluster of practices and events that are likely to occur within a particular pedagogical approach. The next section of the chapter describes this approach, and discusses why it is particularly helpful for EL learners.

Learning Through Apprenticeship

One example of the kind of scaffolded learning discussed in Chapter 1 is learning through apprenticeship. This is the way we learn most naturally. When young children learn to dress or feed themselves, they do so with the guided support of those more skilled helping them little by little to accomplish the task; likewise, when they grow older and learn to drive a car, they develop this ability gradually through doing it themselves with the help of someone more expert.

The notion of apprenticeship in the adult world is one with which everyone is familiar. Nurses, car mechanics, medical interns, housepainters, garage mechanics, hairdressers, fashion designers, teachers, builders, and those engaged in many other occupations all serve apprenticeships of one kind or another, where they learn to become increasingly more expert in their field by working in a real workplace. In my own institution, for example, trainee teachers work in schools regularly throughout their university-based course, teaching collaboratively alongside an experienced teacher who is on hand to monitor their progress, introduce them to the many aspects of the work of a teacher, and give feedback on their progress. During new teachers' first years of teaching, many schools offer further ongoing support in the form of teacher-mentors who continue this apprenticeship process. In similar ways novices in any field (nurses, mechanics, and so on) gradually over time become full members of their particular community.

An important aspect of this learning is that it occurs while participating in tasks that are authentic and relevant in the chosen field (nurses do not need to learn how to assess student learning, nor do builders need to learn to give injections!). In addition the complexity of tasks is carefully sequenced. Apprentices start off with very simple tasks, at first supervised and helped by the expert. As they become able to do these tasks on their own, they are expected to carry out increasingly complex tasks, always initially with the expert's help, until they are finally able to do all the required tasks and activities performed by full members of that particular community.

One of the best-known books about apprenticeship learning is by the researchers Lave and Wenger (1991). They describe five examples of apprenticeship learning in a range of countries, one of which is a study of the apprenticeship of tailors in Liberia. They describe how the training begins with the apprentices' learning to sew by hand, then with a treadle sewing machine, and then learning to press clothes. They make the point that learning processes do not always reproduce the sequence of the production process. In fact, apprentices begin by learning the finishing stages of producing a garment (such as attaching buttons to the finished garment or pressing it), before learning how to sew it and lastly how to cut it. In this way, they understand the end point of the task as a whole, before learning the earlier steps, so that they gain an understanding of how the previous step of the real production process contributes to the next step. In other words, the apprentices learn "mini-tasks" (such as sewing on buttons) in the context of recognizing how these tasks are relevant to the larger task or end product (making a full garment).

While apprenticeship learning varies across different contexts, most such learning shares a number of characteristics. These are listed below. As you read them, substitute *teacher* for *expert* and *learner* for *novice*, and consider how these characteristics differ from those of traditional "chalk and talk" classrooms, where teachers see their role as transmitting knowledge to passive learners.

- Learning is authentic and socially situated, clearly related to the real world.
- Learners can see relevant processes at work.
- Learning is collaborative and shared: the expert and apprentice complete tasks together, in the context of the work of a mechanic, a hairdresser, a nurse.
- The novice is "shown how" and "helped to do." The expert demonstrates and models a task and provides relevant support to the learner until he or she is able to take over that particular task alone. In this way, and over time, the learner moves from novice to more expert, with ongoing monitoring by the expert.
- Once a novice is able to successfully complete a particular task or part of a task, the expert gradually hands over responsibility to the novice, and withdraws the previous help.
- While many basic skills may require repetition and low-level learning, they are practiced *in the context of a larger task or end product*: their purpose is clear and relevant to the apprentice.
- Being an apprentice requires gradually taking on the disposition (attitudes and beliefs) of an expert in the field, and in taking on the particular roles and codes of behavior shared by those who are already part of the particular expert community.
- Apprentices are treated by experts *as the people they will become*; they are identified by others, and see themselves, as potential teachers, nurses, hairdressers, mechanics, and so on.
- Apprentice and expert share the same goals.

Apprenticeship Learning in School

Apprenticeship learning is not of course the only way to learn. In formal learning contexts such as schools and universities we also learn by reading, by listening to lectures, by interacting with a computer, and in many other ways. But many researchers see the overall approach to learning described above as very relevant to the classroom (see, for example, Collins et al. 1991). And, as I will suggest at the end of this chapter, it offers to EL learners in particular many unique opportunities both for curriculum learning and language development.

Like the different fields in which apprentices learn (and as later chapters illustrate), schools and disciplines also have their own culture and language into which learners need to be apprenticed and enculturated. Of course there are important differences between traditional apprenticeship learning and school learning. One of the major differences is that in traditional apprenticeships learners are often learning something concrete or tangible, and so for the learner there is visible and observable evidence of the relevant thinking processes. This is usually not the case in school, where the processes of thinking are often not made visible to students. Collins et al. (1991) argue that in school often too little attention is paid to the reasoning and strategies that experts employ when they acquire knowledge or use it to solve complex tasks. Often there is an emphasis on formulaic methods for solving "textbook" problems or on the development of low-level subskills. As a result, they argue, much school learning remains "inert"—unable to be used—for many students. For this reason, advocates of apprenticeship approaches to pedagogy refer to this kind of learning in school as *cognitive apprenticeship*. Cognitive apprenticeship is concerned with helping students learn to think and reason and solve problems, and emphasizes the need for teachers and students to make thinking visible and explicit:

> In schooling, the practice of problem solving, reading comprehension, and writing are not at all obvious—it is not necessarily observable to the student. In [traditional] apprenticeship, the processes of thinking are visible. In schooling, the processes of thinking are often invisible to both students and teacher. Cognitive apprenticeship is a model of instruction that works to make thinking visible. (Collins et al. 1991, 1)

Making thinking and language visible is of critical importance in the teaching of all students, but has extra significance for EL learners in particular. We will return to this point later at the end of this chapter and in the chapters about the teaching of reading and writing. First, though, let's consider some of the more general implications that this approach suggests for classroom teaching.

Learners participate in "rich" real-world-like tasks

As some of the earlier examples illustrated, many of the tasks in which students were engaged required them to "mirror" the ways of thinking, the ways of using language, and the activities that are characteristic of the discipline. This kind of authenticity was illustrated in Chapter 1 with the example of the two students whose analysis of a fruit drink challenged a large corporation to rethink its advertising. Of course, as all teachers will be aware, it isn't always possible for every classroom task to be as truly authentic as in this example. However, it is important that as far as possible, the teaching of skills and items of knowledge occur in the context of a meaningful broader task which has a relationship to the real world and in which the purpose of lower-level or more decontextualized practice exercises is clear. Two examples of how this might be done are included here.

In the context of a science unit on elements, compounds, and mixtures, the teacher introduced a problem to the year 8 students: the local river had been polluted and the students' task was to discover what substances were in the river. This required students to collect samples of the water and test them to see what substances they contained. In the process of this investigation, students built up knowledge about the scientific techniques used in separating heterogeneous materials (including filtration, decanting, crystallization, and magnetization) and about the concept of solubility. At the end of the investigation the students wrote a scientific report on the substances they found in the river and what the possible causes were. Their reports made use of the scientific language they had developed during the unit.

In this unit, the skills and knowledge that the students needed for this task were in fact mandatory within the science syllabus; however, as with true apprenticeship learning, they were taught not as isolated bits of knowledge but in the broader context of a "real world" task that provided an authentic purpose for the mandated knowledge and skills to be developed and utilized. In the state of New South Wales, in Australia, some schools now contribute data that they have collected to an on-line program known as Stream Watch. This in turn contributes to a database that provides important information to water companies.

Phillip Moulds (2002) gives the following example of work from a year 8 science class. Students were given the task of designing a box for a pizza delivery business that would keep pizzas at a constant temperature for thirty minutes. They were also asked to design an experiment to gather data about how well the box maintained a constant temperature of 45° centigrade, and then to reflect on how the design might be improved. Moulds points out that in this activity students were actively engaged in the learning process, designing a product clearly related to real-world use. The students needed to make use of their knowledge about heat transfer, incorporating information about convection, conduction, and radiation; about what constitutes a "fair test"; and about how the use of test results leads to design improvements.

In neither of these examples was traditional science learning compromised: in fact it was essential for the students to do the tasks. What makes these tasks different from traditional science teaching is the use to which the knowledge is put, the broad context in which the knowledge is gained, and the fact that knowledge is developed as part of a coherent system, rather than as sets of decontextualized and isolated items.

Tasks like these are sometimes referred to as *rich tasks*. They are real-world-*like*, in that they mirror—or imitate—authentic ways of thinking, being, and talking in the world outside the classroom. Imitating, unlike copying or mimicking, does not involve simply reproducing the expert's model, but involves a role reversal by the learner, who begins to act in ways that mirror the expert or adult. If you watch students involved in such tasks, what strikes you most is the enthusiasm and excitement with which the tasks are tackled, perhaps because they are engaged in tasks over which they have some ownership and investment. You will find more about rich tasks later in this chapter.

Thinking is made visible

Making thinking visible is an important aspect of cognitive apprenticeship. As Collins et al. (1991) put it, teachers and students "need to deliberately bring thinking to the surface, to make it visible, whether it's in reading, writing, [or] problem solving."

While experts complete many tasks without consciously thinking about what they are doing, learners need the expert's thinking to be "brought to the surface." They need to be shown explicitly those things that to an expert have become automatic. One example of what this means in practice is the use of the "thinking sheet" described in intellectual practice 3 for supporting students in their design of an experiment. The thinking sheet gave learners an opportunity to make decisions collaboratively in order to plan, make use of prior knowledge, and reflect on how to improve their designs—that is, to mirror and model authentic scientific processes. Through using the thinking sheet, their thinking was made explicit to themselves and to others through talk. And as we are all aware, telling someone about something makes it clearer to ourselves and frequently allows us to see gaps or inconsistencies in our thinking. As well, others' reactions to what we have said may require us to respond by modifying or changing our own ideas. In this case, the thinking sheet provided scaffolding for students to carry out the task itself successfully, and with a greater degree of understanding, than if this planned time for thinking had not occurred. It also constructed a context whereby students used subject-related language for authentic reasons and in a meaningful context.

A year 7 math class also used a thinking sheet to assist them with solving word problems. Most students in the class were EL learners, and word problems often pose difficulties for them not because of the mathematical processes themselves, but because of the language of the problem: EL learners simply may not recognize what mathematical processes are required. In this case the learners as a group were given a thinking sheet with the word problem to be solved at the top. They were asked first to underline the key words in the problem and to give simple meanings for the words. They then solved the problem and finally as a group were asked to write down the process they went through to get to the answer. The group's thinking sheet was used by one of the students to report back to the rest of the class about how the group chose to solve the problem. At this stage the teacher interacted with the students, modeling new language, probing and clarifying what they were saying, and writing up on the board what the students were saying mathematically. The process that the students went through in making explicit their reasoning is a step that is often skipped over or given little time in classrooms where only the "right answer" is considered important.

Talking aloud their thinking also made it much easier for the teacher to check their understanding, just as it did for the teacher in the grade 8 math classroom described in intellectual practice 4.

The editing sheet used to support students in their writing described in intellectual practice 6 is a further example of making visible what skilled writers do intuitively, namely to edit their own work. Here the students were given a list of key questions, together with examples, to guide them to do something even many adults are not skilled in doing!

Observation plays a key role: Learners are given opportunities to observe models of a task as a whole prior to attempting to execute it

In all the classrooms students had a clear idea of what they were aiming at and what the finished product might look like. For example, in the science unit described in intellectual practice 4, students were required to design an experiment to test the truth of common myths. Prior to this, they had watched a *Myth-Busters* (a popular science TV show) video focusing on proving or disproving the hypothesis, *wearing a tongue stud makes it more likely that you will be struck by lightning.* In this very entertaining video scientists set up a series of experiments, using increasingly larger metal studs embedded in a number of constructed "heads," while keeping the charge of lightning constant. (Results were random and the scientists found no correlation between the stud and the likelihood of being struck by lightning, at least not until the size of the stud was increased to about a quarter the size of the head!) While watching the video students made notes on the scientific process that the scientists followed, developing their understanding of dependent, independent, and controlled variables, which they later applied to their own experiments.

Similarly, the TV program on Antarctica described in intellectual practice 2 was modeled on a real program with which all the students were familiar. The Power Point presentations described in intellectual practice 5 were preceded by the children's watching similar presentations developed by another class in the school. Before the children produced the community booklet for new parents in intellectual practice 2, they had looked at other leaflets and brochures, and the teacher had discussed with them the purpose and audience of the booklet and the style of writing this would require. Before writing the discussion text discussed in intellectual practice 6, the students had looked at several models of other texts in this genre.

Abstract tasks or tasks involving low-level skills are situated in authentic contexts, so that students understand the relevance of what they are doing

One of my Ph.D. students recently recounted to me his experience as a young man when he was an apprentice to a barber in his home land of Turkey. He described how one of the first things he was required to do was to shave a watermelon! As he talked, it became clear why: the melon is similar in size and shape to a human head, it is covered with fine hairs, and the action of shaving it imitates the flexible wrist movement

He was required to shave a watermelon.

of a barber as he shaves his customers. This is clearly an "exercise" type activity that if taken out of its context would be utterly meaningless! However, in the context of becoming a barber, it had real relevance and a clear purpose.

So it is with teaching a language: low-level or practice-type exercises without a context have little meaning or relevance to students. An exercise where students turn a number of active sentences (*you mustn't mix acid with water*) into passive sentences (*acid must not be mixed with water*) may help students to master the form and structure of sentences but tells them nothing about how these forms relate to context and meaning, or about the different contexts in which one or the other might be appropriate. The first sentence is likely to be spoken, possibly as a directive from teacher to student in a laboratory setting. The second is more likely to be written and might occur as a set of safety instructions or as part of a written science report. And though the two sentences are closely related in meaning, there is a subtle difference in what is being emphasized: the first is concerned with *you*, the person being spoken to. The second is telling us something about *the acid*. And so while formal practice of these language forms may be useful, it is not sufficient. To excise language from its context and meaning is to tell only half the story. It is like shaving a melon but not knowing why!

And so it is important to teach language in ways that allow EL learners to see the function and meaning of language, not simply the form and structure. Subject-based teaching provides a ready-made context for this. The use and form of the passive voice was an explicit focus of part of the science unit on designing scientific investigations (see intellectual practice 4), because the students needed to use this in their reports. The EL teacher, working collaboratively with the science teacher, taught this explicitly, and the students spent some time locating and underlining the passive verbs in a model report. They also talked about why formal report writing in science usually does not contain references to the actual people who carry out the experiments and how the use of passive verbs allows us to do that. This is an example of how there can be a focus on a single aspect of grammar (including in this case having the students do practice-type exercises) occurring within a broader context in which the relevance of the practice activity is clear.

Assessing Learning Through Rich Tasks

Several examples of rich tasks were described earlier in the chapter. In one such task, students designed a box for a pizza delivery firm that would keep food at a constant temperature. In another, students produced a book about the local community that could be used by newly arrived parents. These tasks were closely linked to the skills, knowledge, and practices of a particular discipline or disciplines and required students to be actively engaged in the learning process. They were characterized by all or many of the features below:

Rich tasks

- Are problem based and require deep understanding.
- May require knowledge related to more than one subject area.
- Result in an end product that is for an audience broader than the teacher and has relevance beyond the classroom.
- Feature a real-world-like setting.
- Can range in length from short-term tasks to long-term multistage projects.
- Allow for end products to be open ended, complex, and authentic and take a variety of formats (text and visuals, performance, multimedia).
- Require collection, organization, synthesis, and transformation of substantial amounts of information.
- Require students to consider alternatives to problems and make connections with other learning.
- Require students to participate in substantive conversation and elaborated written and visual communication.

Because rich tasks are culminating performances, they also serve an important assessment function. They are able to provide evidence that learners have a deep understanding of a topic and are able to use their knowledge in context. Rich tasks are a more appropriate means to assess this than quizzes, end-of-unit tests, and standardized tests (Wiggins and McTighe 2004). These traditional assessments may have a place in assessing the essential knowledge and skills that *contribute to* rich tasks but are not by themselves sufficient to assess the kind of intellectual work that has been described in this chapter. Rubrics can be used to assess rich tasks, with criteria derived from the key features of the task.

Moulds (2002) provides an example of a rich task used in a senior chemistry course. Students were asked to investigate water quality in the Brisbane River by analyzing data from a number of samplings for specific patterns, comparing their results with government standards, and making and justifying recommendations as to how the water quality could be improved. Along the way students completed many smaller tasks that related and led up to the final task, and these tasks required traditional chemistry knowledge about solubility and acid/base chemistry. Rubrics were used to assess and provide feedback to students on these tasks. Moulds comments that from student responses in the final report, it was evident which students had a rich understanding of the key concepts and which had explored ideas at a superficial level.

You will find more about assessing learning in Chapter 8.

Apprenticeship Learning and EL Learners

The approach to learning described through classroom examples in this chapter offers the potential for a challenging and relevant learning environment for all students. But for EL learners it also offers significant opportunities for language development:

- What students hear and what they learn is contextualized. Language is heard and used in a real context and used meaningfully to carry out subject-relevant tasks.
- There are many opportunities, through group tasks, for meaningful interactions in context.
  - Interacting with others, in particular when students are engaged in problem-solving activities, creates an excellent environment for language development (Swain 2000).
  - In small groups, students hear a wider range of language and have more language directed to them than is possible in a whole-class context (McGroarty 1993).
  - Students have more opportunities to interact with other speakers, to take more turns, and, in the absence of the teacher, to take on more responsibility for clarifying unclear wording.
  - In group talk around a task, ideas are often reworded and revised, key words and phrases are repeated, problems are restated, and meanings are refined, all of which give EL learners opportunities to hear similar ideas expressed in a variety of ways; this makes what they hear more comprehensible.
  - Group work often provides an environment in which less confident students feel more comfortable and more prepared to take risks.
- There are opportunities for learning about language in the context of using language.
- EL students greatly benefit from an approach that makes thinking visible and from the explicit teaching that goes along with this.
- EL students are positioned as the people they might become, by taking on adultlike roles. The approach focuses on students' *potential* achievement through explicit support rather than on their current levels of achievement in English, and so allows for teaching to be at an appropriate cognitive level.

Student Voices

This chapter concludes with comments from English language learners themselves. They suggest that students want to be active learners and that they value *thinking* and *doing* for themselves.

Here are the comments of three EL learners after completing the grade 5 math unit on graphs:

> I learned most when I was actually drawing the graphs because then I knew how to draw them.

> I had to think really hard when we were told to do four graphs by ourself [sic] but I really enjoyed it.

> I learned most when we were doing the power point because now I can do [it] at home by myself.

An EL learner in a grade 7 science class comments in a similar way on the value of the students designing, conducting trials, and evaluating their own experiments in a unit on scientific investigation:

> I learned because like we make it ourselves, like we don't copy it from a book because we get to do it . . . instead of just copying it, and it's more fun if you design it and think about it.

The students were also clear about what did not help them! Here are the comments of two students about work they had done in the previous year, which they compare unfavorably to the kinds of active experiences they now have:

> And when we had [grade 7 history] practicals . . . one teacher did most of the work for us and so we haven't done anything on it.

> I was excited when Miss S told us that our new [grade 5] maths theme is about graphs because in my old classes we usually just did times table, addition, and subtraction, so it was good learning about something new.

Students' comments, like the words of the teacher that began this chapter, also reflect the fact that they did not like activities that were too simple, seeing them as a waste of time. Here are three grade 7 EL learners discussing what they find unhelpful for their learning. They are referring to a low-level drill-and-practice exercise that a teacher regularly used:

Student 1:   But with one teacher we get . . . a sheet, and it's got all this stuff in it and then a couple of words along the way she whited out [deleted] a word and then all that happen [sic] is that she read it all out and as she read we fill it in. And that's all that happen [sic] and it doesn't help.
Student 2:   Because like we don't learn from that.
Student 3:   Instead of if you actually do it by yourself.
Student 2:   And we're not actually thinking hard or like what should go in here and why.

Student 3:   You never used your brain!

Student 4:   In the end I know like nothing because it's just, we get these sheets
and there's little blank words and we fill in the blanks. And that's
it and I didn't learning [sic] anything from it. So I was really scared
when the test came.

From the students too, then, comes the suggestion that the most useful learning environment is one in which they are active in their own learning and one that requires more from them than the simple reproduction of knowledge.

The final comment comes from a refugee student from Somalia, who at the time of writing has been in Australia for about three years. He is a superb athlete and until recently this was the only thing in school that he excelled at and the one he enjoyed most. After his experiences in one of the science classes described in this chapter, he commented: "I think science is my favorite subject now." For this student, being treated as the person he could be has given him a new identity, that of the successful student. There can be few more important things that a teacher who has high expectations for students can do than this.

Summary

This chapter has illustrated what an intellectually challenging environment looks like in practice. It has given examples of seven related intellectual practices that occurred in the context of real-world-like tasks that mirrored authentic disciplinary practices. These practices occurred in classroom environments that reflected an apprenticeship approach to learning. Key points included:

- Apprenticeship learning is a natural way to learn and involves collaborative work between "expert" and "novice."
- Cognitive apprenticeship describes an approach to learning and teaching in the classroom that focuses on making thinking visible.
- Apprenticeship learning based on real-life-like tasks offers EL learners opportunities for language development.
- Rich tasks make use of the central ideas of a topic and link school learning to the real world. They provide a way for students to demonstrate their deep understanding of a topic.

To Think About . . .

1. Look again at the seven intellectual practices described here. Are there any practices you would add to these?

2. What additional classroom examples from your own experience could illustrate these practices?
3. How does apprenticeship learning differ from traditional teacher-centered learning? How do the roles of the teacher and students change?
4. In what ways can teachers make thinking visible?
5. In your experience, how does collaborative work help EL learners develop new language?

Suggestions for Further Reading

Collins, A., J. Seely Brown, and A. Holum. 1991. "Cognitive Apprenticeship: Making Thinking Visible." *American Educator* (Winter). Available at www.21learn.org/arch/articles/brown_seely.php.

Gibbons, P. 2008. "'It Was Taught Good and I Learned a Lot': Intellectual Practices and ESL Learners in the Middle Years." *Australian Journal of Language and Literacy* 31 (2): 155–73.

Lave, J., and E. Wenger. 1991. *Situated Learning: Legitimate Peripheral Participation.* Cambridge: Cambridge University Press.

McConachie, S., M. Hall, L. Resnick, A. Ravie, V. Bill, J. Bintz, and J. Taylor. 2006. "Task, Text, and Talk: Literacy for All Subjects." *Educational Leadership*, October, 8–14.

Moulds, P. 2002. "Rich Tasks: Developing Student Learning Around Important Tasks." *Australian Science Teachers' Journal* 48 (4): 6–13.

Newmann, F., and Associates. 1996. *Authentic Achievement: Restructuring Schools for Intellectual Quality*, Chapter 1. San Francisco: Jossey-Bass.

Wiggins, G., and J. McTighe. 2005. *Understanding by Design.* New York: Simon and Schuster.

Notes

1. Some of the classroom examples in this section are based on research carried out in collaboration with the Department of Education and Training, New South Wales, 2004–2006 (see Gibbons 2008 and Hammond 2008).

2. "Display questions" (sometimes referred to as "known-answer" questions) are so called because their purpose is to test what a student knows; thus they are for display purposes only, since the teacher already knows the answer.

3. Chapter 6 describes a range of specific types of writing (or genres) used in different subject areas, of which a discussion is one.

3 | Literacy in the Curriculum
Challenges for EL Learners

> *In the absence of an explicit focus on language, children from certain . . . backgrounds continue to be privileged and others to be disadvantaged in learning, assessment, and promotion, perpetuating the obvious inequalities that exist today.*
> —Mary Schleppegrell,
> *The Language of Schooling*

This chapter illustrates some of the language difficulties faced by EL learners in academic reading and writing. The chapter, together with the chapter on writing, will show how school literacy requires students not only to be able to read and write in a general sense, but, as suggested in the previous chapter, to be able to use a range of subject-specific literacies. You will also find some suggestions in Chapter 4 about how to support EL learners' literacy development in the context of subject learning.

What Does It Mean to Be "Literate"?

Think for a moment about how you would define the term *literacy*. Sixty years ago it was described in the following terms (and note that it refers only to reading):

> Reading means getting meaning from certain combinations of letters. Teach the child what each letter stands for and he [sic] can read. Phonics is taught to the child letter by letter and sound by sound until he knows it—and when he knows it he knows how to read. (Farr and Roser 1979, 13, referring to a 1955 definition of literacy)

Success at school would be much easier for students if that is all they had to do to become literate! This definition suggests that becoming literate is something that once achieved is completed once and for all. Yet all of us can think of examples of how literacy learning goes on throughout one's lifetime. We are always being apprenticed into new forms of literacy (nowadays of course including the multiple modes of technological literacy). Early on in my university career I applied for the first time for research funding.

This kind of writing requires very specific ways of presenting a proposal, arguing for its merit in the broader research and social contexts, and describing the research process and data analysis. Despite thinking of myself as a "literate" person, this form of writing represented for me a new genre requiring new and specific ways of expressing ideas (if the proposal was to be taken seriously and accepted for funding) and a new challenge. As a novice in this writing, I consulted models, talked with others who had more knowledge than I did, and sought feedback on my first draft proposal. In other words, I needed to get explicit help to compose what was for me a new form of writing.

In the same way, we need to recognize that what for us may be familiar forms of literacy, whether reading or writing, may not be so for our students. For them, as the previous chapter suggested, the reading and writing tasks they undertake in the middle years represent unfamiliar ways of using language, and so being shown explicitly how to read and use these new forms of literacy is essential if they are to eventually use them for themselves.

We need also to remember that we all remain, even as adults, "nonliterate" in some areas. Unless you have studied linguistics, you might find the following text challenging:

> The general principle that emerges from this discussion, once again, is that since the trace is being interpreted as in effect a variable, surface structures with traces must meet the general conditions on expressions with variable-like expressions such as the reciprocal phrase "each other." Nothing further need be said, in these cases at least, to distinguish permissible from impermissible applications. (Chomsky 1976, 110)

If you find this text difficult to understand it is not because you are not "literate," but that you are unfamiliar with reading and writing *in this field*. Because it is an unfamiliar discipline (or field), you cannot easily interpret the meaning of the words on the page, even though you can read the passage aloud.

Here is a second example from a science textbook, which, if you are a science teacher, you will find very simple to read and understand. As a nonscientist I have some understanding of the text (in that I can understand the individual words), but I can't claim that I really understand the process that is being described, because I lack the relevant field knowledge: for me the words do not make much meaning, even though they are all familiar to me in other contexts.

> Compact discs use interference of light to store data. The surface of a compact disc is made of pits one quarter of a wavelength deep. Laser light is shone onto the disk. Some light is reflected back to the receiver. The light waves which hit the pits are destroyed, because the crests of the inwards waves line up with the troughs of the reflected waves. The receiver does not detect any light from the pits and they appear black. (Laidler and Sartor 2001, 88)

Being literate in a subject is not only about learning new vocabulary and knowing what those words mean in the context of the subject. It also involves seeing how they link within a broader conceptual framework. Thus we need to have some prior understanding of the key concepts, the "big ideas," embedded in that text. We need always to be mindful that even for fluent readers, written texts do not stand alone. For example, if I am told to "read that text for homework," I may (with difficulty) be able to memorize it but I still won't have any understanding of what I am reading because I have no conceptual "hooks" in my head on which to "hang" it.

Most teachers would agree that simply "parroting" something that has been read without understanding is not learning. Many of the ideas in this book focus on the use of spoken language in the classroom (or "substantive conversations," as this was called in Chapter 1). The reason for this is that providing time for students to engage in talk about disciplinary knowledge gives them opportunities to "talk their way in" to the complex ideas and concepts embedded in a subject, and they are then able to bring that understanding to the texts they read and write.

Literacy in the Curriculum

Language and content are inextricably entwined. Understanding terms like *probability* and *permutation* is inseparable from understanding the mathematical concepts they refer to, just as understanding the term *photosynthesis* cannot be separated from understanding the biological process it refers to. Subject-specific literacy is also closely tied to the ways of thinking and reasoning, and ways of reading and writing, that are valued in a particular subject. As suggested in Chapter 1, each subject "packages" knowledge differently from the everyday, spoken ways of using language. It also packages this knowledge in a different way from other academic subjects: each discipline has its own conventions and patterns of thinking that make it distinct from others. These differences include the reading of different types of texts and the use of different text structures, presentation formats, and ways of organizing language. As we saw in Chapter 1, so much academic language is subject related that it is probably more accurate to talk about *academic literacies* rather than *academic literacy*.

Developing the spoken and written literacy of a particular subject is a key to performing well on tests and assessments in content-area learning. But it is also a key to being an effective and independent learner in any intellectually challenging work. Being subject literate means understanding how the "big ideas" of the discipline are organized and evaluated and is thus related to being able to think and reason in subject-specific ways: think for example of the differences between carrying out an inquiry in science or in history or in social studies. Or consider the differences in what counts as central to the discipline. As a subject teacher, think about how you would answer the question, what is history really about? Or math? Or science?

McConachie et al. (2006) make the point very clearly that to build students' literacy in a specific discipline, teachers must focus on both content and process. They argue that

> to develop complex knowledge in any discipline, students need opportunities to read, reason, investigate, speak, and write about the overarching concepts within that

discipline. Because of time constraints and coverage concerns, many teachers understandably choose to teach either content or process instead of marrying the two. But to build students' literacy in a specific discipline, instruction must do both at once. (8)

However, despite the fact that most educators would agree that language is a central tool for cognitive development in school, as well as for developing subject-related knowledge, it is probably true to say that relatively few subject teachers explicitly focus on the teaching of language in their subject area. One of the reasons for this perhaps is that language is usually not seen as problematic by those who are fluent in it. For many subject teachers, the disciplinary language they read and write and speak is so familiar to them that it is easy not to notice it. Its difficulty may not be recognized by those who are most familiar with it. Much instruction about language in school is in fact implicit or incidental, precisely because many teachers are not used to looking at language itself. And so for many students, learning the language associated with the academic subjects of school is a little like learning a new language without any help! The metaphor of the fish in water is a good analogy: the fish doesn't recognize the water in which it swims. In relation to language and literacy in the subject areas, if subject teachers are not aware of the water (the language) in which they swim, then there may be very negative outcomes for many students, especially those who are unfamiliar with standard English. As one writer has commented, "Because we are immersed in an ocean of academic language daily, it's hard to notice the habits we automatically engage in to comprehend such language. . . . When we become aware of our own habits and strategies, we can model them and make them available to our students" (Zwiers 2005, 60–61).

To illustrate this point further, here is another metaphor. If you think of language as a glass window, then for people who have high levels of literacy in their own subject area, the glass of that window is transparent. Competent users of the language can look through the clear glass and know clearly the "content" of what is being talked (or read) about. The language doesn't get in the way, and the view through the window is clear. But for many students, the glass of that window is not transparent. Imagine it made of frosted glass, so that the content that students see is hazy and unclear: this is often the position for many EL learners if language is not made explicit. And so all teachers need to be able to hold language up to the light, to look *at* it, not *through* it, so that they are better able to support their students in using language appropriately in their subject. Every teacher in every subject needs to think of themselves as a teacher of language.

The visible and explicit approach to language learning and teaching that is advocated in this book begins with all teachers being able to be explicit about what students are required to do *in language* and *with language* in their subject. This chapter and those that follow aim to help you to begin to do this, to start thinking about teaching using a different "lens" and to think about the tasks that you require students to do not just in terms of the content, but in terms of the language needed to carry out the tasks. And so, if you are a subject teacher, think about how language is used in your discipline as you read these chapters. Ask yourself what kinds of thinking and reasoning are valued in your subject, what kinds of questions are asked, what kinds of texts you expect students to read, and what kinds of genres or texts they need to write. If, for example, you have students write a discussion, how do you expect them to structure that piece of writing, how should they present and support arguments and key ideas? If you want them to describe, evaluate, or explain, what kind of wording is appropriate in your subject to do those things? What kind of vocabulary do you expect them to use? How should conclusions be worded? If you are a specialist teacher of EL learners, then consider what the implications are for you in your literacy work with your students. For example, what kinds of texts should your students be reading and writing, and how does the teaching of specific grammatical structures and vocabulary of English relate to subject teaching?

What Makes Academic Language Difficult?

One of the major challenges in developing academic language is understanding the differences between spoken and written language. In this section we will look at the nature of written language in some detail and focus on what may be difficult for EL learners in particular.

Spoken and Written Language

There are important differences between spoken and written language that are potentially particularly challenging for EL learners. In an earlier book (Gibbons 2002) I illustrated how language varies according to the context in which it is used. The context for any piece of language is characterized by three features: what is being talked (or written) about; the relationship between the speaker and listener (or writer and reader); and whether the language is spoken or written (Halliday and Hasan 1985). How we use language in authentic contexts is determined and constrained by these contextual features. Think, for example, of the differences between a social studies text and a biology text. Or imagine yourself chatting with a friend at a party about what you've been doing recently and compare that with how you might respond to questions at a job interview about your work history. Or think about the differences between the way language is used when someone is demonstrating how to conduct a science experiment and the way the same information might be written as part of a scientific report later.

Halliday and Hasan (1985) refer to these contextual factors as *field*, *tenor*, and *mode*:

- *Field* refers to the topic of the text.
- *Tenor* refers to the relationship between speaker and listener (or writer and reader).
- *Mode* refers to the channel of communication, whether it is spoken or written.

Together these three variables constitute what is referred to as the *register* of a text. As children learn language, they gradually learn to vary the language they use according to the context in which they are using it. In other words, they learn to vary the *register* of the language so that it is appropriate for the context. That is just what children do at school of course, when they learn to use the different kinds of language associated with becoming literate in a range of subjects. One of the most significant things they learn to do as they move through school is to learn to talk, read, and write about an increasing range of subjects (or *fields*) in increasingly abstract and impersonal ways (using a more formal *tenor* and expressing what they have learned largely through the written *mode*). The fact that language, by its nature, varies according to context in this way is one of the most powerful arguments to teach EL learners through a program that integrates content and language learning. In an integrated program the curriculum provides a ready-made context for teaching the specific language for learning that is required by learners to participate in mainstream subject learning in authentic and meaningful ways.

An example of how language changes according to context is given in Figure 3.1. The four texts (a text is defined as a piece of complete, meaningful language, either spoken or written) all refer in various ways to the properties of magnets and to which materials are magnetic and nonmagnetic. The left-hand column shows the context in which the language is used, the middle column is the language (or text) itself, and the right-hand column is what the example shows us about the relationship between language and context. The four texts, taken together, represent a speaking-to-writing continuum, referred to in functional grammar as the *mode continuum*.

While the *field* of all four texts is the same (they are on the same topic), there are clearly considerable differences in the way in which the language is used. As they begin to refer to events not shared by listeners or readers, the vocabulary becomes more technical and subject, or *field*, specific; the *tenor* of the texts becomes more impersonal (notice how the personal references to *we* and *our* disappear); and the *mode* varies (the texts become increasingly more explicit and more like written language). Of course, we could continue this mode continuum: consider how magnetism might be written about in a university text book on physics.

As we can see from these four texts, the less shared knowledge there is between speaker and listener (or writer and reader), the more explicit language must become. In text 1 there is a lot of shared information between the speaker and listener—they are in the same situation and share visual contact. But when there are no cues from the visual context (texts 2 and 3) more and more information must be given through language. While EL learners may not have difficulties in talking in a face-to-face context (as in text 1) texts 2 and 3 place considerably more demand on their linguistic resources. And text 4 approximates the kind of academic language that eventually all students will have to control if they are to be seen as successful learners. As Martin (1984) expresses it, "The more speakers are doing things together and engaging in dialogue, the more they can take for granted. As language moves away from the events it describes, and the possibility of feedback is removed, more and more of the meanings must be made explicit in the text" (27).

Context of the Language	Text	What This Shows About Language and Context
Three children are talking face-to-face about an experiment they are doing to find out which of a range of objects are magnetic. They can all see the articles they are taking about, so they don't need to refer to them by name.	**Text 1** Look, *it's* making them move. *That's* not going. *Those* ones are going fast.	The meaning of here-and-now (face-to-face) language depends on the immediate context in which it occurs and includes such things as gestures, body language, or, as in this case, the materials being referred to. For example, if you couldn't see what the children were doing, *it's*, *that's*, and *those* would be impossible to interpret.
One of the same children is informing her classmates what she has learned. She does not have the materials with her. Therefore, for the benefit of the audience, who did not share the experience, she needs to explain what happened through language alone.	**Text 2** We found out the pins stuck on the magnet and so did the iron filings. Then we tried the pencil but it didn't stick.	Language becomes more explicit as less can be taken for granted by the speaker. For example, the speaker now has to refer to the names of the objects used (*iron filings, pins*) and give a more precise description of what happened (*stuck*).
The same learner has now written about what the group found out. The text is further distanced from the original concrete event, because the audience is now unseen. The speaker cannot take for granted shared experiences by the audience.	**Text 3** Our experiment was to find out what a magnet attracted. We discovered that a magnet attracts some kinds of metal. It attracted the iron filings and the pins but not the pencil.	Because written language cannot rely on shared assumptions and experiences, it must re-create experiences through language alone. Thus it becomes increasingly explicit. For example, in this case, for the benefit of the audience, the text needs to explain the context: *Our experiment was to find out . . . .*
This written text is an excerpt from an encyclopedia for children. The text is now about the properties of magnets in general. There is no mention of the specific people and things mentioned in texts 1, 2, and 3.	**Text 4** A magnet is a piece of metal that is surrounded by an invisible field of force which affects any magnetic material within it. It is able to attract a piece of iron or steel because its magnetic field flows into the metal, turning it into a temporary magnet. Magnetic attraction occurs only between ferrous metals.	Written academic language is more abstract and less personal than informal conversational language. Written language is typically "denser" than spoken language, with more information "packed in." (For more information about the characteristics of written language, see the following section about the features of academic language.)

Figure 3.1. From Talking to Writing: The Mode Continuum

Cummins (2000) uses the terms *context-embedded* and *context-reduced* to refer to the distinction between the registers of "everyday" language (like text 1) and the more academic registers of school (like text 4). He has shown that whereas a second language learner is likely to develop conversational language quite rapidly—usually within one or two years—the registers associated with academic learning may take between five and seven years for the learner to develop at a level equivalent to a competent native speaker of the same age (see also Collier 1989 and McKay et al. 1997). These school-related registers, as text 4 shows, tend to be more abstract and less personal and contain more subject-specific language. While most EL learners have little difficulty expressing themselves in more everyday contexts, many may not, without intervention, be able to control the academic registers associated with the later stages of learning in secondary school. This is partly because of the increasing language complexity but also because EL learners are effectively catching up with a moving target: English native speakers are also not standing still in their language development.

One of the classroom implications for recognizing the relationship between spoken and written language that is illustrated by the mode continuum is to provide many opportunities for students to use what Chang and Wells (1988) refer to as "literate talk," that is, talk like text 2. In this kind of talk, students talk about ideas and experiences in a context that requires them to be explicit for the benefit of their listeners. As the mode continuum illustrates, this more explicit language creates a "bridge" between the everyday or face-to-face language and the more abstract and formal language associated with academic literacy.

Two Features of Academic Language

Two features of academic language make it distinct from the everyday face-to-face language with which learners are likely to be familiar. These two features are *nominalizations* and *nominal groups*. Understanding the structure of these two features of written English will help you recognize a major factor in what makes academic language difficult for your students, and so help you support your students in understanding these features in reading and using them when appropriate in their own writing.

Nominalization

Here are examples of two texts that convey similar information (from Droga and Humphrey 2003, 101). Both texts are grammatically correct, and both would be appropriate in certain contexts. As you read them consider how the two texts differ and which one would be more highly assessed as a more appropriate piece of writing in the later years of school.

Text 1

When people **clear** land for houses and roads they **change** the environment. They **destroy** the forest and bushland and then many animals **lose their homes**. More houses and roads will **pollute** the environment even more. Some animals have become **extinct** because their homes have been **destroyed**.

Text 2

Clearing and development of land often results in the **destruction** of the natural habitat of many local species. It may also increase the level of **pollution**. **Loss of habitat** has already led to the **extinction** of many species of animals.

You have probably concluded that although text 1 is quite appropriate for younger learners or as a piece of informal spoken language, text 2 is likely to be more highly evaluated in the later years of school. What are the differences between the texts? If you have looked closely at the language, one of the things you have probably noticed is that many of the verbs in text 1 (the words that describe what people are doing and what is happening) have become nouns in text 2 (they now refer to *things* or *concepts*). These changes are illustrated in Figure 3.2.

This process of changing verbs into nouns is called *nominalization*. Nominalization serves a particular and very important purpose in English: it allows a writer to structure information so that he or she can express abstract ideas (such as *development, destruction, pollution,* and *extinction*). Nominalization becomes increasingly important as students move through primary and secondary school. Textbooks use it to package more information into sentences and discuss subject-based abstract concepts. Increasingly as students move through high school, they are expected to use nominalizations in their writing to demonstrate that they understand the more abstract concepts in these subjects.

However, using nominalizations is not a case of using complex language simply for effect! Rather, it allows the writer to focus on key abstract ideas rather than on persons and events. As a result of using nominalization, the writer of text 2 is able to focus on some key ecological concepts: *clearing and development of land, destruction* and *loss of habitat,* and the *extinction of many species of animals.* Compare this to text 1, where the focus of the sentences is *people* (or *they*), *houses and roads,* and *animals* and their *homes.* This more spokenlike language in text 1, while quite appropriate in the early years of

VERBS (name what is happening)	NOUNS (name things or concepts)
clear	clearing
change	development
destroy	destruction
lose (their homes)	loss (of habitat)
pollute	pollution
extinct	extinction

Figure 3.2. Changing Verbs to Nouns

school, constrains the writer to producing what is basically a sequenced explanation of events. The use of nominalization in text 2, however, allows the writer to focus on "big ideas" or important key concepts, something that isn't possible with the grammatical resources that are used in text 1. This process of nominalization is typical of much written language, because it is very often the general concept or phenomenon we want to talk about, rather than the people and processes around a specific event.

Nominalization is therefore one of the major differences between spoken and written language. Figure 3.2 illustrates the process of turning words that are normally verbs into nouns. But other kinds of words can also be turned into nouns. Figure 3.3 illustrates how verbs, conjunctions, adjectives, and whole clauses or sentences can all be nominalized.

As an educated person, and as a teacher who has probably spent many years studying at a university, you probably consider yourself a good writer. And you probably use nominalization in any formal writing you produce, without considering what you are doing. But this ability to use nominalization develops very late in children's language use. Research has suggested that even most native English-speaking students do not *systematically* use this in their writing until they are about 12 or 13 years old (Derewianka 2003). (And some people may never learn to control it fully, which is one reason even some adults' writing may sound "less sophisticated" or "wordy.") The reason for this late development in young learners, of course, is that this kind of language is mainly associated with written rather than spoken language, and it occurs more frequently in

VERBS educate refract erode	NOUNS education refraction erosion
CONJUNCTION The driver lost his license **because** he was driving too fast. There was a famine **because of** the drought.	NOUN **The reason** for the driver's losing his license was his driving speed. The drought was **the cause** of the famine.
ADJECTIVE The resources were very **scarce** so the school closed.	NOUN The **scarcity of resources** resulted in the school closing.
WHOLE CLAUSE/SENTENCE **The drought was very long and so many people starved.**	**The length of the drought** caused **mass starvation**.

Figure 3.3. Turning Various Words and Groups of Words into Nouns

academic or more formal contexts. It is not until around puberty that learners are exposed to this register on a day-to-day basis through the school texts they read and in the writing they are expected to do. And so for EL learners, learning to manipulate language in this quite complex way is an even bigger challenge.

It is often necessary to first learn a new technical word before it is possible to create a nominalization or general concept. For example, it isn't easy to nominalize a non-technical or "everyday" term such as *spread out* in this sentence from a science text: *Water waves spread out through a small opening.* (We would have to talk about *the spreading out of the water waves.*) However if we replace *spread out* with the more technical *disperse*, it becomes possible to talk about *dispersion.* Here is the text from which that sentence is taken:

> **Refraction** is the bending of waves. Waves that have been bent are said to have been refracted. Water waves are refracted when they move into shallow water. Water waves move slower in shallow water than in deeper water. Water waves spread out, or disperse, through a small opening. This is called **dispersion**. The waves spread out and lose most of their energy. They are much smaller than before. This is often seen in boat harbors and marinas. (Adapted from Laidler and Sartor 2002, 68)

The writers here have used a number of ways to help make this text more accessible to young readers. First, they have used everyday terms (*bend*, *spread out*) to give students a general idea of the concept. They have used an everyday concrete example with which the students may be familiar: *This is often seen in boat harbors and marinas.* And they have introduced more technical terms for the everyday terms (*refract* and *disperse* instead of *bend* and *spread out*), leading to the abstract idea of *dispersion.* So we can see a movement in the language and in the level of abstraction:

> bend → refract → refraction
> spread out → disperse → dispersion (with the concrete example of boats and harbors)

This process allows students to bring familiar everyday language to the learning of the more abstract language needed to express the notions of *refraction* and *dispersion*. And importantly, the writers haven't simplified the text by *avoiding* the use of technical language. Rather, they have used the appropriate terms *refraction* and *dispersion* but made these terms *comprehensible* by using familiar everyday language and concrete experiences as a basis for this more complex and abstract language.

This short example suggests a number of important teaching and learning principles that are relevant for all learners but that have special significance for EL learners learning to read complex texts:

- Go from the everyday, familiar, and concrete to the subject specific, unfamiliar, and abstract.
- Use concrete examples that are familiar to students and that link to their own real-world and out-of-school experiences.

- Use familiar language to talk about these experiences before moving to more specialized subject language.
- In your program planning, sequence teaching and learning activities in such a way that you move *toward* the specialized language of the written texts student will read rather than beginning with the written texts.

Nominal Groups

The other way that written academic language "packages" information (and this is another source of difficulty for students new to a subject) is to make use of a group of words, often a very long group of words, that represent a single thing but carry a great deal of information. Here is an example (adapted from the science section of *The Guardian Weekly*, July 6, 2007) of how such groups are built up (try guessing what it is that is being referred to!):

By itself, a single noun like this gives us very little information:

a beast

But we could extend it to give a more detailed picture:

a fearsome beast

And we can continue adding information until the group of words describing the noun becomes quite long:

a fearsome beast with a beak
a fearsome beast with an 18cm beak
a fearsome beast with an 18cm beak, powerful wings, and a chunky neck.
Icadyptes salasi, a fearsome beast with an 18cm beak, powerful wings, and a chunky neck.
a giant penguin, Icadyptes salasi, a fearsome beast with an 18cm beak, powerful wings, and a chunky neck.
a fossil of a giant penguin, Icadyptes salasi, a fearsome beast with an 18cm beak, powerful wings, and a chunky neck.
Scientists recently discovered <u>a fossil of a giant penguin, Icadyptes salasi, a fearsome beast with an 18cm beak, powerful wings, and a chunky neck</u>.

Extended groups of words like this, referring to a noun, are called *a noun group* or a *nominal group*. Of course a nominal group may be much shorter than this, consisting of just two or three words: the writer could have simply written *a fossil of an enormous penguin*. An easy way to recognize a nominal group is to see if you can replace it with a pronoun like *it, he, she, they*. (And anytime you need to remind yourself what a nominal group is, just think of the penguin!)

A long nominal group.

The article continues, "Scientists recently discovered a fossil of a giant penguin, Icadyptes salasi, a fearsome beast with an 18cm beak, powerful wings, and a chunky neck. The discovery has shaken scientists' understanding of penguin evolution." Here you can see how nominalization and nominal groups have combined to create a very "dense" piece of language and how a nominalization (such as *evolution*) may itself be part of a nominal group (*scientists' **understanding** of penguin **evolution***). The combination of these two features is often the reason for the "density" of much written language, especially in academic or subject-specific contexts. At the same time, nominalizations and nominal groups are important language resources for students to master because:

- They create abstract and technical terms (such as *discovery, evolution, refraction*).
- They "condense" information in texts and so make it possible to be more precise and concise (try, for example, to explain the term *evolution* without using the word, or expressing in everyday language the nominal group *scientists' understanding of penguin evolution*).
- They allow us to talk about a general concept or phenomenon rather than the individual people and processes around a particular event.

Because this dense language carries a large amount of information, it may cause comprehension difficulties for students if the content is not already familiar; this in turn may create barriers to successful reading. Therefore the learning of new concepts must start with classroom talk around what students already know in terms of the content, drawing on the everyday language with which they are likely to be familiar, and with concrete examples related to students' everyday life (see Chapter 4). The development of academic language and the English language standards must become part of broader subject-learning objectives and outcomes.

These examples of the complexity of written language show that academic literacy is very much more than simply decoding and comprehension. They also show that learning the kinds of technical language we find in academic contexts is not simply a question of learning new vocabulary, although this is certainly a significant part of subject-related literacy and helps define each content area. But being literate in a subject also means knowing how to manipulate the forms and structures of "everyday" spoken language in new ways to express more concisely and precisely the complex ideas and concepts that are embedded in the content of a subject and that are essential for learning in that subject. Subject-related academic language is the way it is because of the job it has to do as a tool for making meanings that are relevant and concise within particular disciplinary communities. So the next time you dismiss something as "jargon," remember that it's only jargon when it's part of someone else's discipline!

Summary

This chapter has introduced some key ideas about literacy and the nature of academic language, which show that understanding the complexity of written language requires much more than simple decoding and basic comprehension skills. The chapter also discusses some of the teaching implications for helping EL learners develop more advanced literacy skills. Major points include:

- Literacy is not something learned once: we continue developing our literacy skills throughout life.
- Learning subject-specific literacy needs to be seen as a part of learning subject content, and needs to be explicitly taught and discussed.
- Language varies (in field, tenor, and/or mode) according to the context in which it is used. There are significant differences between spoken and written language.
- The difficulty of academic language is related not simply to unfamiliar vocabulary but to the way that the language is structured—for example, the use of nominalizations and nominal groups that "condense" information and make it possible to be more precise and concise.
- In teaching academic literacy, it is helpful to move from students' concrete or prior experiences and familiar everyday language toward more specialized and abstract subject-specific language.

To Think About . . .

1. How can you use the information about language in this chapter in your work with your EL learners?
2. If you are a subject teacher, what are some of the key literacy demands of your subject?
3. If you are an upper elementary teacher, what are some of the literacy demands faced by your learners in their mainstream work? Make a note of these; later chapters include many related teaching ideas.

4. If you teach older students, look at some examples of the textbooks that are used in your school or class. Identify some specific passages where the language may cause difficulties for EL learners. Make a note of these.
5. What are the implications of the chapter for collaborative planning and teaching between subject teachers and EL teachers?

Suggestions for Further Reading

Butt, D., R. Fahey, S. Feez, S. Spinks, and C. Yallup. 2000. *Using Functional Grammar: An Explorer's Guide*. Sydney: National Centre for English Language Teaching and Research, Macquarie University.

De Silva Joyce, H. 2005. *Developing Writing Skills*. Teacher Resource Book. Sydney: Phoenix Education.

Droga, L., and S. Humphrey. 2003. *Grammar and Meaning: An Introduction for Primary Teachers*. Berry, NSW: Target Texts. Available from www.targettexts.com.

4 | Engaging with Academic Literacy
Examples of Classroom Activities

The research recommends that literacy skills and strategies be taught and used in the context of reading, writing, and learning, rather than solely or primarily practiced in isolation. This is the direct opposite of "skill and drill" worksheets often used for remediation.

—Julie Meltzer and Edmund Hamann, "Meeting the Literacy Needs of Adolescent English Language Learners Through Content-Area Learning, Part 2"

What This Chapter Is About

This chapter discusses principles, strategies, and activities to support student engagement with academic literacy in all curriculum areas. Although these principles and activities are particularly relevant for EL learners, they are equally valuable in supporting the academic literacy development of all students. The first section of the chapter introduces some broad principles for developing academic language in the context of subject classrooms; the second section gives examples of specific activities and strategies that can be integrated with any subject teaching. You will find further ideas for developing reading and writing in Chapters 5 and 6, and for supporting oral language development in Chapter 7.

General Principles for Developing Academic Literacy

As Chapter 3 suggested, academic language and literacy needs to be taught and used in context, an approach that is strongly supported by research (see, for example, Langer

2001; Meltzer and Hammon 2005). This is a very different approach from the decontextualized "skill and drill" exercises taught in isolation and commonly associated with remediation. But there is considerable evidence that the explicit teaching of academic language and literacy, *modeled and practiced in context*, enhances the learning of EL learners (Meltzer and Hammon 2005). There is also evidence that EL learners, like all learners, learn best when the classroom organization includes a mix of whole-class work, group work, pair work, and individual work, along with a mix of direct instruction and student-centered collaborative work. The teaching and learning activities in this chapter and those that follow are based on the principle that there is no single "right" kind of classroom organization or task. What is important is that the task and the classroom grouping are the most effective for the particular teaching focus at that point.

Implement a "Janus Curriculum": Develop Academic Language on the Basis of What Students Already Know

Janus was the Roman god of doors and entrances, always depicted with two faces, each looking in opposite directions. An effective curriculum for EL learners also looks in two directions: at what the students bring in terms of prior learning, experience, understanding, and skills, and at the curriculum outcomes and standards that are your focus. In a Janus curriculum, prior learning and the everyday language with which students are familiar together provide a bridge to new learning and academic language and literacies. New learning proceeds on the basis of what students already know, and this includes connecting school learning with students' personal out-of-school experiences.

Finding out what students already know can include, if it is relevant, letting students tell their own stories. One grade 6 teacher, introducing a text on earthquakes, began by asking students about their own experiences. About a third of the class had had some experience of being in an earthquake, and there followed an interesting half hour of students' stories, in which they described what had happened, what the earthquake had felt like, how they had felt, and the damage it had caused. Personal narratives are a powerful way to engage students and to value what they know, build shared knowledge on which future learning can be developed, and provide opportunities to begin developing topic-specific vocabulary. This is also a context in which the students can use their first language.

The teacher followed up the stories by having the students read a description of an earthquake; because many of the students were from Southeast Asia, and several were from Japan, she chose a passage about the earthquake that devastated Tokyo in 1923. Before they began reading she asked them what words they would expect to find in the passage and wrote these words as a semantic web on the board. Thinking back to their previous storytelling session, the students suggested words such as *disaster, buildings, shake, earthquake, fall down, killed, injured, Richter scale,* and *destroy.* When they had made as many suggestions as they were able (sometimes by using their first language with their peers to determine an English equivalent) the teacher then added, using a different-color pen, additional words that were in the text that she thought might be difficult for the students. These included *aftershock, scale of destruction, tsunami, seismic,* and *victims*. In this way new vocabulary was introduced in context, and the students were now keen to read the text. This introduction generated much discussion and interest in the topic and provided some shared understandings for the more science-focused classes that followed.

Move Toward *Complex Texts, Don't Begin with Them*

Part of what the Janus curriculum means in practice is that teachers think in terms of moving *toward* academic language, rather than beginning a unit with a heavy load of new subject vocabulary and concepts. A difficult academic text is not the place to start! This is especially important for EL learners who are still relatively new to English. Chapter 3 illustrated the notion of the "mode continuum" and suggested that teaching activities be sequenced from those that involve everyday language to those that increasingly involve more written or subject-specific language. *Moving toward academic language* is a similar principle. Most mainstream textbooks are written with the assumption that the students who will read them are already familiar with spoken English. As we know, this is often not the case, particularly when the textbook is laden with unfamiliar concepts and subject-related language. Constantly stopping and explaining words and phrases to EL students as they are reading can disrupt the lesson and, for the student, disrupt the reading process. Rather than giving on-the-spot explanations, it is better to see the text as an end point and to prepare students for reading it by developing an overall understanding of the content first, *before* having students tackle the text alone. As in the textbook example about the refraction of waves in Chapter 3, concepts can initially be introduced using familiar words and concrete examples, together with visuals such as diagrams, illustrations, computer simulations, concrete objects, or other realia. In this context, you can begin to model the more academic language that students will find in the textbook.

I use this approach in my own university teaching, since many of my postgraduate students are studying complex texts in their second language. I usually have a couple of readings to accompany each session, and I have found that the students gain far more in-depth understanding of the readings when they read them *after* the class, rather than reading them as a preparation for the class. My students (and not only those for whom English is a second language) have commented many times that they find complex readings much more accessible when they have already developed some prior insights into the topic during the class, because this prior knowledge provides a "peg" on which to hang the academic language they meet in the reading. Having some knowledge of the topic before they read about it also allows them to take a more critical orientation to what they are reading.

You will find more about making written texts accessible to students in Chapter 5.

Model the Use of Academic Language in Your Interactions with Students

As you talk with students, model appropriate language in your responses to them. Chapter 7 discusses this in detail, but a brief example is included in Figure 4.1. This conversation occurred in an elementary classroom after students had participated in small-group experiments that were designed to show that like poles of a magnet repel and unlike attract. One student is reporting what happened to the rest of the class, while the teacher interacts with him and provides guidance and scaffolding.

STUDENTS	TEACHER
	What were your results, Charbel?
When we put it on one pole . . . um, faces the other one it doesn't stick, but when we turned the other one around, it sticks together.	
	Like that [*demonstrating*]. They attracted to each other, they stuck to each other. Is that right?
[*Nods.*]	Okay, can you then tell me what you had to do next?
When we had, um, the things, the first one, like if you put it up in the air like that, the magnets, you can feel . . . feel the, um . . . that they're not pushing?	
	When you turn the magnet around? You felt that . . .
Pushing and if we use the other side we can't feel pushing.	
	Okay, so when they were facing one way, you felt the magnets attract and stick together. When you turned one of the magnets around you felt it *repelling*, or pushing away. Thank you, Charbel.

Figure 4.1. Bringing Talk Together

everyday and informal ◄————————————————► subject specific		
like this *(demonstrating with magnets)*	stick to, push away *(everyday language)*	attract, repel *(subject-specific language)*

Figure 4.2. "Meshing" Everyday and Academic Language

In Chapter 3 the relationship between spoken and written language was illustrated by the "mode continuum," and it was suggested that students need opportunities to interact in contexts that require the use of more "literate talk." These kinds of conversations provide a bridge between their everyday talk and the more explicit talk associated with academic literacy. Figure 4.1 is an example of what that might look like in practice. Although the learner doesn't at this point take up the subject-specific language himself, you can see how the teacher uses the student's language to model it. She takes up or "appropriates" the language of the student, while at the same time modeling scientific language (*attract and stick together; repelling or pushing away*). She also demonstrates what happens using two bar magnets. In this way she uses language at various points along the mode continuum (see Figure 4.2).

This kind of teacher-student discourse "meshes" everyday and subject-specific ways of meaning, thus building on students' prior knowledge and current language as a way of introducing them to new language. It offers learners several ways of understanding key concepts: in this example this occurred through the teacher's demonstration, through her use of everyday language, and through the modeling of subject-specific language. Typically such talk moves from everyday to academic talk, but may also travel in reverse, as when teachers ask learners to explain key concepts in more everyday ways. This is also important, for we do not want learners simply to "parrot" academic language without understanding.

This Janus-like talk is in fact a common feature of much of the talk between teachers and students in many classrooms, yet teachers are not always consciously aware of what they are doing, nor of its usefulness for EL learners. But being aware of the language we use with students in all classroom interactions is part of being a language-aware teacher. Understanding the relationship between spoken and written language, or between "everyday" and "academic" language, is an important part of this awareness.

Talk About Language: Develop a Metalanguage with Students

Using language to talk about language (often called *metalanguage*) with students is one way of making language more visible. It is often very helpful to EL learners to use some key metalanguage in the context of supporting their reading and writing in your subject. The purpose of this is not simply to name a grammatical structure (which by itself is probably of little use) but rather to draw students' attention to how certain aspects of language function, and how they make it possible to talk about abstract ideas in concise ways. For example, by comparing written and spoken ways of explaining a difficult concept, you can show students how nominalizations and nominal groups make it possible to express complex ideas more concisely and precisely (see the examples in Chapter 3).

When we name something, it is more likely to be noticed, recognized, and used. As Christie (1990) has argued, "To be alert to the ways that one's language works for creating and organizing meaning is to be conscious of how to manipulate and use it" (22). Becoming familiar with terms like *nominalization* and *nominal groups* can provide learners with a resource and a tool for their own reading, writing, and language development. For example, you could get students to underline the nominal groups or nominalizations in a text they are reading. This will help them to recognize the structure of sentences that may otherwise appear very dense. Breaking down language in this way, into manageable parts and into the elements of the sentence, will help make reading easier. Teaching about language in this way is of course much more effective if it becomes something that all teachers in the school do, so that teachers and students share a common language about language.

Integrating Language Activities with Content Teaching

In language learning classrooms, there are broadly two types of language-learning activities:

- *Communicative activities*, where the focus is primarily on *using* language in order to complete a task. Language is used in a meaningful context for authentic purposes.
- *Form-focused activities*, where the focus is on learning *about* language. The activity centers on the language itself.

Using Language: Communicative Activities

In a communicative activity something happens as a result of the language being used; there is an outcome, apart from language learning, such as a problem being solved or a solution found. A key principle in communicative activities is that there should be an "information gap"; that is, the participants do not all have access to the same information and must share their own information in order to complete the task. Thus these activities are structured in such a way that they *require* students to use language in order for the task to be completed. Many of the activities described later in this chapter, such as split dictation and barrier crossword, are examples of communicative activities.

Learning About Language: Form-Focused Activities

Traditional grammar-focused activities are often "exercise-type" activities, the aim of which is to improve students' knowledge about how language works. As far as possible, pedagogic (or grammar-based) tasks should always be in the context of students' developing skills and language knowledge that they will later use in an authentic context. For example, students may learn about the rhetorical structure of a written argument, and the conjunctions used to introduce each point, in order to write a letter to a local newspaper about a contentious issue. Learning about grammar and language usage without a relevant context in which to use the language is likely to be of very limited use (as Chapter 2 suggested, this is like shaving a melon without the context of learning to be a barber!).

Language Activities as a Continuum

Historically there has been much debate about the value of each of these types of activities, and sometimes they have been held up as representing polarized approaches to language teaching. But from the perspective of an integrated content–language program, it is probably much more useful to think of all language-learning activities as ranging along a continuum: on the one hand, those that use language for real-world-like tasks (such as writing a class letter to a newspaper about a local community issue), and on the other, those that are essentially pedagogic tasks that focus more specifically on the form and structure of language (such as a cloze exercise that focuses on subject-specific vocabulary). Both will be useful at particular times, depending on the purpose of the activity. And there are many activities that could be located on the continuum between these two types of tasks.

However, once EL learners are beyond the beginning stages of English, often the most effective language-learning activities are those that encapsulate both aims: they allow for learning *about* language in the context of *using* language. Dictogloss and joint construction, both described below, are examples. These are often the most valuable types of language activities, because they focus students' attention on the language learning that is immediately relevant and useable, while maintaining an equal focus on meaning.

The following activities can easily be integrated into regular content teaching.

Progressive Brainstorm

This is a way for students to share what they already know about a topic at the beginning of a unit:

1. Divide students into groups of four or five and give each group a large piece of paper in the center of which is a circle with the statement, *What we know about [the particular topic]*. Each group has a different-color pen.
2. As a group, students brainstorm what they already know about the topic, writing down the words or concepts they associate with it around the circle (as in a semantic web).

3. After a few minutes, each group moves on to the next group's table, *leaving their brainstorm paper behind* but keeping their particular-color pen.
4. On the next group's paper they add their ideas, using the previous group's ideas as a springboard for things they hadn't thought of earlier, or adding things they think are missing.
5. The groups continue moving until all the groups have contributed to all the papers and are back in their original position.
6. Each group discusses what is now written on their original paper, noting any relevant additions or critiquing anything they disagree with.
7. The papers are put on the wall, and each group briefly reports on any comments they have or anything they have learned from other groups.

A progressive brainstorm helps build shared knowledge in the class and assists the teacher in assessing students' current knowledge and thinking around a topic.

Wallpapering

Wallpapering is another way of brainstorming information or ideas:

1. Give groups of students small sheets of paper on which to write down one thing they know about a topic or one point of view they have about a controversial issue (one point only per paper, in a brief sentence). The papers are anonymous.
2. After a few minutes, one person from each group sticks up the group's papers on the walls of the classroom.
3. Students walk around and read and evaluate one another's ideas. They need to find at least three papers that they can comment on (for example, something they didn't know or something they hadn't considered).
4. Later they can contribute comments as a whole class: *I agree with the one that said . . . ; I didn't know that . . . ; I didn't understand the one that said . . . .* Give the writer of the paper an opportunity to comment.

Semantic Web/Concept Map

A semantic web, or concept map, is a well-known way of collecting, recording, and organizing information. A key word relevant to the topic at hand is written in the middle of a large piece of paper. Students contribute information they know about the topic. It may begin as a brainstorm, with students recalling what they already know and the words and concepts they associate with the key word. Later you may ask students to look for information and ideas that connect with one another. These clusters of ideas can either form the basis of a new map or can be highlighted, a different color for each cluster of ideas. Whenever there is an opportunity, model key academic terms in place of everyday language suggested by the students. The semantic map can also be added to throughout a unit, so that it becomes a visual summary of the key concepts developed. A semantic web, or concept map, is a good way of developing shared knowledge on which future work, such as a piece of writing, can be based.

Dictogloss

A dictogloss (first developed by Ruth Wajnryb 1990) is useful for providing models of academic language. At the same time it gives students opportunities to listen, talk, read, write, make notes, reflect on language use, clarify content, and use academic language for themselves. In a dictogloss, the teacher reads aloud a text on a topic about which students already have some knowledge. It is therefore appropriate toward the end of a unit when most of the ideas and vocabulary will be familiar. The basic purpose is for students, in groups, to jointly reconstruct the text after it has been read to them. The reconstruction should contain the same information as the original, although it does not have to be in exactly the same wording. However, the language does have to be accurate and appropriate for expressing the ideas in the text. The text should be quite short; a piece which takes you about a minute to read at normal speed would be about right. It could be taken from a textbook or be something you have written yourself.

1. Read the text aloud (at normal speed) to the students. They just listen.
2. Read the text aloud a second time, while students listen again.
3. Read the text aloud a third time, still at normal speed. This time the students individually write down as much as they can of the key points and key phrases in the text. Tell them that you don't expect them to write down all the information at this stage, just some key points. Their notes at this stage will probably consist of fragments of information and isolated words. Reassure them that is all that is required at this stage.
4. Once the students have completed their individual note making, they share with a partner what they have written down. In pairs, the students work together to produce a new version of what they wrote individually.
5. After five or ten minutes, ask the partners to form groups of four. The students again work collaboratively to improve on what they were able to produce in pairs. As a group of four, they then rewrite the whole text legibly on a large sheet of paper. Remind them that this final version should have the same overall meaning as the original, with accurate grammar and spelling. However, it does not have to be identical to the original. Typically, students will talk about the information contained in the text, and since they are writing, they are also likely to be talking about the language itself. As students are working, encourage them to use their knowledge of English to check that the grammar of their text is accurate, reminding them, for example, to check the endings of nouns and verbs, subject-verb agreement, and the spelling of technical words.
6. Display all the texts around the room, and then show the original text to the students. Invite them to talk about any differences between the original and their own text; for example, they may have used alternative words or phrases, which can lead to a discussion about whether the meaning remains the same.

Surprisingly, although completing a dictogloss seems a difficult exercise (given that the writing is based on only three oral readings), students are usually very successful in eventually reconstructing the text. This is a good opportunity to remind students of the value of working collaboratively! A dictogloss provides an excellent context for integrating content and language, and for integrating listening, speaking, reading, and writing. It also provides a context for talking with students *about* language in the context of *using* language, as well as a model for a subject-based piece of written language.

Joint Construction

This activity is also described in Chapter 6 in the context of teaching writing and is valuable for focusing students' attention on how written language is structured. Teacher and students jointly write a text together, the teacher scribing on the board and the students contributing ideas and suggesting wording. Joint construction (also called *shared writing*) is commonly used with very young children who are learning early literacy.

In the example below, the teacher is co-constructing the beginning of a narrative about a witch with some elementary students. She acts as scribe and guide, encouraging the children to reread as they compose, writing up their suggestions, deleting or adding words, and reminding them what they know about narrative writing. In these ways she helps students reshape the wording of their initial suggestions.

Teacher:	So we've got our title, and we've talked about what's going to happen. So how could we begin?
Student 1:	*One day.* [*Teacher scribes.*]
Student 2:	No, *once upon a time.* [*Teacher scribes underneath the previous suggestion.*]
Student 3:	*Once upon a time there was a witch.* [*Teacher adds the additional words.*]
Student 4:	*And she lived in a dark wood.* [*Teacher scribes.*]
Teacher:	Okay, let's try another beginning, to see if we can make it more exciting. Remember this is the orientation, so what do we need to do here?
Student 5:	Make the person reading it . . . make them interested.
Student 6:	And they want to go on reading.
Student 2:	And we give details about who and what and where.
Teacher:	Right, so what do you think we . . . ?
Student 5:	*There was a witch who lived in a dark wood.* [*Teacher scribes.*]
Teacher:	Is there another way we could start that sentence? Who's got another idea?
Student 5:	We could say, *In a dark wood a witch lived.* [*Teacher scribes underneath the previous suggestion.*]
Teacher:	Let's read that together.
All:	*In a dark wood a witch lived.*

Teacher:	How does that sound? *In a dark wood a witch lived. . . .* Does anyone want to change that a little bit?
Student 4:	*There lived a witch.*
Teacher:	Let's read it again.
All:	*In a dark wood there lived a witch.*
Teacher:	Which one sounds better: *There was a witch who lived in a dark wood,* or, *In a dark wood there lived a witch?*
Several Students:	The second one.
Teacher:	Why do you say that?
Student 3:	Because it sort of begins with where she lived, and it gives the idea of something scary.
Teacher:	So starting with *In a dark wood* is more effective, you mean?
Several Students:	Yes. [*Teacher crosses out the earlier suggestion.*]
Student 5:	*A bad witch.*
Teacher:	Good. How else could we describe her? What's another way of saying *bad?*
Student 7:	*An evil witch.* [*Teacher adds* evil.]
Student 8:	*An evil witch with green eyes!* [*Teacher extends the sentence.*]
Teacher:	Good, let's reread that and see what it sounds like now.
All:	*In a dark wood there lived an evil witch with green eyes.*
Student 7:	We could say *scary green eyes!*
Teacher:	Yes . . . and now what do we need at the end?
Several Students:	A period.

Joint constructions are also very useful in higher grades, although they are typically used much less often. For example, a teacher could use it to demonstrate to students how to write a science explanation, how to write an introduction to a discussion of a novel, or how to present an argument in a discussion text. The role of the teacher is to act as an editor, discussing with the students how to organize and present ideas; drawing attention to unclear or inaccurate wording, spelling, and punctuation; clarifying meaning; and helping students make improvements by inviting suggestions from the class.

Joint constructions have the advantage of demonstrating both the process and product of writing: they model the process of writing, and they create a final product as a model for students' own writing. Like a dictogloss they also create a context in which teacher and students can talk *about* language—overall structure, conjunctions, sentence grammar, spelling, punctuation—in the context of *using* language authentically. They can also be used to focus students' attention on the differences between spoken and written language so that the formal aspects of language can be explicitly focused on in the context of producing a meaningful text.

The Last Word

This activity (based on Garmston 2005) is an interesting variation on a normal group discussion. It cannot replace such a discussion in all contexts, but has some advantages that regular discussion does not. It is based on a text that students have read, on a topic with which they are familiar. The best kind of text to use is one that may be contentious or on a topic about which students have some opinions and background knowledge. Begin by asking students to underline *one sentence* that is significant to them and about which they have something to say. They may say why they agree or disagree with the sentence or explain why it is significant to them. The most important thing is that they have something to say. They should be prepared to speak for approximately a minute about the sentence they have chosen.

Then, in groups of four, students number themselves 1, 2, 3, or 4. Each group then follows the process described below, moving clockwise around the group.

Step 1

Number 1 reads his or her sentence but *doesn't say anything about it.*

Number 2 comments on number 1's sentence (*not* his or her own). He or she should aim to talk for about a minute.

Number 3 comments on number 1's sentence (*not* his or her own). (If he or she wishes, he or she may build on what number 2 has said or may take a different perspective.)

Number 4 comments on number 1's sentence (*not* his or her own).

Finally Number 1 comments on his or her sentence, incorporating others' ideas and his or her original ideas.

Step 2

Number 2 reads her or his sentence but *doesn't say anything about it.*

Number 3 comments on number 2's sentence (*not* his or her own).

Number 4 comments on number 2's sentence (*not* his or her own).

Number 1 comments on number 2's sentence (*not* his or her own).

Finally Number 2 comments on his or her sentence, incorporating others' ideas and his or her original ideas.

Steps 3 and 4 continue in the same way: first student number 3 and then student number 4 reads his or her sentence, and the others comment as above.

The most important rule is that *there must be no cross-discussion.* Each person should aim to talk for about a minute and must be allowed to have the floor for this time. Explain to the students that there must be absolutely no interruptions! They may encourage the speaker or indicate agreement by nodding, smiling, making eye contact, and so on, but they mustn't say anything. As each round is completed, the group should immediately move to the next person's sentence, still without discussion or comment. At the end of step 4 students could have an informal unstructured discussion.

The first few times you do this activity, make sure students are absolutely clear about the rules, or the activity will fall apart! Until students are familiar with the activity, it is also a good idea to debrief after it is completed. For example, *What did you like/not like? How was this different from regular small-group discussion? Who had the most difficult/easiest role in each round? What was most difficult? Why? How might this activity help your learning?*

What most students comment positively on is that everyone in the group has an equal opportunity and time to speak and to be listened to carefully, unlike a regular discussion, where some students dominate and others say very little. They also like having the opportunity to hear others' comments on their sentence before commenting themselves. (Listening to others *before* you give your own opinion is a useful reversal of what normally happens in an open discussion!) For students who are not confident speakers, being the first person to read their sentence aloud is often a novel experience, since they rarely get the chance to "set the agenda" in other contexts. Moreover, as sentence-chooser, they have the advantage of listening to the three previous speakers before having to speak themselves, and will be supported by this peer scaffolding. However the challenge to speak for a minute (especially if you are the first person to speak after the sentence has been read) may be very daunting for some, and you can make this easier if you allow students thirty seconds of "thinking time" before speaking.

From a language-learning perspective, speaking for a minute, while a challenge, also encourages students to use extended language and make what they say as clear as possible. They tend to produce language that is more "written like" in that it is more complete and well structured. As the mode continuum illustrates (see Chapter 3), well-structured oral talk leads naturally into written language. Again this is less likely to occur in an unstructured discussion where interruptions are common.

Thinking Sheets

A "thinking sheet" is a structured way of having students make their reasoning explicit while they are engaged in cognitive tasks such as solving a problem, planning how to do something, or working out an explanation. It requires them to make their reasoning visible by talking through their thinking aloud. Within the teaching program it provides a planned curriculum "space" in which students talk explicitly about their thinking and explain it to others.

In one year 7 math class, the teacher was concerned about the EL learners' difficulties with understanding the language of math problems. In this example, a group of four students had been asked to solve this problem:

> *The sum of two numbers is 19 and their product is 48. Find the difference between the two numbers.*

Rather than have students solve this individually, they were given a "thinking sheet" to help them articulate their thinking. The sheet included these questions:

- What are the key words in this question? [The students identified *sum*, *product*, and *difference*.]
- Write down another way of saying the same thing.
- What mathematical processes will you need to use: +, −, ×, or ÷?

- Solve the problem as a group.
- Write down the steps you followed as you were finding the answer.

Using the thinking sheet involved the students in considerable subject-related talk as they clarified the question, suggested alternative ways of solving the problem, and made decisions. Once the students had completed the task, a reporter from each group explained to the remainder of the class how the group went about solving the problem. (Other students had solved different, and in some cases more complex, problems.) This reporting was done as a dialogue with the teacher, who asked clarification questions and at times reworded what the student said into more appropriate mathematical language, as in this example:

Student: We timesed it.
Teacher: Right, you multiplied it.

As the reporter was talking, the teacher wrote up the sequence of steps that the group had followed, using both words and mathematical symbols. This lesson led on to an introduction to formal algebra as a systematic procedure for solving similar word problems.

In this case the thinking sheet led to a very different kind of learning process from one dominated by teacher-directed explanation. It helped students develop a language to talk about mathematical concepts, made explicit the mathematical thinking processes involved, and helped students know how to read a math problem.

In schooling, the processes of thinking are often invisible to both students and teacher. Thinking sheets can help make that thinking visible in every subject area. You will find more about thinking sheets in Chapter 7.

Split Dictation

For split dictation you will need to make two versions of a text, each text having different omissions. Choose a text that is related to students' current learning and that will also provide a good model of subject language. (The example in Figure 4.3 comes from a unit on electricity.) In pairs, students must complete the text by dictating to their partner the parts they have and filling in the parts they don't have, so that collaboratively they complete the whole text. This is a barrier game—the partners mustn't show each other their texts.

Barrier Crossword

This is a very useful activity for revisiting subject-specific vocabulary and giving students opportunities to explain the ideas behind complex or abstract words (such as nominalizations, described in Chapter 3). It requires students to work in pairs: partner A and partner B. A barrier crossword is a reversal of the usual crossword: the *answers* are already filled in and the students have to provide the *clues*. Partner A has the answers to all the across words, and partner B has the answers to all the down words.

Partner A

1. A switch _____.

2. _____, you close the circuit.

3. You allow two conductors to touch _____.

4. The bulb in the lamp _____.

5. When you switch off a lamp, _____.

6. _____ separates the two conductors.

7. When the circuit is open,_____ .

Partner B

1. _____ is a device that open or closes a circuit.

2. When you switch on a lamp, _____.

3. _____ so that the current can flow.

4. _____ glows.

5. _____ you open the circuit.

6. An insulator, which may be an air space, _____.

7. _____ the bulb does not glow.

Figure 4.3. Split Dictation (text adapted from Harcourt Science 2006, 482)

(See Figure 4.4 on pages 74–75 for an example.) The partners mustn't show their words to each other, hence the "barrier" designation.

In turn, each student gives his or her partner clues about one of the filled-in words, and the partner tries to guess what the word is. The student who is guessing the word is free to ask questions for clarification. (The word itself must not be mentioned.) When the student guesses it correctly, he or she fills it in. When the word has been guessed, the partners switch roles. This continues until the crossword is completed.

If you make up a crossword like this, choose vocabulary that is related to what students are currently learning about in your particular subject, or vocabulary that you want students to revisit. (There are now a number of Internet sites that will format a crossword puzzle using words you select.) This is a good context for students to focus on the meaning of key words, explaining them in everyday terms without the challenge of producing a formal dictionary-like definition.

Words can be selected from particular subject areas and topics. For example:

Why we need governments: *democracy, government, civics, citizen, rights, responsibility, participation, election.*

Expressing equations and functions: *variable, algebraic, expression, power, exponent, numerator, denominator, unit rate.*

Genres in language arts: *haiku, limerick, novel, novella, discussion, autobiography, folktale, narrative.*

Traditional and Specific Cloze Exercises

A cloze is a text with some words deleted. There are many different kinds of cloze, some of which are described below. When you make deletions, make sure that the first and last sentences remain intact (with the exception of the complete cloze—see the next activity), so that learners have a context in which to read the overall text. To provide extra support for students who need it, include a list of the deleted words.

In a traditional cloze, words are deleted at regular intervals—every seventh word, for example. However cloze activities can also be designed for specific purposes, with only certain kinds of words deleted, such as key subject-specific vocabulary or specific parts of speech (connectives, pronouns). Generally these are more effective for teaching purposes.

In the past, cloze exercises were often used to assess learners' reading skills. However, they are also excellent teaching activities if you allow time for students to justify their answers, because that gives students opportunities to explain their thinking and to reflect aloud on their reading strategies. It helps to put the text on an overhead projector or whiteboard, so that there can be class discussion about appropriate choices. Note that there is sometimes a range of possible words to fill a gap. For example:

A tsunami is a _____ wave caused by an earthquake _____ the sea.

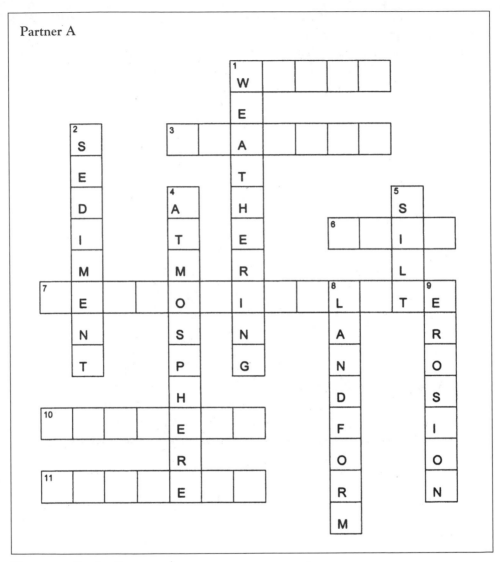

Figure 4.4. Barrier Crossword

Here possible words include *huge, large, gigantic, enormous* for the first deletion and *under, underneath, below, beneath* for the second. However if the word *is, the,* or *by* is missing in the above sentence, no other word is possible because these "functional" words relate to the grammar of the sentence. Allow discussion of the best word where there is a choice, and draw students' attention to those deletions where there is only one correct answer.

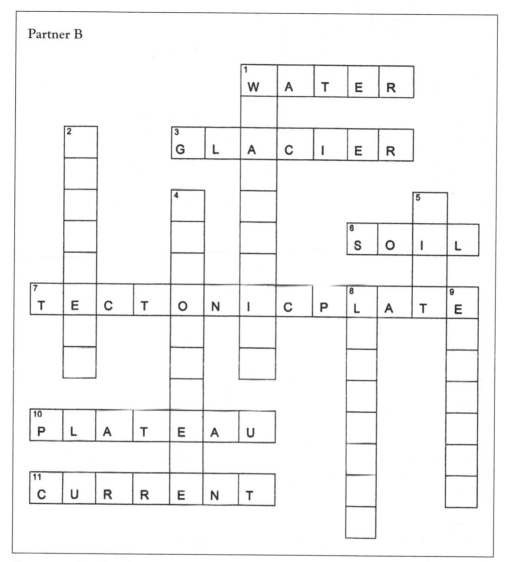

Figure 4.4. (*continued*)

Total Cloze

A total cloze consists only of a title (written in full). The body of the text has been totally deleted; it is made up only of gaps, each gap representing one word of the text.
(The punctuation is also provided.) The text on which the cloze is based must be on
a topic with which students are familiar, so it is better to use this toward the end of a
unit. The text could be a paragraph taken from a textbook or a paragraph you have

written summarizing the concepts or content of a recent topic of study. The text should use appropriate academic language (that is, it should be an appropriate model of written language), so that once it is completed it provides a model of academic writing.

The cloze (the title, the gaps, and the punctuation) is written on the board, and as a whole class, students guess the missing words (in any order). The teacher fills in the words that are correct in the appropriate gap. (Have a copy of the written text in front of you, with each word numbered, with the corresponding number under the correct gap on the board; otherwise it is very difficult to fill in the words quickly and accurately.) The task becomes progressively easier; once the sentences are partially completed, students should be able to predict the remaining words by using their knowledge of the topic, the language associated with the topic, and the sentence structure. Prior to beginning the activity, you could also get students to predict the kind of information they expect to find in the passage, based on the title.

This is a fun activity that students enjoy; typically they become very engaged in reconstructing the text. It is a useful activity for revisiting what has been learned and modeling language. It also gives students practice in prediction, a key skill in reading effectively.

Vanishing Cloze

This is a useful way to have students repeat and practice key language associated with a topic or discipline. Write on the board one or two sentences based on something that you feel students need to rehearse or practice—the definition of a key concept, for example, or a statement associated with a key item of knowledge. Students read it aloud together. Erase one word from anywhere in the text. Students read the whole text again, supplying the missing word. Erase another word and repeat the process. Continue until all the words are erased, so that students are now "reading" from memory. These repeated readings are helpful if the text contains a complex grammatical structure that is significant for students' subject learning (such as a definition) or contains subject-specific vocabulary related to current learning. At those times when very structured language learning is important, this activity provides a context for repetition that is both fun and challenging.

Word Walls

A word wall is a bank of words displayed on the wall of the classroom. These words can be key words in material students are reading; words that are necessary for organizing ideas, such as connectives specific to particular genres (see Chapter 5); words specific to a unit or topic; or high-frequency words useful for EL learners in the class. Students should be encouraged to suggest words to be added. Since they are an easily accessible reference, word walls are a way of encouraging independent and autonomous learning and a useful resource for students when they are writing.

You could also display models of subject language in the room—for example, definitions of terms associated with key concepts; models of and criteria for successful writing in relevant genres; and examples of relevant sentence beginnings (see Chapter 6).

Where might we use this language?	Where might we use this language?
A lot of artists at that time painted pictures of city life.	The melting of the ice caps is a result of global warming.
Magnets attract metals that contain iron.	Famine caused mass starvation.
There was no food and many people starved and died.	Urban scenes were popular among artists of the era.
The ice caps are starting to melt because the earth is getting hotter.	Magnetic attraction occurs between magnets and ferrous metals.

Figure 4.5. Sentence Matching

Sentence Matching

This language-focused activity helps students recognize some of the differences between everyday and more formal language. Students match "more spoken" and "more written" meanings (see the example in Figure 4.5). Choose sentences that are relevant to a particular subject or topic (for illustrative purposes, Figure 4.5 includes a range of subjects). Ask the students to draw lines to link the sentences that have related meanings. Ensure that this exercise is a teaching activity rather than a testing one. Get students, in pairs, to discuss the differences in the language, and then discuss with the whole class what these differences are and in what contexts each might be used.

You could also get students to do a more formal activity by constructing nominalizations from verb forms (see Figure 4.6, Turning Processes into Nouns). Provide an

Process (what is happening)	Noun
attract	attraction
erode	
expand	
contract	
replicate	
refuse	

Figure 4.6. Turning Processes into Nouns

example as shown. Remember to choose words that are relevant to what students are currently learning and also, importantly, to discuss the *reasons* for using a nominalization and the context you might use it in. As we saw in Chapter 3, nominalizations are often used in more formal or written language, because we want to talk about abstract concepts and ideas (like *magnetic attraction*), rather than describe what happened (the *magnet attracted* something).

Bilingual Dictionaries

As concepts are studied in class, encourage bilingual learners who are familiar with key terms in their mother tongue to note new words in English alongside the mother tongue. Or they could note down English words with a mother tongue definition.

Summary

. . . .

This chapter has suggested some key principles for developing academic literacy and has illustrated a range of language-based activities that can be integrated with subject teaching. It has argued that:

- Activities can be placed along a continuum from authentic real-world communicative tasks to more pedagogic form-focused activities.
- The teaching purpose will determine the type of activity and the kinds of grouping used.
- Activities that have a communicative focus and also provide a context for talking about language are likely to be very helpful for second language learning.
- Language-based activities that are designed to develop academic language and literacy are valuable for all students, not only EL learners.

To Think About . . .

. . . .

1. With reference to a group of students you are teaching and to your current teaching program, identify which of the activities you could use and how you would integrate them with the content you are teaching.
2. Do you agree that students need to develop a metalanguage for talking about language? If so, what metalanguage might be necessary for students to know in your own teaching context?
3. Choose one activity that you were not previously familiar with, and use it in one of your classes. Evaluate it in terms of how engaged students were and to what degree it encouraged the use of academic language. If possible, work collaboratively with another teacher.

Suggestions for Further Reading That Describes Other Literacy Activities

Carrasquillo, A., S. Kucer, and R. Abrams. 2004. *Beyond the Beginnings: Literacy Interventions for English Language Learners.* Clevedon, UK: Multilingual Matters.

De Silva Joyce, H., and S. Feez. 2004. *Developing Writing Skills for Middle Secondary Students.* Melbourne: Phoenix Education.

Gibbons, P. 2002. *Scaffolding Language, Scaffolding Learning: Teaching Second Language Learners in the Mainstream Classroom.* Portsmouth, NH: Heinemann.

McKay, P., ed. 2006. *Teaching Creatively Within a Required Curriculum for School-Age Learners.* Alexandria, VA: TESOL.

Meltzer, J., and T. Hamann. 2005. "Meeting the Literacy Development Needs of Adolescent Language Learners Through Content-Area Learning, Part 2: Focus on Developing Academic Literacy Habits and Skills Across the Content Areas." Northeast and Islands Regional Educational Laboratory, The Education Alliance at Brown University. Available at www.alliance.brown.edu.

5 | **Building Bridges to Text**
Supporting Academic Reading

> *For ELLs, whose prior knowledge often does not match what the school expects, the task of constructing meaning from texts is made more difficult as readers meet increasing numbers of words that are not in their listening vocabularies.*
> —Angela Carrasquillo, Stephen Kucer,
> and Ruth Abrams, *Beyond the Beginnings*

What This Chapter Is About

This chapter focuses on how teachers can support EL learners in accessing the meaning of written texts and in becoming more independent readers. As with other chapters, it has an across-curriculum focus. Increasingly as they move through school, students are "reading to learn," as well as "learning to read." Academic reading poses challenges for all learners, in the ways that Chapter 3 described, but there may be additional challenges for EL learners. These have to do with possible greater unfamiliarity (in English) with the content or field of the text, less familiarity with spoken English, or, for some students, with the writing script itself. The difficulty of a particular text may lead teachers in some cases to reject the use of it altogether for EL learners or to provide a simplified version. While these may be appropriate choices in some instances, most obviously in the case of learners who are at the very early stages of learning English, there remains the dilemma referred to several times in this book: ongoing simplification of language is likely to result in students' having little access to the very registers of English they need to develop for learning across the curriculum. Rather than placing a ceiling on what EL students are expected to read, teachers can instead "build bridges" to the text by providing reading activities that will scaffold EL learners' reading. Specifically this support will enable readers to:

- Access the meanings of a text.
- Model reading strategies that are transferable to other reading contexts.

Activities are broadly classified into three types—those that will take place before reading, during reading, and after reading. Examples of each type are provided.

The chapter begins with a brief review of some of the current approaches to the teaching of reading.

What Is the "Best" Way to Teach Reading?

There have been many very different approaches to reading that claim to answer this question, and trying to develop a cohesive approach to the teaching of reading in the classroom is a little like trying to assemble a complex jigsaw puzzle. It is probably fair to say that each of the approaches focuses on one aspect of reading and has something useful to say about what learners need to learn, but none of them alone presents a complete answer. In addition, many approaches and mainstream reading programs do not take into account the needs of EL learners, since most are based on the assumption that learners are already familiar with the spoken form of the language. This section summarizes some of the key perspectives of a range of approaches and offers one way to assemble the jigsaw puzzle.

Traditional, or "Bottom-Up," Approaches

Traditional "bottom-up" or "phonics-based" approaches focus on the basic skills for decoding written symbols. Such approaches begin with the smallest bits of language: the sounds and the letters used to represent them. While a knowledge of the phonic system of English is necessary learning for any reader, we need to remember that it is only one strategy among many that a fluent reader uses. In traditional approaches, learners progress from recognizing simple words in isolation to reading simple sentences that use carefully controlled grammar and vocabulary. Books following this approach, often referred to as basal readers, rely heavily on repetition of (1) whatever sound symbol is the focus of the text and (2) a number of "sight words." Meaning is therefore almost inevitably sacrificed to form, resulting in texts that are often neither interesting nor sensible, and are unlike any authentic spoken language with which young children are familiar. Most teachers, even if they have never used such books themselves, will be familiar with early basal readers such as the *Dick and Jane* books, written in the 1930s (in Australia, the characters were named Sam, Pam, and Digger), and the often strange language they contained:

> *Oh, see Jane. Funny, funny Jane.*

> *Look! The rat ran in the tin. The rat can fit in the tin. Is the rat fat?*

While current basal readers may avoid the extremes of these texts, the basic principles of sight words and a phonics focus remain the same.

A major disadvantage of phonics-driven programs for EL learners is that they offer few links to what these learners already know about their own language or about English. The language of the texts is probably far removed from any spoken "everyday" English with which the learner may be familiar. For beginning EL learners, phonics-based programs present other difficulties, since the English sounds on which such texts are primarily based never exactly match the sounds of their first language. Consequently, reading becomes a very abstract process where unfamiliar knowledge (the sounds of English) is used to teach an unfamiliar skill (reading in English).

Whole Language, or "Top-Down," Approaches

An alternative approach, and one with which a phonics approach is often contrasted, is a "top-down," or "whole language," approach. The primary focus here is on reading for meaning at the level of the whole text—for example, being able to recognize the type of text and its purpose and predict meanings on the basis of one's prior background knowledge of the world and of the language itself. Top-down approaches avoid the limitations of bottom-up phonics approaches and give learners access to a rich range of text models in authentic contexts. However, for some learners, in particular EL learners, top-down approaches may not always include sufficient explicit focus on the language itself, and may not in fact go very far "down."

The notion that readers predict meaning is an important concept in a whole-language approach. Early work by Goodman (1967) illustrates how prediction works, and understanding this helps explain why the reading process may break down for some EL learners. Goodman argues that as they are reading, fluent readers draw on three kinds of knowledge to gain meaning from text: semantic knowledge (knowledge of the world and of the specific content of the text, which in this book is also referred to as *field knowledge*); syntactic knowledge (knowledge of the structure of the language); and graphophonic knowledge (knowledge of sound-letter relationships). Goodman suggests that readers predict meaning in these three ways. In each of the following examples, think about *how* you are able to predict the missing word:

1. Washington, D.C., is the capital of _____ .
2. Here is a wodge. Here is another wodge. There are two _____ .
3. The flag is blue, red and g _____ .

In example 1 you can predict the missing word by using your general knowledge about world geography. Here you are using *semantic* knowledge. In example 2, general world knowledge is of no help, since there is no such thing as a "wodge" in English. But your knowledge of the structure of English enables you to predict that the missing word is *wodges*. Here you are using *syntactic* knowledge: you are probably drawing on analogies with words such as *badge–badges* or *lodge–lodges*. In example 3, the letter *g* gives a clue that the likely word is *green* (as opposed to *yellow* or *black*). Here you are using *grapho-*

phonic knowledge. But your semantic knowledge and syntactic knowledge are useful too: you don't expect that a flag would be gray, even though that fits with the graphophonic clue, and you know intuitively that the missing word will probably be an adjective describing a color. In other words, fluent readers do not need to read every letter or every word. Rather they predict the most likely meaning from context, using different kinds of knowledge.

However, EL learners may not be able to read in this way. They may not have the appropriate background knowledge needed to understand the text, especially if this relates to new or culturally specific knowledge. (For the same reason, you probably had difficulty reading the example of the linguistic text in Chapter 3.) Or they may not have sufficient knowledge of the structure of English to be able to predict in the way that a fluent English speaker is able to. They may, for example, be unaware of the kinds of meanings carried by important "signaling" words such as *although, however, on the other hand, finally,* or *therefore* and so do not recognize how to read the information that these signaling words introduce. These words also often function as connectives that link ideas throughout a whole text, and so failing to understand them means that connections between ideas are lost. EL learners are often unable to locate main ideas or their significance, or recognize the overall organizational structure of the text. Part of the reason for this is that they may be unfamiliar with the meaning and function of these key connectives or signaling words.

Interactive Approaches to Reading

Many researchers now argue that reading is a combination of bottom-up and top-down skills and that successful readers use both predictive and decoding skills depending on the kinds of texts they are reading. Readers also interact with the text itself, drawing on their own personal and cultural experiences to make meaning from it. These personal and cultural experiences are known as *schema:* they are the mental frameworks that we develop as a result of our particular cultural experiences. Applied to reading, schema theory suggests that readers draw on this culturally acquired knowledge to guide their comprehension.

For example, jokes are often hard to understand for a person from outside the culture in which the joke originates. Likewise a political cartoon is not comprehensible if the reader is unaware of the political context that prompted it. Even though the words on the cartoon may appear to be linguistically very simple, the reader will not comprehend the intended meaning without sharing the knowledge of the cartoonist about the situation being depicted. For this reason, books that appear linguistically "simple" may not be comprehensible to readers who do not have the appropriate schema within their schematic repertoire. Conversely, a book that appears linguistically "difficult" may be quite comprehensible for someone who is familiar with its content. For these reasons, what teachers do *before* learners read a text is central to how successfully they will be able to read it.

As a further example of how your schema influences how you interpret text, consider what you are able to infer from these headings. You can predict the kind of text they come from, and some of the content of that text:

The Elephant and the Little Mouse
Further Rent Hikes Likely
Dynamic Manager Required in Busy Company

As readers in an English-speaking Western culture, it is easy to predict that these headings are from three familiar genres, or text types: the first is a children's story, probably with a moral; the second is a newspaper headline; and the third is a job advertisement. We can predict quite a lot of the content too. The story will probably begin with an orientation telling where the story is set and who the main characters are. As the story unfolds, the little mouse, although very small and perhaps scared of the elephant, comes to the elephant's rescue, and in the end they become great friends. The newspaper article will be about rent increases; since the headline refers to "further rent hikes" we can assume that rents have already risen recently. The article will probably also suggest some of the reasons for the increases and who will be most affected. In the final text we would expect to find the details of the position, including the selection criteria, the qualifications required, and the salary range. There will also be a reference number and contact details (perhaps a fax number and a website address).

We can predict all this before we even begin to read the texts themselves. This information is in our heads and is the result of our familiarity with many similar texts that are part of our culture. We "map" this prior cultural knowledge, or schema, onto the texts we read; in this way the reader can be said to "interact" with the text. What schema theory suggests is that meaning does not reside simply in the words on the page but interacts with the reader's "in-the-head" knowledge. If, on the other hand, our previous experiences had not provided us with this cultural knowledge or had provided us with different cultural knowledge, we could not interact with those texts in the same way and would be less able to predict the genre of the texts or their content.

Because they draw on both top-down and bottom-up theories of reading and take into account the role of cultural knowledge, interactive approaches provide a major rationale for many of the reading activities that are described later.

Critical and Social Approaches to Reading

Increasingly, it is important for learners to have the ability to critique and question the texts into which they come into contact, including advertisements, Internet texts, and media reports.

Critical approaches to teaching reading see it as more than the development of the kinds of technical skills discussed so far. All written texts exist in a particular social, historical, and cultural context. No text is "neutral"—whether the arrival of white people in Australia and North America is described as *discovery*, *colonization*, or *invasion* depends on who you are, the viewpoint you hold, and your interpretation of historical events. Different communities or individuals may interpret a text differently depending on their own cultural and social experiences, and this has implications for using texts within a multicultural classroom. In this approach, teaching needs to include classroom discussion on the way that language and the writer's ideology position the reader, how the language does this, and the different "readings" that are possible of a single text. For example, the novel *Nothing But the Truth: A Documentary Novel* (Avi 1991) is written to demonstrate explicitly to its young readers the conflicting interpretations given to the same set of events, as they are reported by the papers, TV and radio, and the participants in the story themselves. It raises many questions about how we should respond to what appears to be "the truth" and the validity of interpretations.

Reading is also a cultural and social practice. The value placed on it, and how it is used, varies from culture to culture. Some EL learners may come from cultures that may not value the reading of storybooks to children but value highly the ability to participate in oral storytelling. Or in their community reading may occur mainly for religious purposes, rather than for gaining information about the world or for recreation. While not in themselves barriers to reading, school orientations toward the purposes of reading may also constitute an additional layer of unfamiliarity for some EL learners, particularly when teachers and schools are unaware of these learners' community literacy practices and are therefore unable to build on their prior experiences and expectations about reading.

Critical and social approaches to reading have little to say about the actual pedagogy involved in teaching initial literacy skills to beginner readers. However, they offer important insights for classroom practice in terms of the selection of texts and the nature of the classroom talk surrounding the texts.

Assembling the Jigsaw Puzzle

In many Western countries there continue to be debates about the best way to teach reading. Often these debates have become politicized, with particular approaches favored or even mandated by governments or local education systems, along with strong claims for the efficacy of the favored approach. But it should be clear from the descriptions above that each approach values a different *aspect* of literacy. And so, rather than looking for a single answer about the way to teach reading, it is probably more helpful to think of each approach as a piece in a jigsaw puzzle, which taken together illustrate the complexity of reading. However, it is often left to an individual teacher to make sense of all the competing claims and put the jigsaw puzzle together.

The work of Freebody and Luke (1990) offers a coherent way for teachers to think about the complexity of reading. They argue that when a fluent reader reads, they take on four "reader roles" simultaneously: *code breaker*, *text participant*, *text user*, and *text analyst*. These four roles together encapsulate some of the major aspects of the approaches discussed in the previous section and constitute a balanced and inclusive view of reading pedagogy.

Reader as Code Breaker

As a code breaker, a reader needs to engage in the "technology" of written script. In the case of English, this includes the relationship between letters and sounds, left-to-right directionality, and alphabetic awareness. The ability to break the code is at the heart of many calls for "back to basics" in reading debates, and it is the major focus of traditional approaches to the teaching of reading. Certainly children's development and ultimate success in reading is likely to be hindered by a lack of knowledge of how to break the code, and a balanced reading program for young children will not ignore these elements. However, as the other roles suggest, while understanding how to break the code may be necessary to being a successful reader, it is far from sufficient in ensuring the successful reading of authentic texts in real social and academic contexts. For EL learners in particular the importance of knowing the code does not justify its teaching in contexts devoid of meaning.

Reader as Text Participant

As a text participant, readers connect the text with their own social and cultural knowledge and prior experiences. In other words they "map" the text onto their own schema and interpret the text in that light. Being a text participant means using this personal and cultural knowledge to predict the likely meanings of the text, in the sorts of ways discussed earlier. As we have seen, these ideas are important in top-down and interactive approaches.

Reader as Text User

As a text user, a reader knows how to participate in the social activities in which the written text plays a major part. The nature of the participation and the ways that texts are used vary from culture to culture: as discussed earlier, texts may be closely associated with religious practices and observances in some communities or seen as a form of leisure in others. The rise of "book groups" in several Western countries, especially among women, is an example of such a cultural practice. The cultural contexts in which learners participate determine their understandings of how written texts are used and of what counts as successful reading. In a longitudinal study with three different sociocultural groups, Shirley Brice-Heath (1983) shows how each group used books differently in the home and how the children from each of the groups were differentially advantaged (or disadvantaged) by these experiences once they entered school. Not surprisingly, the children who were most advantaged were those whose home experiences of books—how they were talked about, their role in everyday life, and the value placed on them—most closely mirrored the talk and values of the school. Social and cultural approaches to literacy are reflected in the reader-as-text-user role.

Reader as Text Analyst

As a text analyst, readers read critically. They understand that the text is a crafted object and recognize what in the text is assumed, implied, unquestioned, or omitted or, in more extreme ways, how language can be used to deliberately manipulate. Critical readers recognize that a text represents one particular view of the world and that however authoritative it may appear, is written by an author who has a particular ideology or set of assumptions. Reading critically is increasingly important in a globalized world with ever-expanding sources of information. The role of the reader as text analyst is central in critical approaches to literacy pedagogy.

Some Reading-Related Activities

These four roles are not intended to represent a developmental sequence. They can all be used at every level of reading; even beginning readers in English can be shown how to predict meaning or to take a critical stance toward the texts they read. But if students are to become literate in the ways that the four roles suggest, then all teachers need to make provision for this literacy development through focused reading tasks and the kinds of talk that accompany texts. As Meltzer and Hamann (2005) have argued, chances to practice reading are not enough. Rather, content-reading instruction needs to be a major focus of content teaching.

One way of orienting students to a text and helping them interact with it is through various kinds of text-related tasks. Activities that are most valuable are those that fulfill two scaffolding functions:

- They support learners in gaining meaning from the *particular* text they are reading.
- They model generic reading strategies that help learners read *subsequent* texts.

Reading tasks usually reflect three main types of reading activities: those that come before reading the text, those that accompany it, and those that follow it (Wallace 1992). The specific purposes for these three types are outlined below, with examples of possible activities.

Before-Reading Activities

Before-reading activities aim to support *overall* text meaning by building up relevant field or topic knowledge and so prepare learners to read the text. Specifically, these activities:

- Prepare learners for potential linguistic, cultural, or conceptual difficulties.
- Activate learners' prior knowledge and understandings.

Once learners have an overall sense of what a text is going to be about, it is much easier for them to make sense of it when they read it. Early research with young EL learners in England (Tizard et al. 1982) showed the advantage of telling stories to children in their first language prior to having them read the stories in English. The researchers found that students were better able to comprehend the English version and could read at a higher level and understand more complex grammatical structures and vocabulary than children who had not heard the version first in their mother tongue. This more complex but comprehensible language also introduced them to more varied and richer models of English.

While in Italy early on in my learning of Italian, I tried a similar strategy. I had attempted to read an Italian newspaper each day, but as a near-beginner this was far too difficult a task, so I began reading the main news items in an English newspaper first. With this prior understanding of what I would be reading about, I read the equivalent news reports in Italian much more easily. Of course there was still much I didn't understand, but having an overall sense of what the whole text was about made what I was attempting to read in Italian more comprehensible. It also meant that the Italian text became a model for certain repeated structures, phrases, and vocabulary, none of which I took notice of when I was simply struggling to understand meanings word by word.

In a similar way, before-reading activities give students an opportunity to find out what the text is about before they read it. They allow students to predict in general terms the kind of text it is, some of the language of the text, and the sorts of information it will contain. Students' predictions may not always conform exactly to the text, but the process of thinking about what the text is likely to contain creates an interest and engagement in their later reading of the text, and makes explicit the predictive processes that experienced readers follow intuitively. In addition, when students go into a text with a misconception, they are more likely to take account of the information presented, because information that runs counter or in addition to our expectations is often more memorable than information that simply confirms what we already know. Finally, if students come to the text with a sense of what it is about, they will be able to minimize the disadvantages of having less than native-speaker proficiency in the language.

At the same time, before-reading activities offer a context for the teacher to engage students in talk about the topic, and opportunities to model some of the grammatical patterns and key vocabulary that learners will later come across in the text and, if necessary, to further build up students' knowledge of the field.

Here are some examples of before-reading activities.

Prediction from a Picture, Diagram, or Other Visuals

Use a picture to illustrate something about the text. (In one class the teacher used a photo of a devastated town that accompanied a text about an earthquake disaster.) In groups or pairs students then brainstorm what the text is likely to be about and the kinds of information it contains. In follow-up class discussion you can assess what learners already know and expand and elaborate on their ideas. (A diagram, graph, map, or other visual image that represents or summarizes the information in the text could be used in the same way.)

Prediction from Key Words, the Title, or the First Sentence

Put up five or six key words from the text (for example, *tremor, aftershock, Richter scale, destruction*) and follow a process similar to the one used in the previous activity. Alternatively, show the students either the title or the first sentence and ask them to brainstorm possible information and key words they think the text might include.

Personal Narratives

Some texts can easily be related to personal experiences. For example, before the students read the earthquake text for themselves, the teacher encouraged students who had a personal experience of an earthquake to share their story with the class. Many students were keen to tell their story, and their personal narratives proved to be very engaging for both the speakers and the audience. Personal narratives are a powerful way to build up engagement with the text, because they are a way of bringing it to life.

Semantic Web

This is another way for the class to share information about what they already know about a topic, and it gives you an opportunity to assess what students know and to model some of the key language of the text. Develop the semantic web (see Chapter 4) on the basis of what you elicit from students. If there are some key words that appear in the text that students do not suggest, introduce and explain them in this context, perhaps writing them up in a different color to identify them as important words to note. (But don't attempt to write up every unknown word, only those that are central to an understanding of the text.)

Reader Questions

After the topic and genre of a text has been established, get students to write down three or four questions they think the text might answer. Questions can be written on the board, displayed around the room, or used in groups. Then give out a copy of the text and allow students one minute to see if the text answers their questions. (Make sure you establish a time frame, because the aim is to have students look only for key information.) Writing their own questions encourages students to interact with the text as they read it. The activity also gives them practice in scanning for particular information before they read the text in detail.

Sequencing Illustrations

If you are using an illustrated text that contains a sequence of events (such as a narrative, a historical recounting, or the description of a process), give students some of the illustrations and ask them to suggest and explain a possible sequence.

Skeleton Text

A skeleton text shows the overall outline of a text but has key pieces of information missing. Students are asked to predict what they think this information might be. Many kinds of texts can be used for this activity. The skeleton text in Figure 5.1 is based on an argument by Jane Goodall (n.d.) about environmental damage. The skeleton version contains only the first and last paragraph, and the words that signal her four reasons for hope. This activity shows students the significance of signaling words (in this case, *firstly, second, my third reason for hope lies in, my fourth reason for hope lies in*) and models how they can use these words to recognize the overall structure of the text. Of course a more complex activity like this depends on students having enough knowledge of the general field of the text to be able to make specific suggestions about its content.

Using the skeleton text in Figure 5.1 as an example, here is a possible process to follow. Prior to reading the whole text, encourage students to use the concluding paragraph to think about what Goodall's four reasons might be. (They are humans' ability to solve complex problems; the fact that nature is amazingly resilient; the energy and commitment of young people toward tomorrow's world; and the indomitable nature of the human spirit.) Once the students have had time to consider what the four possible reasons might be, write up some of their ideas on the board. (These could later form the basis of students' own writing using the text as a model.)

It doesn't matter if the students' ideas are not the same as those of the text: the aim is to engage students in reading the text, not have them produce "correct answers." However, you will probably find that the students' ideas can be related to those of Goodall. You could also add to the students' ideas by eliciting through your questioning some of the reasons that she presents. Again, this activity is an opportunity for you to model some of the language and vocabulary that appears in the text.

Previewing the Text

For some learners it will be helpful to provide some explicit information about what the text contains. Previewing is a teacher-directed activity that provides students with specific information about what they will later read. Previewing helps build up the field of the text and introduces learners to some of the language in it so that they can bring this knowledge to the text when they begin reading.

Depending on the type of text, you may:

- Following the same overall organization as the original, provide a summary of the information in the text using familiar language that students will understand and introducing some key vocabulary.
- Provide a summary of each paragraph.
- Provide the topic sentence of each paragraph.
- In a prior lesson, preteach the concepts and information so that the text summarizes this prior learning (that is, move toward the text rather than beginning with it directly).

As we begin the 21st century, it is easy to be overwhelmed by feelings of hopelessness. We humans have destroyed the balance of nature: forests are being destroyed, deserts are spreading, there is terrible pollution and poisoning of air, earth, water. Climate is changing, people are starving. There are too many humans in some parts of the world, overconsumption in others. There is human cruelty to "man" and "beast" alike; there is violence and war. Yet I do have hope. Let me share my four reasons.

Firstly,

Second,

My third reason for hope lies in

My fourth reason for hope lies in

So let us move into the next millennium with hope—with faith in ourselves, in our intelligence, in our indomitable spirit. Let us develop respect for all living things. Let us try to replace violence and intolerance with understanding and compassion and love.

Figure 5.1. Example of a Skeleton Text Prediction Activity (excerpts from "Jane Goodall Reflects on Working Toward Peace," by Jane Goodall)

- If possible, use the students' first language to explain the key points of the text; in the case of a narrative, tell the story in the students' first language prior to having them read it in English.
- For students who are literate in their first language, provide a bilingual version of the text and have students read this first before reading the text in English.

These strategies enable even very weak readers or early EL learners to follow the text with overall understanding.

Traditionally, before-reading activities consisted mainly of preteaching vocabulary in isolation from the context in which it was used. The sorts of activities described here provide much richer learning opportunities than occur when students are simply taught a list of vocabulary prior to reading a text. Defining words in isolation is insufficient for gaining an understanding of their full meaning, nor does this help learners develop useful predictive strategies to use for reading subsequent texts. New vocabulary is certainly a major learning load for students reading academic texts, but as Wallace (1992) comments, "We learn new words and meanings largely through reading; we do not learn words in order to read" (76). Presenting new vocabulary in the context of discussion around text, especially when that text is itself located within a coherent unit of study, makes this learning more meaningful and encapsulates much more than just the learning of vocabulary.

Time spent on before-reading activities is time very well spent. The better prepared EL learners are to read a text, the more comprehensible the text will be, and the more successful they will be at recognizing the relationship between wording and meaning. Even with good readers, before-reading activities remain important scaffolding for more complex texts.

During-Reading Activities

Fluent readers use a range of reading strategies as they take on the roles identified by Freebody and Luke (1990). During-reading activities aim to make explicit the unconscious processes and practices that fluent readers use. Drawing on the range of approaches described earlier and on the four reader roles, we can describe some of these processes. Effective readers:

- Understand that reading is about making meaning.
- Scan a text before reading it to get a sense of what it contains.
- Understand the purpose of the text.
- Recognize the overall "shape" and organization of the text.
- Recognize which sentence of each paragraph is the topic sentence.
- Read critically, reflecting on and responding to what they read.
- Carry meaning "in their heads" across sentences and paragraphs, rather than reading word by word.

- Recognize the meaning and function of connectives and key signaling words.
- Use schematic knowledge to predict what is likely.
- Look backward and forward in the text for on-going clues to meaning.
- Use a range of reading strategies (e.g., skimming, scanning, close reading), depending on what they are reading.
- Skip over words they do not recognize, or have strategies for working out meanings from context.
- Self-correct by rereading when meaning is lost, perhaps paying closer attention to graphophonic clues.
- Use basic decoding skills when necessary.

Whereas effective readers use most of these processes unconsciously and are constantly interrogating and interacting with the text as they read, struggling readers may need the process to be made more explicit. This is the purpose of during-reading activities. As the label suggests, during-reading activities focus students' attention on the text as they are reading. Here are some examples.

Scanning for Information

Poor readers tend to read word by word and often become bogged down in the detail of a complex text before they have an idea of what it is about. As we have seen, before-reading activities aim to give students access to the general meanings of the text prior to reading it. Once the text is in front of them, it may still be useful to encourage learners to skim the text quickly to develop a clearer idea of how it is organized and what sort of information it contains. Or they may scan it for specific information. Searching down a telephone list, searching a train timetable, or consulting a TV guide are examples of this kind of reading. If students have developed reader questions as a before-reading activity, these questions can also be used for this purpose.

Some learners may have learned to read in only one way, focusing on every word equally and trying to remember every detail. Skimming and scanning activities encourage learners to develop alternative strategies and match these to their reading purpose.

Pause and Predict

This strategy encourages learners to use text already read to predict what is likely to come next. It is particularly appropriate with a narrative text, but could also be used with a text that presents an argument. First, divide the text into appropriate sections with intervening questions at key points that are "natural" breaks in the text. The questions should aim to encourage students to predict what might follow.

You can either read the text to students, pausing at significant moments when it is appropriate to ask for students' contributions, or give out the text piece by piece. Read aloud the first part of the text, then pause and ask the students to predict what might happen next or what argument the writer might present (for example, *what do you think might happen next?* or *what do you think the writer is about to say?*) Allow some time for learners to discuss this in pairs or groups; then ask students for their predictions. Ask them to give a reason for their response. Then either read on to the next part of the text or give the students time to do so for themselves. Ask them to check to see whether their prediction was correct before proceeding in the same way for the rest of the text.

As Wallace (1992) suggests, "What such activities attempt to do is to replicate the process which occurs quite spontaneously in mature readers where . . . we continually use the evidence of what has preceded to predict the continuation of a text" (95).

Margin Questions

These are questions about the text that are positioned in the margins of the page (see Figure 5.2 for an example). The word or phrase or paragraph that the question refers to is precisely indicated. Unlike traditional comprehension questions, margin questions focus not on the content of the text but on encouraging useful reading strategies. In particular they encourage learners to use the available "clues" in the text to work out text meaning. Each question in Figure 5.2 has an explicit rationale and purpose (and in some cases more than one)—see Figure 5.3 on page 96.

Scaffolding a Detailed Reading

Scaffolding a detailed reading provides explicit support on how to read a complex text. The ideas below are drawn from the work of David Rose, who has had considerable success with indigenous Australians who have previously been reluctant readers reading far below age-level expectations (see, for example, Rose et al. 2003). Using this approach (briefly described below), students are able to read texts of a level appropriate to their grade or age level and so have access to models of written academic language. As we have argued throughout this book, an ongoing diet of simplified texts or texts intended for much younger readers fail to provide the very language that EL learners need for learning across the curriculum.

The approach aims to focus learners' attention on the patterns of language in a text and the meanings they express. Unlike many approaches to the teaching of reading, the teacher *gives* information to the students rather than *tests* what they know.

First prepare the students for reading the text, using the kinds of activities outlined earlier in the before-reading section, including giving learners information about the topic and genre of the text. After creating this shared knowledge, read the text, or part of it, aloud with the learners, then hand out individual copies.

Now lead a detailed reading, focusing on the patterns of language and on their meanings within the text. Typically, you will follow the sequence of steps below many times as you and the learners move through the text sentence by sentence. The sentence used as an example here is, *It seemed to me that it was the darkest and blackest night of the year.*

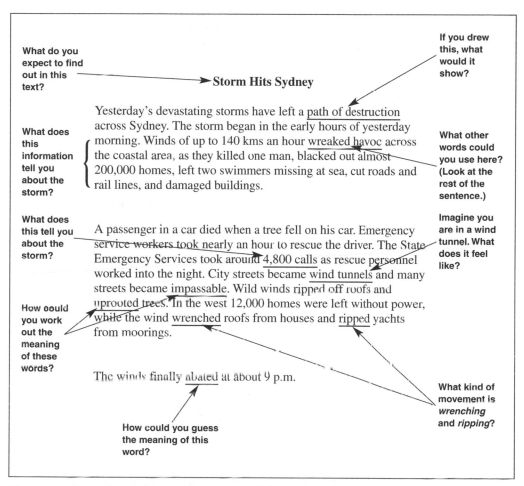

Figure 5.2. Examples of Margin Questions (while-reading activity)

1. Identify a sentence, making sure students know its position in the text (for example, *The next sentence tells us about . . .*).
2. Paraphrase the meaning using language the students will understand (e.g., *The next sentence tells us about the night, and says it was very very dark.*)
3. Ask the students to locate and read the words in the text that represent the meaning of the paraphrase (*the darkest and blackest night of the year*) and then underline them. (When relevant, these underlinings can later be used as a basis for making notes.)
4. Elaborate on the meaning of the wording. For example, you might encourage students to talk about their own experiences of a dark night. When necessary,

Question	Rationale for the Question
What do you expect to find out in this text?	Encourages learner to predict meaning from title.
If you drew this, what would it show?	Asking for a definition, or what a word "means," is a complex task. Learners may know the meaning but be unable to explain it in words. Instead, the learner is asked to visualize meaning (also something that many fluent readers do as they read).[1] The question draws attention to the notion of a metaphorical "path" of destruction.
What other words could you use here? (Look at the rest of the sentence.)	1. It may be difficult to answer "What does this mean?" (And producing a dictionary-type definition is also not relevant here.) Having learners produce an alternative wording is more concrete and focuses attention on meaning in context. 2. The clue to look at the rest of the sentence encourages learners to read ahead for meaning as well as back, and to keep on reading when they don't know a word.
What does this information tell you about the storm?	1. Shows learners the importance of reading several sentences to gain meaning. 2. Shows learners the importance of paying attention to initial paragraphs: they often briefly summarize the overall ideas of the text.
What does this tell you about the storm?	Shows learners that readers make meaning by thinking beyond the text, inferring from what is said.

Figure 5.3. Rationale for the Margin Questions in Figure 5.2

Imagine you are in a wind tunnel. What does it feel like?	1. Shows learners how to read by putting themselves in the text (taking on the role of text participant). 2. A question like "What is a wind tunnel?" may be difficult to answer. It is easier to say what it feels like.
How could you work out the meaning of these words?	Shows learners how to take on the role of code breaker. Illustrates the usefulness of breaking longer words into shorter words and paying attention to prefixes and suffixes.
What kind of movement is wrenching *and* ripping?	Encourages students to guess meaning by using their imagination, prior experiences, and the context in which the word is used.
How could you guess the meaning of this word?	Encourages readers to work out meaning by using the position of a word in the text as a whole. It concludes the description that began in the second sentence: "The storm began. . . ." The word comes at the end and so we can assume it is talking about the end of the storm.

[1] For an interesting discussion of the usefulness of visualizing, see Carrasquillo et al. (2004, 68–69).

Figure 5.3. *(continued)*

further explain any difficult concepts. Accept, affirm, extend, and expand on students' responses.

5. Discuss any significant phrases or words. Here, for example, you might discuss the significance within the text of the wording *it seemed to me*, perhaps by exploring how the meaning of the sentence would change if those words were omitted. Or you could draw students' attention to a more critical reading by focusing on how certain language creates certain effects or how it affects the reader.

This highly scaffolded approach to how meaning relates to the language of the text ensures that all learners can understand the text and at the same time remain engaged with it. In other words, all learners are set up to be successful readers. (The reading can later be used as a basis for writing, using some of the text reconstruction strategies described in the next section on after-reading activities.)

Identifying Paragraph Parts

This activity helps learners recognize the way that information is organized in a paragraph, and so helps them predict what they are likely to read next. It also requires them to sort out the main idea from less important details and so assists them in note-making.

Typically a paragraph has three parts:

- A topic sentence that presents the main idea of the paragraph. Often (although not always) this comes at the beginning of a paragraph.
- A number of sentences that support or add to the main idea.
- A final sentence that often points forward to the content of the next paragraph.

Learners identify the parts of the paragraph, perhaps using different-color pens to mark each part.

Knowing how to read a paragraph also assists learners in their own writing. Often poorer writers use paragraphs quite randomly; a common problem is a large number of very short paragraphs, so that the writing lacks cohesion. This activity is therefore also useful for supporting writing development.

Reading Critically

The role of text analyst is one of the four roles that learners need to develop to function fully as readers (Freebody and Luke 1990). Text-analysis activities require the reader to stand "outside" the text and look at it as a crafted object, rather than see it as a "neutral" vehicle for "content." In other words, reading critically involves recognizing how language works to create a particular view of reality. This is likely to be particularly relevant in subjects like social studies, history, geography, and English. Critical-reading activities are typically collaborative activities that involve much talk around, and about, the text, as students discuss a possible range of interpretations or "readings." They can be used as during-reading or after-reading activities.

As a very clear example of how a writer's ideology is bound up with language, consider this excerpt from *The Illustrated London News*, dated April 24, 1852. The author was writing about (his perspective on) the lives of traditional indigenous Australians:

The mysterious and wonderful arrangements of Divine Providence are brought forcibly to our minds on viewing the modes of life of this peculiar people, existing without a wish beyond hunting the forests and living precariously on food which they obtain by climbing immense gum trees, wholly ignorant that at their roots the most precious metal has been concealed for thousands of years: generation after generation of aborigines has passed away, unconscious of the riches concealed beneath the surface of their native hunting grounds, perchance sufficient to have made them the most powerful race under the sun.

The purpose of the activities below is to help learners become aware of the role language plays in "crafting" the text.

Questioning the Text. Encouraging learners to take a critical perspective toward the text requires asking different kinds of questions from those that might be asked to assess traditional comprehension of the overt meaning, grammar, and vocabulary. Typical questions (see Kress 1985 and Wallace 2003) might be:

- Why has this text been written?
- Who is the reader for whom this text is intended?
- Whose perspective is represented in this text?
- What is not talked about in this text?
- What other ways are there to write about this topic?

Consider how these questions might be answered using the text above. Consider also what knowledge students would need about indigenous peoples in order to bring a critical perspective to the text above. Necessary field knowledge might include that, in common with the aboriginal peoples of North America, Australian aboriginals have a strong spiritual relationship with the land, have lived on the land in sustainable ways for over 150,000 years, have an intricate knowledge of how to obtain food and medicines from the land, and have a highly sophisticated and complex kinship system and a rich spiritual and cultural life reflected in stories and art. None of this is suggested by the text, in which they are presented as "living precariously," "ignorant," and "unconscious" of the wealth of minerals on their land. In fact, in this text we learn more about the values of the writer than we do of the people he is writing about.

Language Analysis. A lot can be learned about the crafting of the text by examining the language "close up." One way to do this is through margin questions (described above); another is through whole-class discussion at the elaboration stage of the scaffolded-reading activity (also described above).

Have students list the words and ideas that are associated with the people in the text above. This can be scaffolded through questions like these:

- What do these words (*existing without a wish beyond hunting the forests, living precariously, wholly ignorant, unconscious of*) suggest about the writer's assumptions of the people he is describing?
- What do these words (*the riches concealed beneath the surface of their native hunting grounds, perchance sufficient to have made them the most powerful race under the sun*) tell us about the values of the writer?

Sometimes even seemingly insignificant words, such as pronouns, can tell a story. For example, what is the significance of the words *our* and *them* in the text?

After-Reading Activities

After-reading activities make use of the now-familiar text as a basis for further language development. They usually require students to return to the text and perhaps reread parts of it carefully in order to complete the activity. Most after-reading activities have one or more of these three purposes:

- To focus learners' attention more deeply on the information in the text.
- To use the language of the text as a model for further language study.
- To allow for a creative or critical response to what has been read.

The following activities aim to have learners focus more deeply on the information in the text.

True/False Statements

Give students a number of statements related to the text, some of which are true and others false. Students decide whether these statements should be labeled with a T or an F and underline the sentence or sentences that support their decision. Make sure that some of the statements require learners to make inferences about the information in the text: they should not be able to find all the answers directly in the words of the text.

Graphic Outlines

Have students represent the information of the text as a graphic outline. There are many "shapes" for graphic outlines, depending on how the information in the text has been organized and presented. Among the commonest are timelines, diagrams representing cause and effect or comparison and contrast, and grids that represent a summary of the information in the text.

Graphic outlines are a good context for giving learners practice in identifying the words that signal overall text organization, referred to here as *connectives*. Connectives are key linking or signaling words that are used to structure the expression of ideas. They indicate the development and sequence of ideas and show the relationship between them. They may be single words or groups of words, and often appear at the beginning of sentences. Some examples of the connectives associated with each kind of text are included below. A fuller list can be found in Appendix 2.

Timelines (examples: the life of Eleanor Roosevelt; the rise of the Aztecs). A timeline can be used with any text that describes a sequence of events happening over time. It can be vertical or horizontal, marked with key events and their dates, using appropriate spacing.

Examples of Key Connectives

in (plus date); *three years later; in later years; two hundred years afterwards; finally*

Dates

Events

Cause and Effect (examples: what causes an eclipse of the sun? the reasons for the great depression). Cause and effect sequences are common in all subjects. In the English language, cause and effect sequences may begin with the cause or with the effect (*as a result of* X, Y *occurs;* Y *occurs as a result of* X). Help learners use the connectives as clues to the correct sequence. Representing cause and effect in diagrammatic form ensures that students fully understand this sequence.

Examples of Key Connectives

as a result, because, when, if, so, therefore, consequently

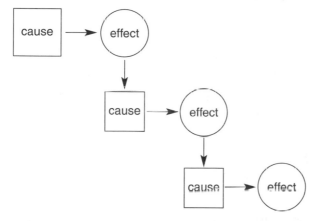

Compare and Contrast (example: what do Buddhism and Jainism have in common, and how are they different?). Similarities and differences are often represented by a Venn diagram; the similarities are listed in the area where the circles intersect.

Examples of Key Connectives

Comparison: *similarly, likewise, in the same way*
Contrast: *however, but, although*

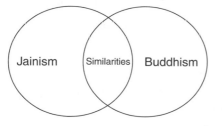

Information Summary (examples: getting fit and staying healthy; types of matter).
An information summary records the key points of a text, together with supporting or
additional details, and is therefore a guide for making notes. Unlike the other examples of graphic outlines, there may be no specific kinds of connectives associated with
general information texts; however, the organization of information is often signaled
by the use of paragraphs (each paragraph focusing on a different aspect of the topic);
the topic sentence in each paragraph (often the first sentence); or the use of subhead-
ings. Some kinds of texts may use connectives for elaborating or restating information
(see Appendix 2).

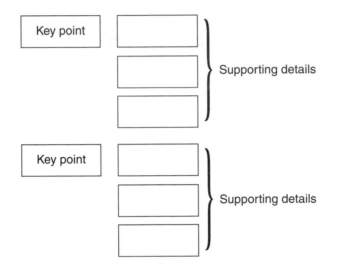

Summarizing the Text

Sometimes it is useful to have students summarize a text. Summarizing is an important
skill, since it requires students to focus on the essential ideas of a text, and is an important strategy for learning from text. However, it is very difficult for learners to summarize a text if they are unable to identify key points, which may be the case if they
have not fully understood the text or if the content is unfamiliar. If you have followed
the suggestions in this chapter, this is unlikely to be the case. However, summarizing
is a complex process, and needs to be modeled with learners—for example, through
questioning that guides learners to focus more explicitly on key ideas. Many textbooks
also have summaries at the end of each chapter that can be used as models.

There are a number of activities that can help learners summarize a text. (Not all
of them will be appropriate for all texts). They can:

- Give a title for each paragraph, write one or two sentences under each paragraph title, and use these sentences as a basis for writing a summary.

- Write down one sentence from each paragraph that they think best summarizes the key ideas of the paragraph. This is the topic sentence and is often the first sentence of the paragraph. Writing down each of the topic sentences in sequence sometimes provides a good framework for a summary.
- In groups, decide on one sentence in the text that best sums up the central meaning of the text. There may be disagreement, but in this process learners will become more familiar with the language and ideas of the text.
- In pairs, tell each other the key points of a text in two or three minutes, then do it in one minute.
- Write the key points of the text in 200 words, then in 100, then in 50. (Depending on the length of the text, the number of words may vary.)

The following activities reflect the second purpose of after-reading activities: they use the language of the text as a model for further language study. (In other words, they use the text for learning about language.) They also create a meaningful context for developing relevant metalanguage.

Cloze Activities

Once students are familiar with the meaning of the text, it can be used as the basis for cloze activities. Cloze activities were illustrated in Chapter 4 and so are not discussed in detail here. You will remember that they may involve the deletion of words at regular intervals (useful for revisiting the text as a whole); total cloze or vanishing cloze; or the deletion of words for a specific teaching purpose (where only certain types of words are deleted). Cloze activities are an excellent way to focus on connectives, since these words cannot easily be explained in isolation. Remember that cloze activities are used here as teaching, not testing, devices; allow plenty of time for learners to discuss the reasons for their choice with others or in a whole-class discussion.

Sentence Reconstruction

With lower-level EL learners, cut up several sentences of the text into individual words, and have students reassemble them. With learners in the early stages of literacy, give oral clues as they are doing this, clues similar to those used in the scaffolded-reading activity described earlier. For example:

> Find the words that start the sentence; they talk about how things seemed to the writer.
> Now find the words that mean "it is very dark."

Go through the cut-up sentences in this way, getting the students to read the sentence aloud after each addition.

This activity focuses attention on the word order of more complex sentences, making clear how each sentence has been built up and how it relates to meaning. The activity also provides scaffolding for possible later writing.

Jumbled Words

With learners in the very early stage of learning literacy, cut up key words in the text into letters and have the learners reassemble them. This activity can be used to focus on a particular spelling pattern and as a model for students to later add similarly patterned words.

Innovating on the Text

Learners, using the text as a basis, maintain the key structures but rewrite it with different content. The new text remains very close to the original, but details are changed. For example, a narrative might feature different characters and places, along with other details and events to make it coherent, but much of the original text will remain unchanged. Other kinds of texts can also be used for innovations—for example, a set of instructions could serve as a model for other instructions.

Innovation on text can also lead to a more critical reading of the original. Using the text above on indigenous Australians, students could rewrite the text from a different perspective, showing how indigenous Australians "saw" the white Englishman who wrote the article. Or an innovation of a traditional fairy tale might include a heroine and hero with very different physical or character traits from those that might be expected in a traditional tale.

After-reading activities may also involve personal responses expressed in other modes, as the two final activities show.

Cartoon or Cartoon Strips

Students turn the text into a cartoon strip. If there is dialogue in the original, this can be added in "speech bubbles." Alternatively the text could be represented by a cartoon with an appropriate caption.

Readers Theatre

This is suitable for narrative texts. Students are each provided with a copy of the text. Then, in groups, each student chooses the dialogue of one character to read, while one student takes on the role of narrator. (Numbers in each group will depend on the number of characters.) The reading can be practiced and later performed. This is a good context for having learners read aloud, since it allows them a chance to practice reading before being asked to do it in front of others (just as adults are likely to do before reading aloud in public). Readers theatre provides a real purpose for reading aloud and also a good context for focusing on pronunciation and performance speaking skills.

Summary

. . . .

This chapter is underpinned by the belief that EL learners should not be left to read difficult texts by themselves. Rather, explicit support for academic reading needs to occur in all content areas, during regular class time. The chapter has argued that reading activities should aim to "build bridges" into the text that the learners are reading, so that they are set up to be successful readers. Major points in this chapter include:

- Learners need to interact with and actively process texts in order to fully comprehend meaning.
- Successful content-area reading depends largely on the kinds of reading activities and explicit reading instruction that takes place around the texts that learners read.
- Reading activities may occur before reading, during reading, and after reading. Each of these kinds of activities has a different purpose to play in helping learners access text.
- Reading activities should aim to help learners comprehend a particular text and at the same time model effective reading strategies.
- There is no one magic way to teach reading: learners need to be shown a variety of strategies to use in reading texts, and take on a range of reader roles as they do so.

To Think About . . .

1. How can you use the ideas in this chapter in your own teaching?
2. The chapter has argued that all teachers need to be responsible for supporting EL learners' reading development. What difficulties do (or might) you or other teachers face in implementing this principle in your own teaching? How can these difficulties be addressed?
3. Depending on your own role (as a content, elementary, or ELL teacher/ supervisor, etc.), what is the most important advice you would give to a content-area teacher about supporting EL learners' academic reading?
4. In what ways do you currently support EL learners in their reading development? Share a success story with a colleague!

Suggestions for Further Reading

Carrasquillo, A., S. Kucer, and R. Abrams. 2004. *Beyond the Beginnings: Literacy Interventions for Upper Elementary English Language Learners*, Chapter 5. Clevedon, UK: Multilingual Matters.

Hood, S., N. Solomon, and A. Burns. 1996. *Focus on Reading.* Sydney: National Centre for English Language Teaching and Research (NCELTR), Macquarie University.

Wallace, C. 1992. *Reading*, Chapters 10 and 11. Oxford: Oxford University Press.

6 | Scaffolding EL Learners to Be Successful Writers

Learning to handle and manipulate the genres of the various school subjects, adapting and modifying them for different purposes, is important not only because it is a necessary part of learning the content of the subjects, but also because it is a necessary part of learning the ways of reasoning and organizing the different aspects of experience that are characteristic of the different subjects.

—Frances Christie and Joan Rothery, "Literacy in the Curriculum"

What This Chapter Is About

This chapter focuses on the ways that teachers can support EL learners' writing development. It describes a sequence of teaching and learning activities designed to apprentice students in the different forms of writing (sometimes known as *text types* or *genres*) that are required across the curriculum. You will find examples of some of these genres in Appendix 3. The chapter also presents ideas about how to scaffold these writing forms so that students are set up for success while becoming independent writers.

The chapter draws from significant work in Australia about the teaching of writing based on the work of linguists and teachers working within the framework of what is known as *functional grammar* (see, for example, Derewianka 2001, 1990; De Silva Joyce and Feez 2004; Droga and Humphrey 2003; Macken-Horarik 1996; Martin et al. 1987). Functional grammar was first introduced in Chapter 3, when we looked at some of the differences between speaking and writing and at the notions of field, tenor, and mode to describe the "style" of a particular piece of language. You will remember that *field* describes the topic or subject matter of a piece of language; *tenor*, the relationship between speaker and listener or reader and writer; and *mode*, the channel of communication, spoken or written. This chapter takes a functional approach in describing the language characteristics of the most important types of written genres in school. It also describes how we can assist students, through specific scaffolding, in learning to use them. This scaffolding takes the form of a particular sequence of activities, known in Australia as the *teaching and learning cycle*. In this approach, teachers take an explicit approach to the teaching of writing while at the same time supporting student autonomy and ownership of the writing process.

Before you read on, think for a moment about some of the characteristics of students who write well in English or in another language. You will probably have identified things such as the following.

Effective writers are likely to:

- Understand the purpose of the writing.
- Understand what they need to do with language so that it is appropriate for the audience and purpose.
- Understand how to organize and structure the overall writing and how this organization differs according to the type of writing.
- Understand that most writing is a recursive process, which requires writers to revise, perhaps reorganize, and edit their work.
- Be aware of the differences between speech and writing and understand that writing is not simply speech written down.
- Draw on models of good writing and know how to go about finding out what they don't know, such as the spelling of a word.
- Know something about the subject they are writing about.
- Make their writing explicit enough for readers to understand their meaning (for example, by anticipating what may need explanation). Anticipation of reader needs may relate to *content* (for example, defining particular technical terms or providing sufficient information) or *language* (for example, making clear what pronouns like *it, he,* and *she* refer to).
- Be confident writers in English or another language.

In contrast, less effective writers may be more concerned with the mechanics of writing, such as spelling, or be overly concerned with "correctness." They may lack the confidence to write at length, be unaware of the differences between different text types, or lack an awareness of audience. Their writing often sounds like speech written down, and it may lack overall organization or structure. They often find self-editing very difficult and are frequently unable to see what editing or revising is needed. And they have probably rarely, if ever, experienced success at writing.

Students who are struggling to write in English as a second language are also faced with a number of additional challenges. Much traditional teaching in school presupposes that learners are already familiar with the language they are learning in and assumes that they have already internalized many understandings about that language. This may not be the case for EL learners. Concepts of print, such as sound-symbol relationships, directionality, and the script or writing system itself, may also be unfamiliar. In Australia, much of the early work around the teaching of writing took place in urban primary schools where many of the students were EL learners. One of the things that the researchers found was that these children tended to write in only one genre: most of their writing took the form of "recounts" (personal accounts of things they had seen or done). While this may be an appropriate starting point for young writers, what concerned the researchers was that this limited (and limiting) form of writing continued throughout these students' primary years: the recounts grew longer but the writers continued to write almost predominantly in this form, rarely venturing into writing factual reports, explanations, instructions, or discussions. This apparent lack of awareness by students of how to produce other important text types, particularly those that demanded more academic language, prompted the researchers to develop the approach described in this chapter.

The approach is based on the belief that all students, not only EL learners, need to be taught explicitly how to control the full range of genres, or text types, associated with writing across the curriculum: unlike learning to speak in one's mother tongue, learning to read and write in these more sophisticated ways is not, for most children, simply "picked up" incidentally. But for students unfamiliar with the language and literacy of school, such as EL learners or those who speak nonstandard dialects of English, this explicit teaching is essential if they are to have equality of access to the dominant written genres that are valued in education.

What Is a Genre?

The term *genre* is often used to refer to different forms of literary writing, such as poems, plays, or novels, or to describe different kinds of films or artwork. These general distinctions can also be subclassified—for example, novels can be separated into a range of genres such as fantasy, romance, historical, detective, or spy novels.

However, within functional grammar the notion of genre has been extended to describe all the language events, both spoken and written, that we participate in as members of our particular society and culture. This broader definition encompasses things such as a marriage service, a lesson, a joke, a seminar, a board meeting, buying a ticket at the railway station, a set of written instructions, a newspaper report, an informal email, a movie review, and so on. In fact, most of what we do in our everyday life, when that involves social interaction with others in the culture, involves participating in a particular genre.

Every genre has a number of characteristics that make it different from other genres:

- It has a particular social purpose and is used to get something done through language.
- It has a particular overall structure or organization.
- It has language features typical of that genre.

Importantly, a genre is shared by members of the same culture and is "recognized" by them as a genre, in that they know how to use it through being part of the culture.

This is one of the reasons why, if you travel to another country, even though you may have some knowledge of the language, you may still find it difficult to understand "how things get done." I remember standing in line for some time in an Italian department store waiting to pay for an item that I was holding (as I would do in Australia and in many other countries). After a while I realized that I should have paid for it first, and then taken my receipt to another counter, where the article would have been sent by the assistant and then wrapped by someone else. I was not, in other words, familiar with this particular genre of buying something. In another culture where bargaining was common, I needed to learn not only the particular language associated with bargaining, but also the rules of how much to offer and the social "etiquette" of bargaining appropriately. Without understanding this, the would-be buyer may be seen as impolite or arrogant (and may also be less successful in paying an appropriate price!).

Of course, when you are familiar with something, you don't need to think about how to do it: someone who has grown up in a culture knows the social rules implicitly. But if you are not yet part of the culture and haven't yet developed this implicit knowledge, then having someone tell you how to take part is very important: it may save a lot of time and many painful mistakes! As Lisa Delpit (1998) has argued, "Unless one has the leisure of a lifetime of immersion to learn [the rules of the culture], explicit presentation makes learning immeasurably easier" (283). This explicit teaching is especially important as learners begin to use more formal academic registers.

In this chapter we will focus only on written genres, limiting these to some of the most important genres used in school. To illustrate the three key aspects of genres mentioned above (social purpose, organization, and specific language features), we'll look first at two common school genres, narrative and argument.

Narrative

The traditional tale of the *North Wind and Sun* is used as an illustration.

Social Purpose

The purpose of narratives is to entertain, but like other traditional tales this story is also intended to teach and offers a moral (gentleness may be more powerful than strength).

Organization

Traditional Western narratives follow a typical organizational pattern. They begin with an *orientation* that introduces the characters and sets the scene, often giving details of when and where the story takes place. Then there are a number of *events*, which lead to a problem or *complication* that sets up some kind of tension. Finally there is a *resolution*, where the problem is resolved in some way. These four stages are illustrated in Figure 6.1.

Once upon a time the North Wind and the Sun were arguing about which of them was more powerful. "I am more powerful" said the Wind, "because my breath is very strong." "But strength is not the only power there is," replied the Sun. They argued for a long time, each of them claiming to be stronger than the other. To settle the argument they decided they should have a contest to see who was the most powerful.	Orientation *sets the scene, gives details of who, when, where*
After a while they noticed below them a man walking along the road. It was a bitterly cold day and the man was wearing a long, thick, warm coat. They decided to settle the argument by seeing who could most easily make the man take off his warm coat. "Do you see that man?" asked the Sun. "Let's see who can make him take off his coat." "That's easy," laughed the North Wind. "I can easily blow his coat off his back!" First the cold North Wind blew hard, trying to blow the man's coat off his back.	Events *relates a sequence of events*
But the man just wrapped the coat more closely around himself. Then the North Wind puffed and puffed, and blew harder and harder, but the man wrapped the coat even more tightly around his body. Finally the North Wind gave up his attempt, exhausted. "Now it's your turn," he gasped to the Sun.	Complication *introduces a problem or difficulty*
The gentle Sun shone out warmly. Soon the man grew warm and unbuttoned his coat. The Sun shone and shone, and after just a few minutes the man took off his coat. And so in the end the North Wind had to admit that the Sun was the stronger of the two.	Resolution *relates how the problem is resolved*

Figure 6.1. Organizational Structure of the Narrative *The North Wind and the Sun*

Language Features

This short story shows many of the typical language features of a narrative:

- It is sequenced in time, and this is signaled by a range of time connectives (see Chapter 5 and Appendix 2): *once upon a time, after a while, first, then, finally, soon, after a few minutes, in the end.*
- It uses the past tense.
- It uses many "action" verbs—verbs that describe what happens—*noticed, blew, wrapped, gave up, shone, unbuttoned.*
- It contains dialogue and uses a number of "saying" verbs—verbs that introduce the dialogue and express what the participants say—*said, asked, replied.* Sometimes these saying verbs also indicate *how* something is said: *gasped, laughed.* (Many narratives also use "thinking" verbs that give us information about what the participants are thinking or feeling, such as *wondered, remembered, thought, felt, disliked, loved, adored.*)
- It uses descriptive language to describe people and things—*bitterly cold* day; *long, thick, warm* coat; *cold* North Wind; *gentle* Sun—and to describe how actions occur—*easily, harder, tightly, warmly.*

Argument

If we compare this description of a narrative with a different genre—an argument—it is clear how distinctive each genre is. Again we will look at the social purpose, the organizational structure, and the particular language features.

Social Purpose

An argument seeks to persuade the reader to agree with a claim or point of view made by the writer. Central to a well-written argument are the contentions and evidence used to support the writer's view.

Organizational Structure

Typically an argument begins with the author's *statement of position*, sometimes accompanied with a *brief preview of the supporting arguments* to follow. This is followed by *each supporting argument in turn, together with supporting details or evidence.* The argument concludes with *a reaffirmation of the writer's position.* These stages are illustrated in Figure 6.2.

Language Features
- It is sequenced logically, with connectives used to introduce and sequence each of the three arguments (*first, in addition, finally*) and to introduce the concluding statement (*therefore*).
- It uses the simple present tense to make generalizations about the topic.

Old-growth forests are a priceless resource to our planet, and should be protected. There are a number of reasons why they are so important. They have great environmental value, they play a vital role in maintaining a healthy global climate, and they contribute to biodiversity and so to all life on earth.	*Statement of position, and preview of following arguments*
First, they are home to a great many species of plant and animal life. These species depend for their survival on complex ecological relationships that have taken many thousands of years to develop in the forest environment. When old trees are logged, the habitats and food chains they provide will not return for many hundreds of years. This will inevitably lead to the extinction of many plants and animals. In addition, scientists have become increasingly aware of the role played by forests in the global climate system. For example, the loss of trees in the Himalayas has contributed to flooding in Bangladesh. Humans have already caused the world's climate to change, and it is the forests than can help to restore balance to this system. Finally, old-growth forests contribute to biodiversity. Scientists believe that life on earth cannot survive without a great variety of species. Each old tree in an old-growth forest supports an ecosystem of enormous diversity, and so each tree that is logged contributes to the extinction of life on the earth as we know it.	*Arguments (here there are three), each with supporting evidence or details*
It seems obvious that no economic argument in support of logging can possibly justify the destruction of trees in our old-growth forests. It is therefore vital that we protect this priceless resource for our future.	*Reaffirmation of writer's position*

Figure 6.2. Organizational Structure of the Argument *The Importance of Old Growth Forests* (text adapted from De Silva Joyce and Feez 2004, 146)

- It uses field-specific (technical) vocabulary: *old-growth, global climate, biodiversity, ecological, habitats, food chains, extinction, ecosystem.*
- It uses evaluative vocabulary and language that suggests the writer's stance, voice, or attitude, especially in the initial statement of position and in the reaffirmation at the end: *priceless, vital, healthy, obvious,* no economic argument *can possibly justify.*

Implications for Teachers

An analysis of school genres, as in the two examples above, reveals the grammatical challenges to EL learners and therefore helps teachers recognize where learners may need support. The two genres illustrate that simplistic statements about what counts as "good writing" (i.e., using identical criteria for both) are not sufficient to guide students in their writing. The analyses show that what might be good writing in a narrative is not the case in an argument. Technical vocabulary is absent from the narrative, yet it is essential in the argument so that the writer's voice carries authority and because the writer needs to talk about the scientific evidence as support for the claims he or she makes. The structure of the two pieces is also very different, and the way that the writing is sequenced requires different kinds of connecting words. Thus the social purpose of the writing affects all aspects: its overall structure, the kinds of connectives used, and the grammar and vocabulary. Writing involves writing *something*, producing a written product of some kind, and that product cannot be divorced from its purpose and from the context in which it will be read.

Understanding the purpose, organization, and language features of the kinds of writing we require from students is essential if we are to give EL learners the guidance and scaffolding they need to be successful. If teachers have an explicit understanding themselves of what an effective piece of writing in a particular genre looks like, it is much easier to make this explicit to learners. That is why it is important for all teachers, not only EL teachers, to be able to identify the key genres used in their own subjects or teaching contexts. Appendix 3 identifies the features of a range of school genres in the same way that the narrative and argument genres are analyzed above. You will find each genre described in terms of its social purpose, its organizational structure, and its typical language features. As in the examples above, the language features include the kinds of connectives or conjunctions that are used to link ideas across sentences and paragraphs, along with any other relevant aspects of language. Some of these genres are more likely to occur at the elementary levels, others at early or later middle or secondary levels. Some will occur in all curriculum areas, others will be specific to particular subjects. Here are some important points to note as you refer to this list of genres:

- The list represents only some of the most common genres used in school. It is *not* a definitive list of all the genres used in every subject! There will be some that you know are important in your own subject area or teaching context that are not included. If this is the case, add them, and try to describe them using the same headings.

- Each genre should be thought of as a *prototype*, because often there are variations in how the genres are used. For example, a short story writer might choose to begin with the resolution of a story and then present the action as a series of flashbacks. Or she may choose to incorporate multiple complications and partial resolutions to maintain tension and suspense. Fluent writers may play with genres in many ways, but they and their readers understand what this variation is based on. Or a text may be a hybrid genre: for example, within an argument the supporting evidence for a claim may take the form of a short personal recount, or it may contain an explanation. It is not unusual for one genre to be embedded within another in this way, and you will find many examples of "hybrid" genres in all the textbooks learners read. Nevertheless an understanding of how to use the prototype genres included in Appendix 3 is an excellent and necessary basis for more creative or demanding writing and for developing an understanding about the relationship between grammar and meaning.

- The genres should not be thought of as *prescriptive*: they are not a set of "rules" about how to use the language. Unlike much traditional grammar, they come not from a set of rules about what constitutes good writing, but from an ongoing analysis of valued educational writing in actual usage. Thus they are *descriptive*, in that they describe how successful writers actually use language in authentic writing contexts and, most important, how this language varies depending on its context and purpose.

- Genres are not static. They change according to the demands of the culture and society, so that new genres are constantly being created and old ones discarded. Emails and text messaging are examples of these new genres. And increasingly, in the kinds of electronic texts found on the Internet, verbal and visual elements work together in dynamic ways previously not possible.

- The list of genres in Appendix 3 is for teacher information and is not intended to be shared with students in this form. A pedagogical approach based on genre theory is the subject of the next part of this chapter. It describes some of the ways teaching about genres can be translated into classroom practice.

Introducing and Scaffolding Genres in the Classroom

Let's look now at how these principles and information about writing can be put into practice. The approach described below is particularly relevant for content-based language teaching and is a very valuable way of integrating the development of curriculum knowledge with explicit language teaching. It also integrates listening, speaking, reading, and writing.

The Teaching and Learning Cycle

In this approach, usually known as the teaching and learning cycle (or sometimes, the curriculum cycle), the particular genre on which the teacher is focusing is introduced, modeled, and practiced in a series of four stages: building the field, modeling the genre, joint construction, and independent writing. Each stage has a particular teaching purpose, which is described briefly below.

Stage 1: Building the Field (Developing Knowledge of the Topic)

This stage is primarily content focused. The aim is to build up information about the writing topic itself, so the focus is primarily on the information or "content" of the text that the students will eventually write. For this reason it may be relevant for students to use their first language for some activities at this stage of the learning sequence. In the field-building stage students will also become familiar with the key vocabulary associated with the topic.

Sometimes students in school are expected to write on topics they know very little about, and as a result their writing lacks authority and may sound unsophisticated. Knowledge of the topic is essential for factual texts, but this does not apply only to factual writing. Narrative writing too depends on the author's knowing his or her context well: a science fiction writer, for example, usually draws on some recognized scientific information even while constructing fantasy from it. In one interview, J. K. Rowling, the author of the *Harry Potter* series, described how she developed a detailed history of each of her characters' lives before beginning the books. As she pointed out, much of this information about her characters may not always have been directly referred to in the novels, but this background allows an author to write from an authority that produces fully rounded characters and coherence within the novel. In other words, a writer needs to know more than may actually be shared with the reader.

Stage 2: Modeling the Genre

This stage is primarily language focused, specifically on the form and function of the particular genre students will be writing. In this stage the aim is for the students to become familiar with the purpose, organization, and language features of that genre (refer to Appendix 3 for teacher information).

Stage 3: Joint Construction

This stage is both content and language focused. An example can be found in Chapter 4. The aim is for the teacher and students to write together, collaboratively constructing a piece of writing in the chosen genre, discussing as they do so both the validity or relevance of the information or content and the appropriateness of the language. (It is similar to what is sometimes known as *shared writing*.) Joint constructions illustrate both the process and product of writing and take account of both relevant content and the form of the genre. The joint construction imitates a very natural process in child oral language development. Young children learn to talk by interacting with parents or caregivers, perhaps older siblings, and friends, and often in the course of the talk the child's conversational partner will reword or "recast" what the child is trying to say into more appropriate language, as in this example with a twenty-one-month-old child:

Child:	I goed park.
Father:	Yes, you went to the park today, didn't you?
Child:	Went park today.
Mother:	And who took you?
Child:	Grandma. Went park today.

What the child says in the final line represents an increase in clarity and content from what he says initially. This development is the result of the parents' contributions to the conversation, and these are contingent on—responsive to—what the child is trying to talk about. At the same time it remains the child's "story," based on what he wants to recount. In this sense this is a jointly produced text, created by both child and parents collaboratively. Teachers play a similar role in a written joint construction.

Stage 4: Independent Writing

At this stage students write their own text in the chosen genre.

Examples of Teaching and Learning Activities for Each Stage

Let's assume you have chosen a particular genre on which to focus within a unit of work. This is the genre that the students will eventually use themselves in their independent writing during the final stage. For the purposes of the description below, we'll refer to this as the *focus genre*. It's important to choose as the focus genre a text type that is relevant to the particular unit of work—for example, the writing of a science report in a science unit focusing on experimental design, or a short narrative in a literature unit, or an argument in a social studies unit about an aspect of conservation.

Stage 1: Building the Field

Everything you already do when developing curriculum or subject knowledge with students is relevant to this stage; if you are working on a particular subject and topic, you will already be building the field (that is, developing subject knowledge). If you are a subject teacher, all the teaching and learning activities you would normally use in the content classroom, including practical tasks, discussions, IT use, excursions, and all the speaking and reading activities, contribute to this stage. As you can see, this stage encompasses a lot of speaking, listening, and reading and may involve practical activities.

Within your regular program you could also include some of the language-based activities in Chapters 4, 5, and 7, all of which can be easily integrated into regular content teaching. In addition, here are some other language-based activities that may also be integrated with subject teaching and so be useful for building the field (not every activity below is appropriate for every subject or topic or level):

- Let students share what they already know about the topic, through a *semantic map*, *wallpapering*, or a *progressive brainstorm* (see Chapter 4). Allow the use of students' first language, since the primary aim in these activities is to have students reflect on prior learning.
- Read about the topic using a range of sources and some of the before-reading, during-reading, and after-reading activities suggested in Chapter 5. *Jigsaw reading* is a particularly valuable activity, since it requires all students to contribute orally to shared group knowledge while reading at an appropriate individual level.
- Develop a *word wall* or *word bank* about the topic where topic-specific vocabulary can be displayed. Encourage students to add words as their learning progresses throughout the topic (see Chapter 4).
- Have students *interview an expert* about the topic where appropriate.
- Organize *excursions* to relevant sites or to museums at the beginning of the topic, so that there is a shared experience on which to build new language.
- Watch relevant videos or DVDs. Provide a structure for students to note relevant information as they watch. For example, give a list of questions for which students must listen for the answers. To encourage oral communication when using videos, put students into pairs, with partner A answering one set of questions, partner B a different set, so each student has different information at the end. After watching the video, students share what they have learned with their partner.
- Provide a structure to summarize the ongoing learning of the class—for example, information displayed on a *graphic outline* such as a *timeline* or an *information grid* (see Chapter 5).
- To revisit or reinforce subject learning, use a *dictogloss* or a *total cloze* (see Chapter 4).
- Use a *picture dictation*. This is a listening activity in which students have a number of individual pictures that they must put into the correct order as they listen to you read a description of a sequence aloud. For example, you might read an explanation of the water cycle as students place relevant diagrams in the correct order.
- Use a *barrier crossword* (see Chapter 4) to develop or revisit topic-related vocabulary.
- Encourage the use of students' first language for learning by having same-language students work together in any of the above activities, and by encouraging students to make bilingual notes.
- Have students keep their own dictionary of subject-specific words, and encourage students to do this bilingually.

- Use *picture/sentence matching* activities relevant to the topic. Students match a series of pictures or diagrams to appropriate sentences. This could be based on a book that is being used in class. This is a useful activity for lower-level or beginning EL students. Adapt language where necessary.

Stage 2: Modeling the Genre

This stage aims to build up students' language knowledge about the focus genre. You need some good model texts to illustrate the organization and language features of the genre. These can be commercially produced, written by you, or written by other students. Put at least one of the texts in a form large enough for the whole class to see so that you can talk about it more easily. Power Point presentations make it very easy to highlight key features of the genre and its overall structure. This is a good context for using metalanguage to talk with students about the features (terms such as *organizational structure, connectives, verbs, nominal groups,* and so on).

Here are some suggestions for activities that focus on the structure and language of the focus genre:

- Display a model and read it to the students. Discuss with them the purpose of the genre.
- Give groups of students several different examples of the focus genre, and ask them to decide how they are alike.
- Draw attention to the way the text is organized. You could have the students mark each of the stages on their own copy.
- Focus on the key language features (see Appendix 3), drawing on the models to show examples. Have students highlight these themselves on their own copies.
- Have students do a *text reconstruction* in pairs. In a text reconstruction students sequence jumbled sentences into a coherent text. Ask them to explain the sequence they choose. Alternatively, for a more challenging activity, jumble up two texts.
- Use a *dictogloss* (see Chapter 4) taken from an example of the focus genre. This will provide another model of the text type, and can also be used to revisit subject content.
- Use a *split dictation* taken from one of the model texts to focus on language features (see Chapter 4).
- Develop a *cloze activity* (see Chapter 4) taken from a model text, deleting words that typify the genre, such as connectives or key grammatical features (e.g., past tense in narratives, imperatives in instructions).
- Display information about the genre (e.g., its purpose, structure, and key language features) on the wall.

Stage 3: Joint Construction

At this stage the previous two stages are brought together. Using the knowledge they have developed about the content in stage 1 and the focus genre in stage 2, students begin the task of writing. In a joint construction, however, they do not write alone, but jointly with you. Typically, as we saw in the example in Chapter 4, you'll help students reshape the wording of their initial suggestions.

Ask students to contribute ideas about what to write, while you act as scribe and guide, suggesting wording or discussing with students how the writing might be improved. "Think aloud" during this process: *That's not very clear, is it? Could we use another word in place of* and *here?* Throughout the process, together with your students, constantly reread what has been written; reorganize ideas; improve wording; or make corrections to grammar, spelling, and punctuation. Discuss language and how it is used while students are actually engaged in composing the text.

By the time the writing is completed, it will probably look quite messy, with deletions, corrections, and changes evident. What this stage demonstrates for students is the *process* of writing: writers reread and revise what they write; they don't "get it right" the first time. What it also demonstrates is the *product* of writing: the result of the joint construction is another example of the focus genre that students will finally write individually during the final stage of the cycle.

The topic of the joint construction is usually one that relates to the topic being studied but will not be exactly the same topic that the students will eventually write about. For example, if the final task is for students to write a science report, then the joint construction will also be a science report, but it will not be on the same experiment that students will eventually report on in their individual writing.

Stage 4. Independent Writing

At this stage students are writing independently. By now students should have developed knowledge about the topic, become familiar with the major features of the genre, and participated in a joint construction with you as their guide, so this independent writing has been strongly scaffolded. Learners should now be able to write with confidence, drawing on their experiences and learning in the previous three stages.

During this stage:

- Encourage the students to refer to the models they used in stage 2.
- Remind them to write an initial draft (more than one if necessary) and edit and revise their writing. (Remind them of the process of writing demonstrated in the joint construction.)
- Encourage reflection and autonomy by providing them with an editing sheet to remind them of the key features of the focus genre (see the following section and Appendix 3).
- Encourage them to show their writing to a partner and get feedback.
- Confer with individual students as necessary.
- Remind them that the final version is for public display and needs to be correct and well presented.
- Encourage students to share their work with people outside school.
- For early EL learners who may need more scaffolding, provide a scaffolding framework (see Figure 6.3).

Title: _____

Say what this discussion is about, and give your opinion.

The topic of this discussion is . . .

Many people argue that . . .

However, in my opinion . . .

Give your reasons for your opinion (your arguments).

There are a number of reasons why this is the case.

First . . .

In addition . . .

Moreover . . .

Finally . . .

Now give other people's reasons for disagreeing with your opinion (the counter-arguments).

On the other hand, some people argue that . . .

In addition . . .

It has also been suggested that . . .

Give your conclusion. Remind the reader of your view and summarize your reasons.

However, overall it can be argued that . . .

because . . .

Figure 6.3. Scaffolding Framework (Argument)

What perhaps most sets this approach apart from some other ways of teaching writing is the amount and quality of the scaffolding provided. Students are set up for success because this scaffolding (stages 1, 2, and 3) is "front-loaded"—provided *before* students begin writing alone. It integrates subject content and language, while at the same time integrating listening, speaking, reading, writing, and some research and study skills. Thus it can provide a framework for the development of language and literacy in academic contexts.

Using a Genre Framework for Assessment

Knowledge about genre is also a useful tool when assessing writing. Most teachers have had the experience of being faced with a poor piece of writing and finding it difficult to know where to begin and how to help the student. Having a systematic way of approaching this helps you see what students are able to do, as well as where they need help. The framework in Figure 6.4 lets you record information about each individual student's areas of strength and areas in which more guidance is needed. The information obtained can be used as you plan future programs and may also form a basis for more formal reporting to other teachers or parents. While it is not intended to be used in this form directly with students, it does provide you with a basis for giving clear oral feedback to students about their writing (see the next page).

The framework contains seven sets of questions to ask yourself as you assess a student's piece of writing. Working from left to right, the sets of questions are ordered systematically, beginning with a focus on the whole text and working "top down" toward a focus on the mechanics of writing. Thus the first set of questions (*general comments*) addresses how far the piece as a whole makes meaning, the second focuses on the genre, the third on the overall structure of the genre, the fourth on connectives, the fifth on vocabulary, the sixth on sentence grammar, and the seventh on punctuation and spelling. The questions under each of the headings may not all be relevant for every piece of writing you assess, but they are intended to demonstrate the sort of information you should consider. Punctuation and spelling are last not because they are not important but because if a piece of writing is poorly organized or ungrammatical and also has poor spelling, then having students correct their spelling still results in a poor piece of writing, albeit with correct spelling! It is better to revise at the level of the whole text first and deal with spelling later (and this reflects what most effective writers do).

A brief written comment on each area is usually sufficient. Some teachers have found it useful to note, for their own record keeping, areas of strength in black ink and areas of need in red ink. Over time, as the student writes other pieces, your comments will gradually build up to become a profile of an individual writer, with strengths and language learning needs identified. The framework may also be simplified so that it

1. General Comments	2. Genre Type	3. Overall Organization	4. Cohesion (connectives and reference words)	5. Vocabulary	6. Sentence Grammar	7. Punctuation and Spelling
Is the overall meaning clear? Are the main ideas developed? Does the writing reflect the writer's other classroom language experiences (e.g., what she or he has read or talked about)? What is your overall impression compared with other things the learner has written?	What kind of genre is this? Is this appropriate for the writer's purpose? Has the writer written this text type before?	Is the overall structural organization appropriate to the text type? Are any stages missing?	Are the ideas linked with the appropriate connectives (*these will vary with the genre*)? Is there appropriate variety of these connectives? Are pronouns (e.g., *he* and *she*) used correctly? Do pronouns have a clear referent (e.g., is it clear what words like *he, she, this, there,* etc. are referring to)?	Is appropriate vocabulary used? Is there appropriate semantic variety (e.g., a range of "saying" verbs in a narrative text)?	Is the sentence grammar accurate (e.g., subject-verb agreement, correct use of tenses, correct use of word order)?	Is the punctuation appropriate (e.g., paragraphs, dialogue, headings and subheadings, commas, periods)? Is spelling accurate? If the writer does not yet produce correct spelling, what does he or she know about spelling (e.g., evidence of sound/symbol correspondence)?

Figure 6.4. Question Framework for Assessing Writing

becomes an editing sheet for students to use themselves. For example, an editing sheet to use with a narrative could contain questions like:

- Will my audience understand what I have written?
- Are all the parts of the narrative included (orientation, events, complication, and resolution)?
- Have I used a range of time connectives to sequence what happened?
- Have I used dialogue?
- Have I used a range of "saying" verbs?
- Have I used the past tense correctly?
- Have I described people and things clearly for my audience?
- Does the punctuation make the meaning clearer?
- Have I used correct spelling?

Editing sheets could be developed for each of the genres, based on the descriptions given in Appendix 3. Ensure that you focus attention on the overall text first, before spelling and punctuation.

Using this approach for assessment also helps you give useful oral feedback to students that they can act on in future. Here are some excerpts from a conversation a teacher had with a student about a story the student had written:

The overall organization of your narrative was very good, and you used a good range of action verbs to describe what happened. I like the saying verbs you chose as well: *shouted, yelled, whispered.*

Next time you write a narrative, try to use a range of time connectives. Can you see you used mostly *and then*? That doesn't give the reader much information, does it? What other time connectives could you have used? [At this point, you can direct the learner to a book you have shared, as a model, or perhaps you have a word wall with appropriate connectives listed.]

Figure 6.5 (page 124) is a piece of writing from a grade 6 student. He had been in Australia about twelve months at the time of writing and was literate in his first language (Greek). The writing is a retelling of a narrative read to the class by the teacher (the folktale *The Princess and the Pea*). As you read it, use the framework to make comments, and note what the student *knows* and *can do* and the specific language areas with which he needs help. (Figure 6.6, page 125, is an example of a teacher's assessment of the same text.)

Some Commonly Asked Questions About Using the Teaching and Learning Cycle

Here are some of the questions that teachers ask when they begin to use this approach, along with some possible answers.

A long long time ago is the greek have a king with adult prince.

One day his fathere said to him "you got to marry so he said he going to choose his a girl to marry for himself. He go around the country greek to find the girl but he haven't find her yet. He go home and he so sad. One day he was sit in his room and look outside, it was storm day and thunder, Sudenly he heard the door knock he open the door and he she the girl and she said she was a princess, He bring he inside the room. In the morning he going to tell his fathere about that. And his mother said "I going to made a bed for her sleep and I put a little peanut under the twenty pillow for he sleep that way. If her can't sleep she was a princess and the night came every body sleep and in the morning, every body have a breakfast. The Queen ask the princess "Have you got a good sleep? The princess said "No! I haven't got a good sleep, I think like a very big stone under my head. And every body laf and said the Queen try to test you see you a real princess and they are marry.

Figure 6.5. Writing from a Grade 6 EL Learner (reproduced as written)

How do I choose which genre to focus on with my learners?

There are two ways to do this. If you are working in a subject area, then select a genre that is relevant to a particular unit of work. In this case the content area "drives" the choice of genre. If you are a specialist language teacher, you could select a genre that you know your students are less familiar with. In this case you will need to select appropriate content to provide a context for the writing. At the elementary level, there may be a whole-school approach to the teaching of key genres, so that different genres may be the focus of different grade levels (although every genre will also need to be revisited throughout the grades). Generally, early genres include personal recounts, narratives, information reports, procedures, explanations, and arguments, with more analytical genres occurring in the middle years.

How long does it take to complete the whole teaching and learning cycle?

The cycle will last throughout a whole unit of work; it is not intended to be used within a single lesson! Of course, students won't "finish" learning about the genre in a single cycle. In a regular curriculum, any genre will occur many times over in the course of a student's school career, and students will over time gradually become more proficient in using it in increasingly sophisticated ways.

Do I need to go through all four stages once students begin to be familiar with a particular genre?

No. The cycle is intended to be used flexibly. Once students have become familiar with a genre and are able to use it with some confidence, it may be possible to skip stages 2

1. General Comments	2. Genre Type	3. Overall Organization	4. Cohesion	5. Vocabulary	6. Sentence Grammar	7. Punctuation and Spelling
Good. Clear and easy to understand. Reflects understanding of story read to class. Ideas could be more fully expanded.	Narrative	Good. All part of narrative included, could be expanded.	Good. Appropriate use of time connectives (a long time ago, one day, suddenly, in the morning). Referents not always clear, pronouns sometimes confused	Appropriate, shows uptake from story.	Needs help with tense, especially past tenses. Needs vocabulary for saying verbs.	Needs help with (1) paragraphing (2) setting out of dialogue.

Figure 6.6. Teacher's Assessment of Student Narrative

or 3, or cover them very briefly. However, it will probably be necessary to remind students again of the models and refer back to their previous writing. And it will always be necessary to ensure students have sufficient knowledge of the *field* of their writing.

How can I make use of my students' first languages in this approach?

Students' first languages can be used at various points throughout the cycle, although since the ultimate aim is to enable students to write in English, the final independent writing is usually in English (but see the following question). Students' first languages can be used to build up field knowledge, providing they also have access in English to the same information so that they develop key vocabulary. In stage 2, there may be some interesting discussion around how different cultures structure their writing differently or use different styles. (For example, you could compare a business letter in Spanish and English, or examine the way an argument is structured in Spanish, Chinese, or Arabic compared with English.)

If I have students with very little knowledge of English in my class, how do I give them extra help within this approach?

As far as possible it is better to have students engaged on the same key tasks and to offer different levels of scaffolding, rather than have them engaged in separate lower-level tasks. But this may not always be possible when students are beginners. Depending on the student's level, you could:

- Encourage students to write in their first language. With the aid of another speaker of the language (unless you speak the learner's language), produce an English version as well, so that the student has a bilingual version.
- Provide a *writing framework* (see Figure 6.3). This illustrates the organization of the genre and has sentence beginnings at key points. Frameworks can be made very simple for beginning EL learners, although the overall organization should be retained. If students need more help, you could also provide them with some complete sentences to copy onto the framework. Younger learners can cut these up and stick the sentences onto the framework instead.
- Get students to sequence pictures that tell a story or show a sequence of processes. Have them write sentences under each picture describing the sequence.
- Write a sentence or two summarizing an important piece of learning for the unit as a whole. Cut the sentences into individual words and jumble them, and let the students sort the words back into the right order. It's important that even at the very beginning stages of learning English, EL learners have opportunities to be engaged in tasks that are related to what the class as a whole is doing or learning.

- Use a dialogue journal. This is an ongoing written conversation in which you ask a question and the student responds (and vice versa). This could be related to the topic the students are studying or something the student wants to know about.

How do I find time to do all this if I am a subject teacher?

Time is much less an issue if you integrate literacy teaching with content teaching using some of the strategies in this chapter and others. Good literacy teaching isn't something added to an already crowded curriculum: it isn't the icing on the cake, but the ingredients of it! As earlier chapters have suggested, it isn't really possible to teach content without addressing language, since the language is the means by which subject knowledge is realized. So rather than being concerned with "covering content," it is better to think in terms of "uncovering the subject"—that is, making the ways of using language and the ways of thinking in the subject explicit to your students. And this in turn will help develop understandings about literacy that are transferable to new contexts and new learning. You should also consider that spending time on scaffolding language pays off in terms of very much reducing the time you would spend on correcting and grading—you will find that the students produce much-better-written assignments.

If I am a subject teacher, why can't I leave teaching about genre to the EL specialist?

An EL specialist knows a lot about language and ways of teaching it, but cannot be expected to be familiar with the content and key genres of every subject area, especially at the higher grade levels. And in reality, even if some students in the school have direct access to EL specialists, many will not and will be in mainstream classes without specialist support. It is for this reason that the *every teacher is a teacher of language* principle is such a critical one for all schools. And, as we have seen, we cannot separate learning subject content from learning language. Ideally, however, EL specialists and mainstream or subject teachers will work collaboratively on teaching programs.

If I am an EL specialist, what is my role in this approach?

You have a very important role as a language specialist in supporting content teachers as they teach specific genres, as well as teaching genres to any students you work with directly. In the approach described in this chapter, you may be involved in any of the following activities, depending on the way the EL program operates in your school:

- Directly teaching basic key genres to a group of early EL learners.
- Working with individual faculties to develop integrated writing programs.
- Supporting teachers who are not EL specialists in identifying the key features of key genres in their subject or general teaching.
- Designing language-based teaching and learning activities for use at stages 1, 2, and 3 of the cycle.

- Assessing EL learners' writing and identifying language needs.
- Working alongside subject teachers in the classroom to provide in-class support to EL learners.
- Being an advocate for first language use at relevant points in the cycle.
- Conferring with EL learners as they are engaged in their independent writing.

Summary

This chapter has introduced the notion of genre, along with ways of teaching it across the curriculum. It has shown how:

- Genres are cultural in nature and differ in terms of their social purpose, overall organization, and specific language features.
- Written genres that are valued in school need to be explicitly taught, since they are central to learning and to successful student outcomes.
- The teaching and learning cycle naturally integrates content or subject teaching with language and literacy teaching.
- The cycle also integrates listening, speaking, and reading with writing.

To Think About . . .

1. With reference to a group of students with whom you work, identify the overall strengths of their writing and the language areas in which they need support. How could the teaching and learning cycle described in this chapter be used with these students?
2. In relation to the teaching of writing, what differences are there between the ways that students in your institution are currently taught and the approach described here?
3. If you are a subject teacher in middle or high school, identify some of the key genres used in your subject. Refer to Appendix 3 and add any genres not listed there that are relevant to your teaching.
4. If you are an elementary teacher, what genres would you focus on with students in grades 5 and 6?
5. If you are an EL specialist, in what ways might you use this approach with your EL learners? Which genres would you focus on first with low-level and newly arrived EL learners?
6. How could this approach be used throughout your school?

Suggestions for Further Reading

••

Derewianka, B. 1990. *Exploring How Texts Work*. Sydney: Primary English Teaching Association; Portsmouth, NH: Heinemann, 1991.

De Silva Joyce, H. 2005. *Developing Writing Skills*. Teacher Resource Book. Sydney: Phoenix Education.

De Silva Joyce, H., and S. Feez. 2004. *Developing Writing Skills for Middle Secondary Students*. Book 2. Sydney: Phoenix Education.

Droga, L., and S. Humphrey. 2003. Grammar and Meaning: *An Introduction for Primary Teachers*. Berry, NSW: Target Texts. Available from www.targettexts.com.

Martin, J. 1990. "Literacy in Science: Learning to Handle Text as Technology." In *Literacy for a Changing World*, edited by F. Christie. Hawthorn: AU: Australian Council for Australian Research.

Schleppegrell, M. 2004. *The Language of Schooling: A Functional Linguistics Perspective*. Mahwah, NJ: Lawrence Erlbaum. (See Chapter 4.)

7 | Planning Talk for Learning and Literacy

Spoken discourse has an essential role to play in mediating the pupil's apprenticeship into a discipline, both as a medium in which to respond to and prepare for work on written texts and . . . as an opportunity for "talking their way in" to ways of making sense of new information.

—Gordon Wells, "The Centrality of Talk in Education"

What This Chapter Is About

This chapter focuses on how classroom talk can create a language-learning-rich context for EL learners. The two functions of spoken language in the classroom identified by Gordon Wells—to provide a bridge to written literacy and to make sense of new knowledge—are central to learning across the curriculum. Throughout this chapter there are many examples of what this means in practice when many students in the class are EL learners. The chapter begins by discussing what kind of talk is supportive of second language learning and continues with a discussion of implications and strategies, first for teacher-student interactions and then for student-student interactions.

What Kind of Talk Supports Second Language Learning?

The cartoon on the following page shows a teacher talking to a young EL learner. It's pretty clear that not a lot of communication is going on here! Consider the nature of the teacher's responses to what the child is saying and what the child might be learning and feeling in this interaction. What advice would you give the teacher?

Form-Focused and Meaning-Focused Talk

The teacher's responses are focused solely on the *form* of the language, not on the content and meaning of what the learner is saying. The student is probably learning that this conversational situation is not one he wants to repeat—better to say nothing at

all next time! And in this situation he is probably not learning the language forms the teacher is insisting on. As his body language suggests, he is probably feeling increasingly embarrassed or inadequate as the interaction continues. He says less and less: the teacher effectively closes down the interaction through her interventions.

Talking with students is critical to what they learn. How we respond and what we say not only helps (or fails to help) their academic learning, it also constructs them as learners in particular ways: as worthy conversational partners and successful learners or as people whose ideas are not listened to. Our talk with students is never "neutral," and never just about the "content" of what we are teaching.

In comparison with the teacher talk in the preceding cartoon, here is a conversation in which a very young child (Nigel) is learning about language. While Nigel had been feeding a goat at the zoo, the goat tried to grab and eat a plastic lid Nigel was holding. The keeper had explained that eating the lid wouldn't be good for the goat. Later at home Nigel retells the incident to his mother and father:

Learning Language—A Collaborative Process

Nigel: Try eat lid.
Father: What tried to eat the lid?
Nigel: Try eat lid.
Father: What tried to eat the lid?
Nigel: Goat . . . man said no . . . goat try eat lid . . . man said no.

Later

Nigel: Goat try eat lid . . . man said no.
Mother: Why did the man say no?
Nigel: Goat shouldn't eat lid . . . [*shaking his head no*] good for it.
Mother: The goat shouldn't eat the lid. It's not good for it.
Nigel: Goat try eat lid . . . man said no . . . goat shouldn't eat lid [*shaking his head*] good for it.

(Halliday 1975, 112)

Notice how different this conversation is from the interaction in the cartoon. The parents focus primarily on the *meaning* of what Nigel is saying, while at the same time still providing strong support to help him make it more explicit, grammatical, and complete. But this support, unlike the cartoon interaction, is in the service of meaning and leads not to closing down the conversation but to extending it. First the father prompts Nigel to tell his listener what he's referring to (*what tried to eat the lid?*). Later the mother responds to Nigel's extended version (*goat try eat lid*) by asking a question to extend the story and providing the wording that Nigel is attempting (*it's not good for it*). While Nigel doesn't at this point take up that wording, he does produce at the end of these two short conversations a retelling of the event that, unlike his initial attempt, could be understood by someone who had not shared in the original experience.

This ability to reconstruct, through language alone, an event not shared by a listener represents a significant step in early child language development. What has helped Nigel here is the nature of his parents' responses that are finely tuned to his immediate learning needs and to his intended meanings. What he finally says has not been produced by Nigel alone, nor have the parents "taken over" his retelling: rather, this interaction has been co-constructed collaboratively by Nigel and his father and mother.

Factors That Facilitate Second Language Learning

It is not difficult to see which of the two examples above is likely to be more support-ive of language development. If we look at the past twenty or so years of second lan-guage acquisition (SLA) research, we can hypothesize why this might be the case. SLA research has suggested a number of factors that contribute to second language devel-opment. They have clear implications for the kinds of spoken language that support second language development and thus for the kinds of classroom contexts that are most learning rich for EL learners.

Comprehensible Input

Comprehensible input is associated with the work of Steven Krashen (1982), who ar-gues that being able to comprehend what is said (or written) is central to successful lan-guage learning. Comprehensible input, however, is not necessarily simplified input. There are many ways to make language comprehensible: by initially using a learner's mother tongue, orally or through written texts, to teach content; by using visuals such as pictures, diagrams, and graphic outlines; by drawing on previous experiences or learning; through practical demonstrations and experiences such as science experi-ments or excursions; through gestures or mime; by using symbols such as chemical or math symbols; by using interactive dynamic multimedia texts; by expressing ideas in more than one way; and in many other ways.

Krashen suggests that comprehensible input should be ahead of what a learner can actually produce, since language comprehension is always ahead of language produc-tion. Krashen describes this kind of input as *I* [input] + *1*. What this means in practice is that teachers need to use, as far as possible, authentic specific subject language but make it accessible to learners in the sorts of ways suggested throughout this book, rather than resorting to ongoing simplification of language.

Comprehensible Output

Merrill Swain (2000, 1995) has shown that comprehensible output is also essential for language learning. Comprehensible output refers to the learner's *use* of language. Learn-ers need opportunities to take part in extended interactions rather than being consis-tently asked to provide one- or two-word answers to questions. Unlike what happens when we listen or read (activities that do not require the learner to actually produce lan-guage), speaking requires learners to pay attention to what they are saying and how they are saying it, for the benefit of their listeners. This requires them to process the lan-guage at a deeper level. Swain argues that the most useful kinds of interactions are often those that involve "problem-solving dialogue," where small groups or pairs of students focus on solving a problem collaboratively. This may be related to a problem or ques-tion located within the content of a curriculum area (solving a mathematics problem or making recommendations about an environmental issue, for example) or be specifi-cally language-based (the dictogloss activity described in Chapter 4, for example). Swain argues that using language in interactions with others is not simply an *outcome* of the learning that has already taken place but is itself a source for *new* learning.

"Stretched" or "Pushed" Language

Swain also suggests that comprehensible output can lead to "stretched" or "pushed" language—those times when a learner is pushed by a particular situation to go beyond their comfort zone. If you have learned a second language yourself, you will have experienced certain times when you are aware that your current language skills are not adequate for the situation in which you find yourself. As a very early learner of Spanish, I needed to make some complicated changes to a trip and was trying to exchange my existing ticket. My Spanish was not up to this task, but I did eventually make myself understood, albeit in very poor Spanish! In Vygotskian terms I was operating at the outer boundaries of my zone of proximal development, and it was a struggle! Yet it is often these moments of struggle, when there is a "press" on our language resources and our current language skills are being stretched or pushed, that are critical learning moments. We are likely to notice what our interactant says, for example, since it is immediately relevant to our needs, or we may remember what to say next time, or having rehearsed saying something once we are better able to do it again. And if the communication breaks down entirely we are pushed to rethink how we have said something and perhaps use alternative ways of wording it. Using language that is beyond the learner's comfort zone is necessary at times if there is to be new learning. Of course, in the classroom this shouldn't involve emotional stress for the learner: along with creating situations that will result in learner language being pushed comes providing the sensitive and finely tuned scaffolding offered by a teacher or more advanced peer. (We can observe a similar process at work as Nigel grapples with the telling of his story with the support of his parents.)

Negotiation of Meaning

As learners engage in conversations either with peers or with more expert users, meanings are constantly being negotiated through clarification questions, confirmations of meaning, and adjustments to what has been said. Below two young EL students are engaged in a find-the-difference barrier game. Their task is to find six differences between two almost identical pictures. They are sitting back to back, so they are not able to see each other's pictures. Both pictures show a calendar on the wall of a classroom, but with different dates.

Student A:	Do you have a calendar on the wall [pronounces *calendar* with a stress on the second syllable—calendar].
Student B:	A what?
Student A:	A calendar.
Student B:	What is that?
Student A:	A calendar—it's got days and numbers on it.

Student B: Oh, a *calendar*! [*now understanding*]
Student A: Yeah, a calendar. [*pronouncing the word correctly*]

Negotiation of meaning does not occur only in situations involving early second language learning. It occurs at all levels, including in highly educated talk between native speakers. You will probably remember many occasions involving discussions or problem solving where meanings or ideas are collaboratively refined, and those participating need to clarify what they said or ask others to clarify or confirm.

Models of Appropriate Language

Learners need models of the language that are appropriate to the contexts in which they find themselves. School contexts, as we have seen, require both the spoken and written registers and genres of the various subjects; the registers needed to talk appropriately to teachers or other members of the school community; and knowledge of how to participate in classroom conversations. Collaborative student-centered group work plays a central role in developing this range of communicative functions, and the group often provides important peer scaffolding. But as we have seen in Chapter 3, academic language is unlikely to be simply "picked up," and group work cannot by itself provide models of language that students have not yet experienced. If students are to go forward in their language development, the teacher's role in modeling appropriate academic language and selecting resources remains essential. This book provides many examples of the ways that language can be modeled in the context in which it will be used.

A Well-Developed Mother Tongue

Over the past thirty years there have been numerous studies that report a clear association between bilingualism and students' linguistic and cognitive growth (Cummins 2000). A well-developed first language supports the development of a second, particularly when first language development includes literacy. As Cummins has argued, "Conceptual knowledge developed in one language helps to make input in the other language comprehensible" (39).

An effective English language program does not close off options for the use of other languages in the classroom, nor should it lead to a one-way journey away from family and community. The use of the students' mother tongue in the classroom, in addition to the kind of English language teaching described in this book, supports the academic and intellectual development of EL learners by providing contexts in which learners are better able to participate in curriculum activities using the full range of their available linguistic resources. In addition, the use of the mother tongue helps to provide a more positive affective classroom environment, one where students' cultural and linguistic identities are acknowledged and strengthened.

Underpinning many of the ideas in these and other current SLA studies is the importance of dialogue that occurs authentically in situations where learners participate to solve real problems or get something done. If you refer again to Chapter 2, you will notice that all the examples in the high-challenge classrooms associated with academic achievement involve a great deal of spoken language, but that this talk occurs in the context of authentic curriculum tasks, not in a separate language lesson. In other words, language is used for a real purpose, not merely to rehearse it. This is a central principle in creating a language-learning-rich classroom for EL learners and one that needs to be considered in the design of tasks involving spoken language. The remainder of this chapter illustrates some of the classroom implications of this principle.

Making Teacher-Student Talk a Context for Language Learning

This section describes five ways to make teacher-student talk more supportive of EL learners' content and language learning. They are:

- Extending teacher-student exchanges.
- Giving students time to think.
- Appropriating and recasting student language.
- Encouraging literate talk.
- Making reasoning explicit.

Each of these is discussed below, after we first look at how classroom talk has traditionally been conducted.

Traditional Classroom Talk

There is one very common and pervasive pattern of teacher-student interaction that is used the world over and has been observed by many language researchers for over 140 years (Hoetker and Ahlbrand 1969; Mehan 1979; Van Lier 1996). Known as initiation-response-feedback (or initiation-response-evaluation) (IRF/IRE), it typically consists of three "moves": (1) the teacher initiates a question (a "display" question to which he or she already knows the answer), (2) a student responds to the question, and (3) the teacher gives positive or negative feedback on the student's answer. Here is an example:

Move 1 (Initiation)	Teacher: What are these called?
Move 2 (Response)	Student: Compasses.
Move 3 (Feedback/Evaluation)	Teacher: A pair of compasses, good.

The IRF exchange may serve a number of useful purposes. It enables the teacher to quickly check the students' current knowledge or understanding or demonstrate a logical sequence of steps (such as talking students through the solving of a math problem). Well-planned IRF questions may also probe students' thinking at all levels.

However, if this is the major pattern used by a teacher, it is clear that there will be few opportunities for EL learners to *use* new language. Overuse of the IRF patterns fails to create the sorts of contexts for talk suggested by the SLA research discussed earlier. The student's response is typically very brief and hemmed in between the teacher's initiation and feedback; there is little opportunity for extended student output, stretched language, or negotiation of meaning. Each individual student's response is evaluated on its own rather than being treated as a part of an extended and substantive conversation. And often the teacher's feedback has the effect of closing down the exchange, preventing any further exploration of thinking or opportunities for language use by the student (as illustrated by the cartoon at the beginning of this chapter). Nystrand and Gamoran (1991) suggest that this kind of exchange is at the heart of why life in schools is "emotionally flat" (257).

Extending the IRF Exchange

Despite the potentially limiting effects of the IRF exchange, it can be modified to create increased opportunities for student participation and learning. Below, an example of a basic IRF structure is followed by a modified version where the third move allows a more extended response by the student.

Example 1: The IRF Exchange

Teacher:	What is the circumference?
Student:	All the way round.
Teacher:	Right, remember it's called the perimeter of the circle.

Example 2: Extending on the IRF Exchange

Teacher:	What is the circumference?
Student 1:	All the way round.
Teacher:	All the way round what?
Student 1:	The circle.
Teacher:	Can you say that again? Remember that word we used yesterday to describe all the way round? The . . . ?
Student 1:	Oh! Peri. . . .
Student 2:	Perimeter.
Student 1:	Perimeter.
Teacher:	Right. So the circumference is . . . ?
Student 1:	The perimeter of the circle.
Teacher:	Right, the circumference is the perimeter of the circle.

One of the differences between these two examples is that the description of a circumference (*the perimeter of the circle*) is provided by the teacher in the first instance but by the student in the second. In the second example the teacher has allowed the student several opportunities to respond, has prompted the student with a clue about the word (*that word we used yesterday*), and so has given the student more time to *think* about what to say. Too often teachers provide answers to their own questions or "recast" (reformulate) a student's answer too soon, as in Example 1. Learning in a second language, while you are still developing that language, often requires more processing or thinking time than is frequently given in teacher-student talk.

Giving Students Time to Think

One way of allowing more thinking time for students is to increase "wait time" (the time teachers wait between asking a question and getting a response). Research has shown that even two or three seconds extra wait time can lead, for all learners, to more extended, more complete, and better-formed answers (Dillon 1990).

Alternatively, you can ask a question of the whole class and allow learners thirty seconds of "thinking time" before calling on a student to respond. This encourages all the students to think through an answer. A similar strategy is to let students in pairs tell each other their answer before asking a student to share his or her answer.

As Example 2 illustrates, one effective way of increasing student thinking time is for the teacher to slow the overall pace of the discourse, holding back from immediately providing the desired wording and instead giving the students more opportunities to produce it themselves. This happens when teachers "probe" a student's response by asking for clarification or additional information or invite the student to restate the answer. This often requires some teacher scaffolding.

Example 3, below (from Gibbons 2002, 35), also illustrates the positive effect that "holding back" can have on a learner's language. In this grade 4 class where almost all students are EL learners, the students have been studying magnetism. Lindsay has discovered that if she places a sheet of aluminum foil between a bar magnet and a nail, the magnet still attracts the nail. Here she is explaining this to the rest of the class. Notice how the teacher again slows down the pace of the conversation by delaying the third move of the IRF sequence, and the difference this makes to Lindsay's explanation. (In this exchange, each dot represents a one-second pause.)

Example 3: Holding Back the Third Move

	STUDENT	TEACHER
1		What did you find out?
2	If you put a nail . onto the piece of foil . . and then pick it . . . pick it up . . the magnet will . . . . that if you put a . nail . under a piece of foil . and then pick . . . pick the foil up with the magnet . . . still . . still with the nail under it . . . it won't . . .	
3		It what?
4	It won't . . . it won't come out.	

5	What won't come out?
6 It'll go up.	
7	Wait just a minute…can you explain that a bit more, Lindsay?
8 Like if you put a nail and then foil over it and then put the nail on top . of the foil . . . the nail underneath the foil . . . . Miss, I can't say it.	
9	No, you're doing fine. I can see.
10 Miss, forget about the magnet, um, the magnet holds it with the foil up the top, and the nail's underneath and the foil's on top and put the magnet in it and you lift it up . . and the nail will, um, hold it, stick with the magnet and the foil's in between.	
11	Oh, so even with the foil in between . . . the magnet will still pick up the nail. All right, does the magnet pick up the foil?
12 No.	

The effect of the teacher's interaction on Lindsay's language is very clear. The hesitations evident in Lindsay's first attempt disappear, and what she says is increasingly explicit and clearer to the listeners, as was Nigel's story after talking with his parents. In fact, Lindsay's talk becomes more "written like" (see Chapter 3 and the discussion of the mode continuum), and what she finally says in Turn 10 will stand her in much better stead for any subsequent writing task than her original attempt. Having rehearsed and articulated her experiences and ideas with the teacher and rethought her original attempt, she will be much better prepared for writing. In fact, the children's learning journals in this classroom (in which they made notes about what they had learned each day) consistently reflected the co-constructed talk between student and teacher, using words and phrases from the spoken interaction.

Also note that the teacher's initiation is not a question to which there is only one answer but is close to a genuine question (unlike many of the questions teachers ask). Lindsay is invited to tell the class what she discovered, but it is left to her to decide what this will be. If you are a second language speaker, entering a conversation on your own terms in this way is usually easier than having to respond to a question about a topic already predetermined by the teacher. Note, too, the encouragement given by the teacher, who assures Lindsay at a moment of struggle that she understands what she's trying to say (*I can see*).

Also significant is the fact that each group of students in the class had carried out related but different experiments. This organizational structure for the lesson created a genuine communicative situation: the students were interested in listening to what other groups had done, and Lindsay had something she wanted to share. Throughout the interaction, the teacher treats Lindsay as a worthy conversational partner who has something worth listening to rather than as a mere displayer of received knowledge. When a teacher shifts roles in this way, more extended responses from students are much more likely. As Dufficy (2005) points out, "When responsibility for talk is more equally shared, the mindful teacher must inevitably engage with what children consider important at the time. . . . When teachers rush to cover a topic, opportunities to assist children to develop dispositions to engage with challenging academic work are lost" (75).

Appropriating and Recasting: Borrowing and Reformulating Student Language

In Example 4, below, taken from the grade 7 science classroom described in Chapter 2, the teacher and students are talking together about a video that showed how scientists tested the hypothesis *wearing a tongue stud makes it more likely that you will be struck by lightning*. In this interaction the teacher is developing the students' understanding of the notion of *replication* and its importance in designing valid scientific experiments. This is a good example of the "Janus curriculum" mentioned in Chapter 4, where something familiar to students in their everyday lives (the wearing of body jewelry) is used as a basis to develop scientific thinking and language. Paying attention to the words and phrases in bold type, note how the students' contributions to the discourse, worded in everyday ways, are clarified and extended by the teacher through the modeling of subject-specific language.

Example 4: Building on Student Contributions—Appropriating and Recasting

Student 1: They have to do it [*the experiment*] **many times** so they can see if there are any changes.

Teacher: Yes, so they can see if they get similar results.

Student 2: And see if the myth is busted. It wasn't getting busted but then they **kept doing it** until it got busted.

Teacher: So they did the experiment **many times**. Your experimental method should be **repeated a number of times**, too—so that a more accurate conclusion can be made. This is called **replicating** the experiment. . . . Okay, so they **repeated** their experiments many times.

Student 3: They **kept on doing** it.

Teacher: They **kept on doing** it. And this is what you have to do as well in your experiments. You have to **replicate** the experiment; you're going to **repeat** it several times, **replicate** it. And why do we have to do that? So that we get . . . ?

Student 2:   An accurate . . . ?
Student 3:   So that we get more accurate *results*.

One of the things the teacher does here is to use the students' language as a basis for modeling new language. In her own talk she appropriates, or takes up, the students' wording (she repeats *did many times* and *kept on doing it*) and then recasts, or reformulates it (she provides *repeat* and *replicate*). Thus the students have access to the scientific term *replicate* through the use of increasingly more technical language that has been based on familiar language: *kept doing it → did many times → repeat → replicate*. In the later part of the lesson, the teacher nominalized the verb *replicate*, referring to it as *replication*, and this term was subsequently used by the students themselves when they began to design their own experiments.

As we saw in Chapter 4, this kind of teacher-student talk "meshes" an everyday meaning with a subject-specific meaning, thus building on students' prior knowledge as a way of introducing them to new language. Such talk—referred to in Chapter 4 as "Janus-like"—is not uncommon in the talk between teachers and students, yet teachers are not always consciously aware of its usefulness for EL learners. Being aware of the language one uses with students in all classroom interactions is part of being a language-aware teacher.

Encouraging Literate Talk: Building a Bridge to Written Language

Encouraging literate talk means giving learners opportunities to use the kind of spoken language that is closer to written language and providing them with a chance to "rehearse" this more complete and explicit language in talk with others. This was illustrated in Chapter 3 in the discussion about the mode continuum, that is, the continuum from face-to-face spoken language to formal written language. As a reminder, here are the same four texts again, based on the topic of magnetism:

1. Look, it's making them move. That's not going. Those ones are going fast.
2. We found out the pins stuck on the magnet and so did the iron filings. Then we tried the pencil but it didn't stick.
3. Our experiment was to find out what a magnet attracted. We discovered that a magnet attracts some kinds of metal. It attracted the iron filings and the pins but not the pencil.
4. A magnet is a piece of metal that . . . is able to attract a piece of iron or steel because its magnetic field flows into the metal, turning it into a temporary magnet. Magnetic attraction occurs only between ferrous metals.

As Chapter 3 pointed out, using "language while doing" (like text 1) is for most EL learners not alone a sufficient preparation for writing. There is a big leap in the language between texts 1 and 3, and so rather than expecting learners to move straight from one to the other, we need to provide a language "bridge" between them. That bridge can be thought of as "literate spoken language," where the student, perhaps in interaction with the teacher, makes events, ideas, or information explicit through language alone, as the student does in text 2. One of the ways to do this is through "sharing," where students retell to someone else what they have learned, what they have done, or what they think or feel. In a previous book (Gibbons 2002) I have described one example of this as "teacher-*guided* reporting," since the success of this activity with EL learners often depends on the teacher providing the kind of finely tuned contingent support that we have seen in the examples. In these guided interactions, as we have seen in the examples in this chapter, learners are given the support they need to make their language more complete and explicit enough for a listener who may not have shared the speaker's experience or knowledge. Making explicit the language one uses is also, of course, one of the major requirements of formal writing.

Making Reasoning Explicit

In the example below, a grade 7 student is explaining to the teacher how his group went about solving this math problem:

> Helen buys 12 oranges and receives forty cents change from seven dollars. How much does each orange cost?

Almost all the students in the class were EL learners, and although generally their math skills were appropriate for the grade level, they frequently had difficulties with language-based problems. The class had also recently begun to study algebra, and the teacher wanted to hear their reasoning as they solved the problem. For these reasons he asked students to explain the process they had used, not simply produce the right answer. As in example 3, the teacher has taken the initial activity (the "doing") a step further by having student reflect on the process.

Example 5: Making Thinking Explicit

Eddie:	First we did 12a equals seven dollars take away forty cents.
Teacher:	Yes, you've written 12a. Well, what does the a mean for that though?
Eddie:	The a equals the item of the oranges.
Teacher:	So you mean . . . ?
Eddie:	Twelve oranges, so that equals the items.
Teacher:	Can you explain that again?
Eddie:	We're making up the cost of each orange to find out how much one orange costs.
Teacher:	What you are saying is a is the cost of *each* orange?
Eddie:	Yes.
Teacher:	So how about we write in here, "Let each orange cost a." Right? [*Student nods.*] Now what did you do with seven dollars?

Eddie: Yes, and then we . . . 12*a* equals six dollars sixty.

Teacher: Sorry. Backtracking, what are we taking away, subtracting? Why are we taking away forty cents?

Eddie: In the question, it says that we have change, and if we got six dollars sixty . . . like how much does one orange cost—fifty-five cents . . . times 12.

Teacher: So you're saying, pay the seven dollars and you get forty cents back. What did you do next?

Eddie: So 12*a* equals to . . . equals six dollars sixty.

Teacher: And then?

Eddie: We changed that to 660 cents. And 660 divided by 12.

Teacher: And so we get *a* equals the cost of each orange?

Eddie: Fifty-five. Then we did a check.

Teacher: Great. So you went and checked.

Eddie: And we did 55 times 12. That equals six dollars sixty.

Teacher: Terrific. So you went back and did a check step. Thank you, Eddie. Has anyone else got a different equation? I actually thought of arranging the equation in a different order. Has anyone done it differently? Yes, Katie?

Katie: We had 12*a* plus forty equals seven dollars.

[*Dialogue continues.*]

As Chapter 2 suggested, making thinking explicit plays an important role in learning. Cognitive apprenticeship is concerned with helping students learn to think and reason and solve problems and emphasizes the need for both teachers and students to make thinking visible and explicit. This is what we can see happening here. Although the problem is quite simple, the teacher's emphasis on having learners explain orally how they solved it allows him to check on their reasoning and also provides the students with a model they can later use for tackling more complex problems. In addition, this kind of talk often provides opportunities for a teacher to provide a model of new academic language by recasting what a student has said. Note how this teacher builds on Eddie's explanation of the function of the *a* in the equation to provide a more math-appropriate expression:

Eddie: We're making up the cost of each orange to find out how much one orange costs.

Teacher: So how about we write in here, "Let each orange cost *a*."

Key Features of Supportive Teacher Talk

In his work with teachers in Mexico, Mercer (2000) examined teacher talk in classrooms where there was a focus on scaffolding students' learning. He noted that the talk of more effective teachers could be distinguished by three characteristics:

- They used question-and-answer sequences not just to test knowledge but also to guide the development of understanding, often using *why* questions to encourage students to reason and reflect.
- They taught not just subject content but also procedures for solving problems and making sense of experiences. This included demonstrating problem-solving strategies, explaining the purpose of classroom activities, and encouraging children to make explicit their own thinking process.
- They treated learning as a social communicative process by encouraging students to take a more active role in classroom events, relating current activity to past experience, and using students' contributions as a resource for building new shared knowledge. (160)

The examples included in this chapter also demonstrate these characteristics and suggest how teachers can make their regular talk with students a more learning-rich experience for English language learners. In summary, here are some key points to think about in your own interactions with EL learners:

- Slow down the discourse: provide "thinking time" by extending wait time, allowing students to think through their answers before responding to your question, and holding back the third move.
- Exploit the third move and extend the IRF sequence by probing student responses.
- Listen to what students are saying (not only for the "prescripted" answers you have in your head) and respond accordingly.
- Consider the ratio of your "display" questions to questions to which you do not have a preconceived answer.
- Set up situations in the classroom where students have a chance to be the expert (because they know about something that others don't).
- Treat learners as successful conversational partners.
- Allow time and opportunity for thinking processes to be made explicit through talk.
- Ensure that all students are given opportunities and support to speak.

Making Talk Between Learners Worthwhile

Group work offers many opportunities for language development. First, as we have seen in previous chapters, collaborative tasks provide opportunities for meaningful interactions in context. As discussed earlier in this chapter, interacting with others, especially when students are engaged in problem-solving activities, creates an excellent environment for language development (Swain 2000). In addition, in group situations students hear a wider range of language and have more language directed to them than is possible in a whole-class context. They have more opportunities to interact with other speakers, to take more turns, and in the absence of the teacher, to take on more responsibility for clarifying misunderstandings or rethink how they have expressed something. In group talk around a task ideas are often reworded and revised, key words and phrases are repeated, problems are restated, and meanings are refined—all of which give EL learners opportunities to hear similar ideas expressed in a variety of ways and so make what they hear more comprehensible. Finally, group work is likely to provide an environment in which less confident students feel more comfortable and are more prepared to take risks.

Designing Tasks for Talk: Planning for Substantive Conversations

As all teachers are aware, effective and collaborative talk does not occur simply because students are sitting in groups. The tasks in which learners will participate need to be designed so that talk is necessary: a well-designed task should require talk, not simply invite it. This is one of the principles behind many traditional communicative activities, when different group or pair members hold different information that they must share in order to complete the task (see as examples the barrier crossword and split dictation activities described in Chapter 4). These kinds of tasks, as Chapter 4 suggested, are most relevant when they are located and integrated within a broader and more complex task that has some value to the learner and is wherever possible related in some way to life and experiences outside school. Perhaps most important is the need for students to be engaged in a task. And the kind of task that is most likely to be engaging is one in which there is some intrinsic value to the learners, the rationale for doing it is clear, and the learners have some agency over how the task will be completed.

All the activities and tasks described in Chapters 4, 5, and 6 involve students using spoken language, and create meaningful contexts for the use of academic language. Below are some additional strategies for encouraging substantive conversations between students, all of which can be integrated into a range of subject areas.

Thinking Sheets

Thinking sheets were illustrated in Chapter 2 in an example in which a planning sheet provided scaffolding for designing an experimental process. A second example was given in Chapter 4 in which a thinking sheet led to student talk about solving a word-based math problem. You will recall that thinking sheets

- provide an overall structure and purpose for students to solve problems collaboratively;
- help students make their own ideas explicit and hence open to scrutiny and perhaps modification;
- are likely to encourage substantive conversations;
- provide an opportunity to engage in meaningful subject-related language in a relevant context; and
- provide scaffolding for a subsequent activity.

Normally only one or two copies of the sheet are given out to a group of four or five students, to encourage the sharing of information and ideas rather than individual work. Thinking sheets are often forward focused: they are not only valuable as an activity in themselves but also scaffold the next activity. For example, in the science class students clarified their understanding of the significance of variables and later used this understanding as they designed their own experiment. In the math example, the students talked about how to solve the problem prior to explaining how they went about it to other students and to the teacher.

Jigsaw Groups

This organizational structure is familiar to many teachers. It is often associated with reading but provides many opportunities for learners to use more academic spoken language, or literate talk, and to take part in substantive conversations. In groups of four or five, students research one aspect of a topic and become "experts" in it (each group in the class researches a different aspect of the same topic). Later the class breaks up into new groups, each group comprising one person from each of the expert groups, so that every member of the group now has particular information about the overall topic that the others don't share. Each student shares with the group what she or he has learned, and the other group members take notes and ask questions. The outcome of this process can be a jointly produced group report, or the activity can be used as a basis for more in-depth study or individual work.

Here is an example of how jigsaw groups could be used, based on the topic of the Renaissance. Focusing on the question of how the Renaissance changed Europe, different groups could research the changes in art, literature, science, and religious beliefs. In a large topic such as this, these subtopics could be further broken down, with different groups looking at the work of Michelangelo, Leonardo, or Brueghel or the writing of Shakespeare or Dante. As members of each group will later need to share what they have learned, they will need to prepare a set of notes and/or visuals that present and summarize key points. You could also incorporate a thinking sheet to help them focus on the key ideas of their topic and plan what they will later share.

Once the new groups are formed and students have shared what they have learned in their "expert" groups, the activity could be extended into a more in-depth study by the whole class. Again, students could use a thinking sheet to guide them to make sense of the overall information they have now received. In the example above, this could focus on the overall impact of the Renaissance on how people began to see the world in a new way. Students could be asked to consider such questions as:

- What does all this tell us about how people's thinking and beliefs changed?
- Why do you think writers began to write in their national languages instead of Latin?
- Why do you think artists chose different sorts of subjects for their paintings than they had used in earlier times?
- What common ideas have we found in the topics we have researched?

Alternatively, students could be asked to evaluate some key statements about the "big ideas" of the topic and to decide on their validity. For example:

The Renaissance led to a focus on individuality.
New ideas about art, science, and humanity were the result of the rediscovery of ancient Greek and Roman knowledge.
Without increased trade between Italy and the Middle East, the Renaissance might not have occurred.

Jigsaw groupings require large amounts of spoken language and can be used flexibly with a range of English language levels. At the first stage of the task, when students are becoming "experts," it may help beginner or lower-level EL learners to work in pairs so that they can later help each other when sharing their information with others. Mother tongue resources could also be included at the initial stage of finding out information. A thinking sheet can help students locate significant facts or ideas and find and summarize key information (for example, by asking key questions or drawing their attention to the topic sentences of each paragraph). This will later provide scaffolding for the sharing stage of the task.

Paired Problem Solving

This activity requires two pairs of students to solve one of two problems. Having come to a solution, the two pairs cross-question each other about their solutions to the respective problems prior to solving the same problem for themselves. This activity is particularly relevant when it involves having students design and make something.

One such problem (described in Des-Fountain and Howe 1992) was based on a book that students had read. It required students to create a paper boat able to float and carry twenty marbles. Manzeer, an EL learner, participated in one of the pairings. He was able to describe the process he and his partner went through, including their early failures. In their first attempt, the boat had fallen apart in the water; as Manzeer explained it, "It looked like a bit of food; it was all cut up." His participation in the making of the boat also supported his understanding of the later discussion between the pairs about what could have been improved in the design. The conversation between the children provided him with rich models of language, including how to make a suggestion: *Do you think you should have done . . . ? Maybe you could have . . . . Perhaps it would be better if you . . . .* In addition to having access to this new language in a meaningful context, Manzeer was working at an appropriate cognitive level, since the task was quite challenging and demanded critical thinking and problem-solving skills.

Activities for Beginning EL Learners

As I have argued throughout this book, EL learners should as far as possible participate in the same or equivalent tasks as other students. What differs is the degree and type of scaffolding that is provided for them (and in some cases the language in which they are working). In Chapter 6, for example, we saw how a genre approach to teaching writing can accommodate low-level learners by using a range of scaffolding. However, some EL learners who are at the very early stages of learning English may still be unable to participate in more complex tasks. For these learners, more traditional communicative activities, provided they are integrated with the particular focus topic, can build up confidence and language knowledge. Below are some examples of activities that can be easily integrated and require the use of some subject-specific language. (For other examples see Gibbons 1993 and 2002.)

Find the Difference

You need two pictures that are basically the same but have some differences, some of which may be minor. You can create these by making two photocopies of a picture or diagram and then making changes to one of them using white-out and/or drawing in any additional details, and then photocopying it again. Try to make changes that relate in central ways to the particular topic—for example, a piece of key equipment missing in a diagram of a science experiment. The task is for the learners to find the differences and note what these are. They should be told how many differences there are, and they may ask questions of each other or take turns to describe their own picture, but they mustn't show their partner the picture. It is likely that this activity will lead to students asking questions, naming and describing objects in their picture, and describing the position of objects. If students don't know all the names of the objects in the picture, they may describe them. Additional scaffolding can be provided by having key vocabulary for each picture listed at the top.

Picture Sequencing

For this activity you will need a set of pictures or diagrams that show a predictable sequence—the life cycle of a butterfly, for example, or the water cycle or the key events in a narrative or historical recount. Students work in a small group or in pairs, each student having one or more cards. This is also a barrier game—the students mustn't show anyone else their picture. In turn, they describe each picture, and as a group they decide on the correct sequence. Once the order has been established the cards are laid down in that order from left to right. This could lead to a writing activity describing the sequence.

Picture-Sentence Matching

Provide pairs of students with a set of picture cards and a set of sentences that describe or explain the cards. Student A has the pictures, student B the sentences. Neither must see the other's cards. Student A describes a picture to student B, and student B chooses the sentence that matches it.

For example, in a history unit the pictures could illustrate what happened in a particular historical event, while the sentences tell the story in words. When they have matched all the pairs, the students decide on an appropriate order. In a history unit on the Renaissance, the picture cards could show paintings from Medieval and Renaissance times, and the sentence cards could briefly describe each painting. Having matched picture and sentence the students could then sort them into the two types of painting.

Picture-sentence matching activities bring together visual concrete images and related academic language and so are especially supportive for beginner EL learners.

Word-Picture Matching

Younger or preliterate learners can match key words to pictures. For example, in a unit on the properties of matter, students could cut out magazine pictures that represent the three states of matter (gas, solids, and liquids) and label the state both in their mother tongue and in English.

Inquiry and Elimination

Within your subject area, choose a large picture showing a range of objects that are related, such as a set of flags (geography), a set of animals (geography or natural science), or a set of paintings (history or art). Alternatively, use a set of names (countries, for example) or a set of symbols (chemical symbols, for example).

Students, in pairs, take turns (silently) choosing a picture/name/symbol. Their partner must guess the item chosen by asking questions that can only be answered by *yes* or *no*. Restricting the number of questions allowed to five or six encourages students to avoid random questioning and ask broader questions before specific questions in order to eliminate as many options as possible. For example, the answer no to the question *Is this the flag of a country in the Northern Hemisphere?* immediately reduces the options to countries in the Southern Hemisphere.

This activity encourages the use of subject-specific language, logical thinking, and questioning.

Criteria for Well-Designed Tasks

A number of principles underpin all the tasks described above. A well-designed task aimed at second language development illustrates all or most of these criteria:

- There is a real need to talk.
- Language is used for an authentic purpose.
- The task is embedded in a curriculum topic.
- The task is engaging and relevant to what the students are learning.
- The task is cognitively demanding, at a level appropriate for the grade.
- The task requires participation by all members of the group.
- The task requires learners to use stretches of language.
- There is often a built-in "information gap," since the students hold different information or opinions.
- There is a clear outcome for the task, such as the solving of a problem or the sharing of information.

Teaching About Talk

Besides being mindful of task design, teachers also need to consider the ability of students to work in a group. No matter how well-designed a task or program might be, it is unlikely to be effective if students do not know how to work effectively in groups. The interpersonal skills of working collaboratively need to be taught, even to older learners (and to some adults!). In his work with elementary teachers in the U.K., Mercer (2000) found that raising children's awareness of how they talk together, and how language can be used in collaborative activities for reasoning and problem solving, had positive effects on their ability to use language to think together critically and constructively. He and his colleagues and the teachers they were working with designed a series of "talk lessons" that focused on learning about talk and learning to use it effectively with others. In these lessons the children developed their own sets of ground rules for talk: *we talk one at a time; we respect one another's opinions; we give reasons to explain our ideas; if we disagree we ask "why?"* (The teachers also modeled these behaviors in their own talk with the children.) In debriefing discussions at the end of each lesson, teachers reviewed with the class what they had learned about "good ways of talking to each other, and the useful ways that helped you find out what other people were thinking" (164).

Compared with a control group that had not taken part in the talk lessons, there were striking differences in the quality of the children's talk. Those who had taken part in the lessons participated more fully, spent more time on making joint decisions, discussed issues in more depth, sought out one another's views, checked for agreement in the group, made relevant information explicit for others, and made their own reasoning visible in the talk.

All learners will benefit from this kind of explicit discussion about talk and thus will gain more from collaborative tasks. But it is especially helpful to EL learners. The interpersonal dimensions of language are in reality rarely taught even in language classrooms, except in very general ways; teachers usually focus far more on the academic aspects of language learning. Yet EL learners, who may also be experiencing new ways of learning and a different teaching and learning culture, may find taking part in collaborative work a new and challenging experience and be unsure what is expected of them. Being shown how to do this appropriately is important scaffolding if EL learners are to participate in learning tasks successfully.

Summary

This chapter has shown how teachers can use more contingent forms of teacher-student talk that create contexts for talk that are "language-learning rich," and are integrated with subject learning. It has illustrated ways in which some central conditions for second language learning can be created in both teacher-student and student-student talk. It has shown how:

- Traditional patterns of teacher-student talk can be modified so that opportunities for language learning are increased.
- Substantive conversations between learners are likely to occur through the use of particular types of tasks.

The chapter has also described:

- Criteria for effective teacher-student talk.
- Criteria for task design.
- Some tasks and activities for integrating spoken language with subject learning.

To Think About . . .

1. How can teachers become more aware of how they talk with students?
2. For what teaching purposes do you think the IRF/IRE pattern can be useful?
3. What other kinds of interactional patterns are common in your classroom?
4. How do (or could) you support EL learners to participate in classroom talk?
5. What group activities in this chapter could you adapt for use in your own subject area?

Suggestions for Further Reading

Dufficy, P. 2005. "'Becoming' in Classroom Talk." *Prospect: An Australian Journal of TESOL* 20 (1) [Special Issue: *Rethinking ESL Pedagogy. Sociocultural Approaches to Teaching and Learning*]: 59–81.

Echevarria, J., and A. Graves. 1998. *Sheltered Content Instruction: Teaching English Language Learners with Diverse Abilities*, Chapter 7. Needham Heights, MA: Allyn and Bacon.

Freeman, Y., and D. Freeman. 1998. *ESL/EFL Teaching: Principles for Success*, Chapter 6. Portsmouth, NH: Heinemann.

Gibbons P. 2002. Scaffolding Language, *Scaffolding Learning: Teaching Second Language Learners in the Mainstream Classroom*, Chapter 2. Portsmouth, NH: Heinemann.

Gibbons, P. 1993. *Learning to Learn in a Second Language*, Chapter 3. Portsmouth, NH: Heinemann.

Gibbons, P. 2003. "Mediating Language Learning." *TESOL Quarterly* 37(2): 247–73.

Mercer, N. 2000. *Words and Minds: How We Use Language to Think Together*, Chapter 6. London and New York: Routledge.

8 Planning for a High-Challenge, High-Support Classroom
Setting Up EL Learners for Success

Our national educational goals include supporting adolescents to develop . . . "advanced literacy." If this outcome is truly essential to the development of competent independent EL learners who can participate fully in our democratic system, then we need collectively to develop the will and resources to support teachers and schools to enact these practices effectively, regularly, and systematically.

—Julie Meltzer and Edmund Hamann,
Meeting the Literacy Development Needs of
Adolescent Language Learners Through
Content-Area Learning, Part 2

What This Chapter Is About

This chapter focuses on the process of planning and implementing a teaching program. It begins with a look at two major ways in which scaffolding can be enacted in the classroom, and continues with suggestions about how to approach the planning of an integrated (content and language) program. It concludes with a summary of some key principles to consider in developing a classroom program that provides both "high challenge" and "high support" for EL learners.

As Chapter 1 pointed out, the large majority of English language learners will spend most if not all of their school lives in the mainstream classroom. As numbers of English language learners increase, subject teachers are increasingly expected to take on the dual role of teaching both content and language. As has been argued throughout this book, the regular curriculum in fact has the potential to provide rich and varied opportunities for learners to develop the language that is most relevant for effective participation in school: the whole curriculum can be conceptualized as a resource for language learning. But if these potential opportunities are to be realized, and are to become real affordances for learning, then, as we have seen, the explicit planning and teaching of language—especially academic language—needs to occur across the whole curriculum in the context of content teaching.

Earlier chapters have illustrated how this might look in practice and how all teachers can be teachers of language. We have seen how academic language can be made accessible to EL learners without recourse to ongoing simplification, how the written genres of school can be explicitly scaffolded, and how classroom talk can provide many contexts for the kinds of spoken language that will support the development of the academic registers of school. The book has also illustrated that having high expectations of what students are capable of, and providing intellectually challenging programs for all students, goes hand in hand with teachers knowing how to scaffold the development of students' academic language.

In summary, an effective learning environment for EL learners requires the following conditions:

- Teachers understand the language demands of their own subject (or of the content areas they teach) and are aware of how language is used in the subject.
- Subject content and language are authentically integrated in a well designed and academically rigorous program.
- Teachers are aware of the best conditions under which a second language is learned.
- Teachers hold high expectations of what is possible.
- Teachers know a range of language-based strategies that provide explicit support for EL learners.

Under such conditions the mainstream classroom can become a highly effective learning context for English language learners. These conditions are thus key areas for whole-school development.

Designed Scaffolding and Interactional Scaffolding

The notion of scaffolding was introduced in Chapter 1 to describe the temporary, future-oriented, targeted help that supports learners in developing new knowledge, skills, and understandings that are transferable to new contexts. Scaffolding is the support required if learners are to engage in learning in their zone of proximal development. In a classroom context, it is useful to think of scaffolding as operating at two levels: *designed (macro-) scaffolding* and *interactional (micro-) scaffolding* (Hammond and Gibbons 2005).

Designed scaffolding refers to *planned* support—those activities consciously selected to scaffold learning (for example, all the activities described in this book could serve as scaffolding in a subject-based program). Designed scaffolding is therefore "preplanned" before any teaching takes place. *Interactional scaffolding*, on the other hand, is not planned. Opportunities for interactional scaffolding arise in the spontaneous, ongoing talk between teacher and students or between students. In teacher-student talk, as Chapter 7 illustrated, this kind of scaffolding is contingent on what a student says.

For EL learners, both levels of scaffolding are important. The integration of content and language and the selection of appropriate scaffolding activities are central to a well-designed program. As the planned teaching program is enacted in the classroom, teacher responsiveness to what students say is critical if learning is to occur. As Edwards and Mercer (1987) have suggested, "It is essentially in the discourse between teacher and pupils that education is done, or fails to be done" (101).

Although it is possible to discuss each of these two levels of scaffolding separately, they are also clearly related: worthwhile and relevant interactional scaffolding is most likely to occur in the context of a well-designed program. Without the existence of a carefully planned program, interactional support can become a hit-or-miss affair that may not contribute much to the overall learning within a unit of work.

The following sections provide more detailed explanations of what each of these levels looks like in practice. Examples have been drawn from the work of Hammond and Gibbons with elementary and secondary subject teachers in schools with high numbers of EL learners (Hammond and Gibbons 2005).

Designed Scaffolding

In planning a unit of work, decisions need to be made about a number of areas. Effective content-based EL programs are likely to include the following characteristics.

Programs build on students' prior knowledge and their current language skills (both their mother tongue and their second language), while at the same time embracing new content and language goals

An effective program embraces both students' starting points and broader curriculum goals and standards. As pointed out in Chapter 4, this dual focus on what students bring to learning and what they need to know means that a content-based language program has a Janus-like quality. In the year 7 mathematics program referred to in Chapter 4, the solving of word-based math problems began with students' commonsense trial-and-error strategies for solving them, using informal nonmathematical language in English or their mother tongue and "commonsense" thinking. This became the basis by which the teacher introduced learners to algebra as a system used to solve similar problems, together with the appropriate mathematical language.

Clear and explicit program goals are shared with the students

Each time a new unit of work is introduced, outcomes and expectations are explained to students. Questions like *why are we learning this?* and *why is this important?* are discussed. There is also space for students to pursue their own questions—deciding how to solve a problem, for example. As a result, students have a clear idea of the purpose of the overall unit of work. Teachers also explain the purpose of teacher-directed activities and how these fit into the overall program. For example, in one elementary classroom, explaining the purpose of a thinking-sheet activity led to a discussion on the value of collaborative talk for learning.

Tasks are sequenced so that each task serves as the "building block" for the subsequent task

Careful sequencing of tasks enables students to move step by step toward more in-depth understanding of more complex concepts. As Chapter 3 suggested, planning a sequence of tasks that require a gradual shift along the mode continuum is one way to move from familiar everyday language toward the abstractions of academic texts. The relationship *between* sequential tasks (not simply the value of the tasks themselves) is particularly significant for EL learners who are learning to use increasingly more abstract and academic language.

The year 7 math class referred to above is an example. Student were first asked to locate and define what they saw as "key words" in a language-based problem. Students underlined the words *sum, product,* and *difference* and defined these using everyday language (*sum means add, product means multiply, difference means we subtract*). This activity became a support structure (or scaffolding) for the next task, which was to solve the problem. This in turn served as scaffolding for the next activity, which was to record step by step how the problem was solved. This written record then became the scaffolding for the following task: a reporter from the group, in interaction with the teacher, explained how the group solved the problem. The teacher then recast the student's explanation, which was couched in informal language, using more mathematical language. This whole sequence of activities in turn became the scaffolding for an introduction to the formal study of algebra.

A sequence of interrelated activities like this represents a very different kind of learning from one-shot, individualized attempts at problem solving (in which there is often no explicit attention paid to language) and the teacher-directed explanations and rules that learners are often expected to memorize. Here the students are constantly engaged with language and content-based problem solving within a sequence of activities that served as scaffolding for both math and language learning.

A variety of organizational structures is used (pair work, group work, individual work, teacher-directed whole-class work)

Much educational discussion to date has focused on the relative merits of *teacher-centered* versus *learner-centered* learning. However, the reality of the classroom is more complex than this polarization suggests, because teachers' and students' roles are not always uniform. In contrast to a "centering" view, a sociocultural view of learning sees an active role for both teacher and learners, where the degree of expert support by the teacher will vary depending on the purpose and nature of the task and the nature of the scaffolding required by the learner. In a well-designed program, therefore, a range of organizational structures will be used, because at different points in their learning students will need differential support. Teachers can provide more or less support for the whole class or for specific groups or individuals as needed, while at other times, groups or individuals can work independently.

The curriculum is amplified, not simplified: Teachers use "message abundancy"
One of the most important ways in which teachers make information comprehensible for EL learners is by giving similar information in a variety of ways, some of them non-linguistic. Rather than trying to simplify information, amplifying the curriculum means finding as many ways as possible to make key information comprehensible. This may include:

- Beginning by using informal language accompanying hands-on experience (such as a science experiment, an excursion, or a math activity) and then reflecting on what has been learned in a teacher-guided debriefing, with the teacher modeling subject-specific language.
- Displaying key information visually throughout a unit of work (the ongoing recording of new learning on a chart, for example).
- Using graphs, maps, photographs, diagrams, graphic outlines, semantic maps, and pictures to represent key information in alternative ways.
- Using appropriate prereading activities before students read complex texts.
- Presenting familiar and concrete examples as a basis for discussing abstract concepts.
- Using videos, movies, or the Internet to present key information multi-modally.

I refer to this amplification of meaning as "message abundancy," meaning that key ideas are presented in many different ways. For EL learners, this means they have more than one opportunity to understand key content. EL learners often complain that teachers talk too quickly. However, it may not be the *speed of a teacher's speech* that is a problem but rather the *speed at which information is given*. Students learning in a second language need more time to comprehend new information than students learning in their mother tongue; in a fast-paced classroom EL learners may still be trying to make sense of one piece of information while the teacher has already moved on with another key idea. Slowing down the pace at which information is presented will not only support the learning of EL learners but is also likely to assist many other learners.

Consider the "message abundancy" in the following example. In the science classroom described in Chapters 2 and 7, you will remember that the students were focusing on the processes of scientific investigation. As part of their learning they needed to understand the notions of *controlled*, *dependent*, and *independent variables*. The teacher provided a range of ways to help the students understand these concepts:

- The students watched a *Myth Busters* video showing a concrete example of what scientists did to develop a valid experiment.
- The teacher discussed with students what they had learned, writing up their responses in *blue* on the whiteboard (e.g., *the scientists kept the size of the heads the same*).
- As the students talked, she recast what they said using the scientific terms and wrote up the technical terms in *red* beside the students' responses (e.g., *controlled variable*).
- Scientific definitions of the three kinds of variables were displayed on a wall chart throughout the unit of work, and the teacher drew the students' attention to these charts.
- In groups, the students put this learning into practice by identifying the variables involved in another shared experiment.
- Students designed their own experiments, identifying the variables they chose to use.

The EL learners in the class therefore had many opportunities to understand the notion of a *variable*, compared with a more content-driven, less "message abundant" classroom.

In the above example, the rich opportunities offered to students to develop both the key concept and the scientific language were the result of

- participating in an initial shared experience and a concrete example of the key concepts (the video);
- hearing *everyday* alongside *academic* language in interactions with their teacher;
- seeing key points written on the board;
- having the differences between everyday and technical language highlighted through color coding;
- having access to a chart giving formal definitions;
- getting practice in putting concepts into practice; and
- using the learning in a new context.

Talk often occurs around a written text

There are many opportunities for students to talk together in groups working on collaborative activities, and these activities are often mediated by a teacher-designed text (such as a thinking sheet; see Chapter 7) or set of questions related to a text (such as margin questions; see Chapter 5). These texts or questions provide a structure for group learning and often become a significant point of reference in a unit of work. Such teacher-designed texts can be quite simple (a brief set of instructions) or more complex (a planning sheet for a complex task), but they all provide a structure to help students think about and reflect on the task they are completing, and support students' ability to work more autonomously.

There are planned opportunities for talk about language

All effective programs include opportunities for teachers and learners to talk *about* language—that is, to use metalanguage. For example, teachers draw students' attention to the features of genres they are writing (their overall structure and key grammatical patterns and vocabulary), the differences between talking and writing, and to key signaling words and complex nominal groups in the key texts they read (see Chapters 4 and 6). The development of this kind of metalinguistic awareness helps students engage in a critical analysis of their own and others' language. As Chapter 4 has argued, metalanguage is an important tool for both teachers and students; it focuses students' attention on the role of language in learning. Often EL learners have a greater awareness of language than their monolingual peers, and helping them develop a metalanguage for the academic features of English builds on this bilingual awareness.

Interactional Scaffolding

The second level of scaffolding is interactional (or "contingent") scaffolding. The features of supportive talk are discussed in detail in Chapter 7; therefore, only key points are included again here. In their talk with learners, teachers provide scaffolding through the way they respond to what students say. Thus how a teacher responds is contingent on the learner's contribution to the interaction. In scaffolded interactions, teacher-talk is characterized by all or many of the features below. Teachers:

- Listen to learners' intended meanings, not for a "prescribed" answer.
- Build on learners' prior experiences.
- Recap what has been said at regular intervals, to remind students of key points.
- Appropriate students' responses and (when appropriate) recast them into more technical or academic wording.
- Engage in longer exchanges with students than occur in a three-part IRF sequence, and so provide opportunities for students to say more or rethink how they have expressed something.
- Allow learners more time to respond (by asking them for further explanation of their ideas, for example).
- Allow adequate wait time in a variety of ways.

Many educators have acknowledged the centrality of interactional scaffolding for learning. Van Lier (1996) argues that "even though it does not show up in lesson plans or syllabuses, this local interactional scaffolding may well be the driving force behind good pedagogy, the hallmark of a good teacher" (199). Likewise Wells (1996) suggests that it represents "the craft of teaching" (84).

Interactional and designed scaffolding, used in tandem, are the means by which EL learners are able to participate in academically challenging learning. Rather than reducing the curriculum and requiring less from students, a well-scaffolded program allows EL students to become the learners they have the potential to be.

Five Steps for Planning an Integrated Program
••

This section presents a general overview of a process to follow in developing an integrated program. A more detailed checklist follows. The five steps described here are based on the assumption that you have already decided on the "content" you wish to focus on in a particular unit of work.

Step 1: Note what you already know about your students' language strengths and their language learning needs

Begin by reflecting on the students in the class; consider in broad terms what they are already able to do in English and in their mother tongue. Identify what your prior experience with the students has suggested about their language learning needs in English: think about the broad areas in which you've noticed they have difficulty. For example, you may have noticed they find it difficult to locate key ideas in a text, or that they are unable to structure a particular genre appropriately in their writing, or that they write in very informal, "spoken like" ways. Or there may be particular grammatical structures that they do not use appropriately or correctly, such as the expression of past time or connectives for temporal sequencing.

Much of this information will come from your informal assessments of learners, as you evaluate how effectively they can complete the day-to-day listening, speaking, reading, and writing tasks of the classroom—for example, through observations, interactions with students, informal checks for understanding, and student self-assessment. You may also gain information from more formal assessments: student project evaluations, class tests, and (possibly) standardized tests.

Step 2: Identify the language that is central to the particular topic you plan to teach

As we have seen, language cannot be divorced from the content that is being taught. To identify this language, think of the tasks you want students to complete, and ask yourself, *What language will students need to know and use in order to participate in the planned subject-focused learning activities?* For content teachers, this is often a difficult question to answer, because it requires viewing the program through the lens of language as well as subject knowledge (usually not something subject teachers are accustomed to doing). But the more specific you are able to be about the language of your subject, the more targeted support you will be able to give EL learners and the more linguistic tools all students in the class will have for learning. There are more specific suggestions about how to identify the language of the topic or content later in the chapter.

Step 3: Select the key language on which you will focus

In a single unit of work it won't be possible to focus on all the language you have identified in step 2. Decide the most critical and relevant language to focus on, taking into

Science Objectives	Language Objectives
Students will develop an understanding of what constitutes a scientific method. They will carry out independent investigations to prove or disprove common myths. They will develop understandings about the kinds and functions of variables and the need for replication in the context of developing a method; carrying out practical experiments; observing, recording, and interpreting results; and drawing conclusions. They will complete an experimental report detailing their investigations.	Students will write an experimental report, using: • An appropriate organizational structure. • Appropriate grammar (nominalizations and nominal groups, cause and effect structures, passive voice as appropriate). • Time connectives • Correct technical vocabulary (*controlled, dependent, independent variable; replicate, replication*).

Figure 8.1. Integrating Content and Language

account any notes you made in step 1 about learners' language needs. Consider what student language learning needs can *sensibly and realistically* be addressed in this unit of work. For example, if you have already noticed that students have difficulty with the language of a science report and the particular unit includes the writing up of an experiment, then you may decide to spend time on this. If you have noticed that they also have difficulty accessing key ideas in complex texts, you may decide not to focus on that specifically at this time but to include a focus on reading in a later unit of work. The decisions about what language you will focus on will enable you to define specific language objectives for the unit, to accompany the content objectives. Figure 8.1 is an example taken from the science unit about experimental design discussed in Chapters 2 and 7.

Step 4: Design or choose activities to present and use the focus language

Next you need to decide what activities you will use in order to focus on the language you have identified in step 3. These will be activities that are relevant to *both* the language focus you have decided on *and* the subject content that students are working on. For example, depending on the language focus(es) you have chosen, you may decide to use a dictogloss to model the introductory paragraph of a discussion, or a split dictation to model the overall structure of a procedural text, or a sentence-matching activity to illustrate the difference between spoken and written language. Of course, the field (subject content) of these activities will be related to the topic of the particular unit of work in which they occur. Earlier chapters include many examples of language-based activities. Many of them can also be used as informal assessment activities.

Step 5: Evaluate the Unit of Work

After completing the unit of work, consider how you might evaluate it. In relation to EL learners, it will be useful to consider such questions as:

- Did the unit of work build on EL learners' existing knowledge (of content and language)?
- Did the EL learners demonstrate that they have developed new concepts, new levels of understanding, and new language? What evidence is there of this?
- What syllabus outcomes/standards did EL learners demonstrate?
- Did teaching and learning activities extend EL learners beyond what they could already do?
- Was adequate scaffolding provided for all learners to enable them to participate in learning tasks?

A Framework for Thinking About Language in a Subject-Based Classroom

These five steps provide a framework for thinking about how a teaching program can be inclusive of EL learners. This section, which looks in more depth at how content and language can be integrated, provides prompts that assist in identifying the language embedded in the content of the unit and the language demands that the planned content will place on learners.

The second of the five steps outlined above, identifying the key language embedded in the particular topic, is a complex task but is central to the notion of integration. The questions in this section are intended to make this task more concrete. Of course not all questions will be relevant at all times; they are intended as a general framework for thinking about how language and content are related. While some questions may not be relevant to your situation, you may think of others that are particularly important in your academic area or in the institution in which you work. Working with other members of your faculty is a valuable way to develop an understanding of what language and genres are central to your own discipline and what key questions need to be asked. If possible, also work with another language-aware teacher, such as a specialist ELL teacher.

It has been suggested that in most learning contexts, learners ultimately remember only about one tenth of what they have studied. If you think back to your own school or university experiences, you will probably only remember a very small amount of the information you were once familiar with. But what stays with you are the "big ideas" and the skills, concepts, and understandings you learned along the way. This is the "10 percent we walk away with" (Wiggins and McTighe 2005). Given that learning is so much more than remembering discrete facts, it is important that teachers make decisions about the key learning they want students to retain: the central concepts, ideas, understandings, knowledge, and processes that represent the 10 percent their learners will walk away with. Wiggins and McTighe refer to this as the "enduring understanding" of the topic. And so it is important for teachers to be clear about the big ideas of the topic—both in relation to content and to language—before they begin to translate this into classroom practice.

It is also important to consider how this central learning will be assessed. One way to do this is to decide on the assessment tasks at the same time you decide on the big ideas. These culminating assessment tasks were referred to as *rich tasks* in Chapter 2, and their characteristics were described there. They are culminating demonstrations, or products, that require students to engage intellectually with the subject. The information booklet for recently arrived migrant families, also described in Chapter 2, is an example of this kind of task.

Once the culminating rich task has been designed, it then becomes possible to "backward map"—that is, to plan the teaching and learning experiences that will lead up to the rich task (Wiggins and McTighe 2005). As Moulds (2002) suggests, "There is a strong relationship between the final assessment task and the learning experiences that students complete *prior to the task*" (10, emphasis added). Backward mapping is a particularly important tool for teachers to use with EL learners, because, as described earlier, an effective EL program requires teachers to make decisions at the planning stage about the language outcomes of a unit of work and then decide on the language-based activities that will lead to these outcomes.

Therefore, before starting to develop a unit of work, consider the following questions:

Decide on the "big questions" in the unit (see Chapter 2)

- What are the key concepts and big ideas you want all learners to understand and to be able to use?
- What rich task (or other kind of assessment task) will you use to assess students' understanding of these big ideas and key concepts?
- What do students already know about these ideas and concepts?
- How can you introduce the key concepts in language that is familiar to students, drawing on their own experiences?
- How are these concepts and ideas expressed in the academic language in your subject?

- What can individual EL learners contribute to the learning of everyone in the class (e.g., because they have special knowledge about or interest in the topic)?
- What classroom activities can you use to introduce this new language and link it with what students already know?
- Using backward mapping, what general sequence of activities will lead up the final assessment task?

Consider how spoken language can be used to support both content and language learning (see Chapter 7)

- How will you provide opportunities for students to use language with one another to talk through complex ideas or concepts (i.e., to have substantive conversations)?
- What opportunities are there for learners to work collaboratively in groups on subject-related tasks?
- Are there structures in place that will help ensure that substantive conversations occur (e.g., thinking sheets)?
- Are group tasks worth doing for their own sake?
- Are students given opportunities to pose their own questions?
- Are there planned times for teacher-student interactions about what students have learned?
- Are there opportunities for talk about learning and about language?
- In what ways will you make complex or academic language more comprehensible?
- How and at what point in the unit will you model academic language in your own talk?

Identify what texts students will read (see Chapters 3 and 5)

- What aspects of the language of the texts might cause difficulties for your students?
- Are there conceptual or cultural aspects of the text that may be unfamiliar and hinder learning?
- How can you address these difficulties and help learners access the texts?
- What before-reading, during-reading, and after-reading activities will help learners access these texts?
- How will class work help learners understand the reading they will be doing?

Identify the writing you expect learners to do (see Chapter 6 and Appendix 3)

- What kinds of genres will learners be expected to write?
- Are you able to be explicit about the language features of the genre you want students to write?

- If this is the first time learners are being asked to write in this way, how will you deconstruct the genre, and what topic will you choose for the joint construction stage?
- What extra scaffolding will you provide for those students who need additional support to help them complete the writing successfully?

Sequence activities broadly according to the mode continuum (see Chapters 3, 4, and 7)

- How will you sequence the teaching and learning activities so that learners begin with familiar (probably spoken) language and then move toward the new academic language?
- What opportunities are there for EL learners to use "literate" spoken language prior to writing tasks?

Assessing Learning

Most teachers, to a greater or lesser extent, need to take account of an educational context in which high-stakes standardized tests and calls for increased accountability are increasing. While most educators of EL learners are well aware of the potentially discriminating effects these tests may have on students, this is in reality the context in which the education of culturally and linguistically diverse learners takes place (see Cummins 2000 and Abedi 2005 for further discussion). As suggested in Chapter 2, such tests may assess what students know about essential knowledge and basic skills, but they are not able to assess learners' deep understanding of a topic nor their abilities to transform and apply core concepts in meaningful contexts. Nor can they provide the immediate, individualized, nuanced feedback (Sarroub and Pearson 1998) that teachers need to teach responsively and that students need if they are to understand their achievements and areas of challenge.

It is worth noting that the kinds of practices described throughout this book do not negate the importance of basic skills and traditional knowledge: indeed, for the intellectually challenging work advocated here, traditional disciplinary knowledge is essential. In addition, as the book has illustrated, a great deal of attention is paid to the development of reading and writing and to the explicit teaching of language. In such a curriculum, where knowledge and language is put to use in context, it is in fact more likely that learners will develop the kinds of skills that standardized tests claim to measure. But they will also learn how to apply what they have learned and become more autonomous learners and problem solvers.

To gather the most comprehensive information about students' learning, teachers must use multiple forms of assessment. These might include teacher-analysis of a piece of writing, teacher-created assignments and tests, portfolios, spoken presentations, multimedia presentations, completion of concept maps, and reading logs. If criteria are shared with students, then the assessment also becomes a means for learning (as suggested in Chapter 6). Involving students in developing criteria and rubrics makes the learning goals of the activity explicit and so places more autonomy and responsibility for their learning on the learners themselves.

Learning in the Challenge Zone

This book began by arguing that all educators need to maintain high expectations of what English language learners are able to achieve. These high expectations are realized when students are learning in their "challenge zone" and engaging in intellectually worthwhile tasks. In Chapter 1 this challenge zone was characterized as learning in an environment that has both high intellectual challenge and high teacher support. While there is no one-size-fits-all or ready-made answer about how to create this kind of learning environment, this book has argued that it must be one where EL learners are given

- opportunities to engage in worthwhile subject-based rigorous tasks;
- targeted and specific academic language support in all curriculum areas; and
- a curriculum where their current identities, languages, skills, experiences, and existing knowledge are used as the foundation for new learning.

A major implication of this high-challenge, high-support classroom, as illustrated throughout the book, is that all teachers of EL learners need to understand how academic English works and how it varies according to context, and know how to use a range of language-teaching strategies in the context of subject teaching.

But teaching is about far more than a checklist of strategies and technical knowledge. Successful outcomes for EL learners depend ultimately on the kinds of relationships that are formed between teachers and learners, and the views teachers hold about English language learners and the communities they come from. How teachers view their students, and ultimately how their students are constructed as learners, depends on the teachers' assumptions and beliefs about knowledge; about teaching and learning; and about the kinds of classroom roles they take on, and the roles they offer to students. As Cummins (2007) argues, we need to ask ourselves to what extent particular classroom practices "construct an image of the English language learner as intelligent, imaginative, and linguistically talented" (4).

Teachers' assumptions and beliefs are a major driving force behind most decisions made in individual classrooms and can have either enabling or constraining effects. For example, a teacher who sees knowledge as a commodity that can be transmitted from teacher to students as a kind of ready-made package is not likely to devote much "airtime" to listening to and building on students' ideas and prior knowledge. A teacher who sees learning as something that occurs solely within an individual rather than between individuals is not likely to set up the kinds of collaborative group work that facilitates language development and deep subject knowledge. A teacher who sees a subject as a body of content to "cover" is not likely to be thinking about the literacy demands embedded in the subject. And a teacher who sees EL learners as language "deficient" is unlikely to take the trouble to find out what a student knows in his or her first language, or to encourage the kinds of higher-order literacy engagement that are fundamental to school success.

Teachers' "ways of thinking" can therefore have a profound effect on the educational outcomes of their students. Behind the many strategies and tasks described in this book lie some important beliefs and assumptions that reverse the kinds of constraining thinking described above. Here, in brief, are some of the ways of thinking that create opportunities for EL learners to engage in learning in the challenge zone:

- *Their teachers think about EL learners as the people they can become, not simply as learners with limited English.* This emphasis on students' learning *potential* rather than on their current abilities, and the consequent raising of expectations of what is possible, are especially important for EL learners, whose cognitive and conceptual understanding may outstrip their English language development, or, conversely, where abilities in English may potentially impact subject learning.

- *Their teachers are less focused on "covering content" and more focused on "uncovering the subject."* Most teachers feel that they are under pressure to cover a certain amount of work with their students, and while this may be largely unavoidable in the senior years of school, it is much less so in the middle years. A shift of focus toward uncovering the subject means that teachers make explicit to learners the ways of using language, the ways of thinking, and the ways of meaning that are valued in their discipline. These are the enduring tools that help students "learn to learn" and that provide a strong basis for increasingly complex subject learning in the senior years.

- *Their teachers are reflective practitioners.* Reflective practitioners think critically about their own practices and avoid the temptation to locate the causes of underachievement in the students or in their home backgrounds. Rather, they take a critical perspective on pedagogical and assessment practices that are not inclusive of linguistic and cultural diversity. The questions at the end of each chapter in this book are intended to provide a starting point for such reflection.

- *Their teachers see a culturally diverse classroom as a resource, not a problem.* The last twenty years have been characterized by mass movements of migrants and refugees across the world that have resulted in a wider cultural mix in most cities than ever before, and in increasing diversity in schools. It is becoming ever more important for people to be able to navigate difference and talk across cultures. Classrooms where there is multicultural diversity mirror the broader society and, through the kinds of collaborative learning described in this book, create opportunities for all students to look beyond cultural difference to a recognition of what they share, and to take this understanding into the world beyond school. As Wells (2007) has said, "Who we become depends on the company we keep and on what we do and say together" (100).

When students are treated as capable learners, when they are actively engaged in challenging tasks and in literacy learning, and when they are given opportunities to use knowledge in meaningful ways with others, EL learners not only achieve at higher levels, but also expand their academic and personal identities, and their own beliefs about what is possible. This book has offered some suggestions about how that can become a reality in the classroom.

Suggestions for Further Reading

Carrasquillo, A., S. Kucer, and R. Abrams. 2004. *Beyond the Beginnings: Literacy Interventions for Upper Elementary English Language Learners*, Chapter 7. Clevedon, UK: Multilingual Matters.

Gibbons, P. 2006. "Steps for Planning an Integrated Program for ESL Learners." In *Planning and Teaching Creatively within a Required Curriculum*, edited by P. McKay. TESOL Language Curriculum Development Series. Alexandria, Va: TESOL.

Dong, Yu Ren. 2007. "Integrating Language and Content: How Three Biology Teachers Work with Non-English-Speaking Students." In *Bilingual Education: An Introductory Reader*, edited by Ofelia Garcia and Colin Barker. Clevedon, UK: Multilingual Matters.

Appendix 1

....

Summary of Teaching and Learning Activities

Self-editing criteria sheet	Chapters 2 and 6
Rich tasks	Chapter 2
Modeling academic language in talk	Chapters 3 and 7
Talking about language	Chapters 4 and 7
Progressive brainstorm	Chapter 4
Wallpapering	Chapter 4
Semantic web/concept map	Chapter 4 and 5
Dictogloss	Chapter 4
Joint construction	Chapter 4
The last word	Chapter 4
Thinking sheets	Chapters 4, 7, and 8
Split dictation	Chapter 4
Barrier crossword	Chapter 4
Traditional cloze	Chapter 4
Specific cloze	Chapter 4
Total cloze	Chapter 4
Vanishing cloze	Chapter 4
Word walls	Chapter 4

Sentence matching	Chapter 4
Turning processes into nouns	Chapter 4
Bilingual dictionaries	Chapter 4
Prediction from a picture (before reading)	Chapter 5
Prediction from key words	Chapter 5
Personal narratives	Chapter 5
Reader questions	Chapter 5
Sequencing illustrations/diagrams	Chapter 5
Skeleton text	Chapter 5
Previewing the text	Chapter 5
Scanning for information (during reading)	Chapter 5
Pause and predict	Chapter 5
Margin questions	Chapter 5
Scaffolding a detailed reading	Chapter 5
Identifying paragraph parts	Chapter 5
Reading critically	Chapter 5
True-false statements (after reading)	Chapter 5
Graphic outlines	Chapter 5
Summarizing the text	Chapter 5
Sentence reconstruction	Chapter 5
Jumbled words	Chapter 5
Innovating on the text	Chapter 5
Cartoon strips	Chapter 5
Readers theatre	Chapter 5
The teaching and learning cycle (overview)	Chapter 6

Building the field	Chapter 6
Modeling the genre	Chapter 6
Joint construction	Chapter 6
Independent writing	Chapter 6
Using an assessment framework for writing	Chapter 6
Extending the IRF exchange	Chapter 7
Giving students time to think	Chapter 7
Making reasoning explicit	Chapter 7
Using jigsaw groups	Chapter 7
Paired problem solving	Chapter 7
Find-the-difference barrier game	Chapter 7
Picture sequencing	Chapter 7
Picture–sentence matching	Chapter 7
Word–picture matching	Chapter 7
Enquiry and elimination	Chapter 7
Amplifying the curriculum: message abundancy	Chapter 8

Appendix 2

Types of Text Connectives (Signaling Words)

Text connectives show the relationship between the ideas in a text. They often occur at the beginning of a sentence or paragraph and "signal" the sort of information that will follow. Each genre tends to use a particular kind (or kinds) of connectives. For example, a narrative will typically use time connectives, whereas a discussion is likely to use connectives to sequence ideas, contrast ideas, summarize, add information, or elaborate. Connectives serve an important function in structuring and organizing the text as a whole (see Appendix 3).

Indicating time Examples: then, afterward, in the end, later, until that time, next, at the same time, finally, after a while, previously	**Sequencing ideas** Examples: to start with, first, second, third, finally, most important, last
Indicating cause and effect Examples: therefore, as a consequence of, consequently, as a result, due to, because of this, so	**Summarizing and concluding** Examples: in brief, in conclusion, to conclude, to summarize, to sum up
Adding information Examples: in addition, again, furthermore, similarly, also, as well, besides, above all	**Clarifying or elaborating** Examples: in other words, for example, for instance, more precisely, to illustrate, that is, to put it differently
Comparing Examples: similarly, likewise, in the same way, in the same manner	**Contrasting** Examples: however, nevertheless, on the other hand, on the contrary, yet, conversely

For more information, see de Silva Joyce and Feez (2004) and Derewianka (1998).

Appendix 3: Typical Features of Some Written School-Related Genres

(Based on the work of Martin and Rose 2008, de Silva Joyce and Feez 2004, Schleppegrell 2004, and Macken-Horarik 1996)

(1) Personal/creative genres

Genre/Example	Purpose/Description	Typical Organization	Typical Connectives or Conjunctions That Help to Structure the Text (See also Appendix 2)	Typical Language Features
Personal recount *Our class excursion to....*	Retells a sequence of events, drawing on personal experience	1. Orientation (tells who, where, when, etc.) 2. Series of events (3. Personal comment)	Text focused around a time line, with ideas linked through time connectives (*later, in the afternoon, afterward; many years later*)	Action (doing) verbs (*arrive, go, run*); may also include verbs of thinking/feeling and saying — Past tenses to refer to past time — Typically one person as major participant (*yesterday I went with my class to*)
Narrative *A science fiction story*	Recounts a sequence of events with complicating action(s) that result in a climax and resolution	1. Orientation 2. Events 3. Complication 4. Resolution	Text focused around a time line (although events may not always occur in strict chronological sequence) Time connectives (as above), although sometimes these may remain implicit	Action or doing verbs (*arrive, go, run, fight, stop*); thinking/feeling verbs (*think, feel, hear, wonder*); saying verbs (*said, replied, shouted, whispered*) — Past tenses to refer to past time — Several people/characters as participants — Nominal groups, especially in description — Adverbs introduce information about manner (how something is done) and may express judgement

173

(2) Factual genres

Genre/Example	Purpose/Description	Typical Organization	Typical Connectives or Conjunctions That Help to Structure the Text (See also Appendix 2)	Typical Language Features
Information report *Fossil fuels*; *Marsupials of Australia*; *Types and uses of graphs*	Relates a set of facts, gives generalized information about a class of things (focuses on classes of things rather than individuals)	1. General statement identifies the topic and may define or classify it 2. Descriptions of key attributes (types, uses, characteristics etc.), often under individual subheadings	No explicit connecting words Structure of genre often indicated in the text through headings and subheadings	Relating verbs to describe and classify (*is/has*) Adverbials of place (where) and manner (how) Vocabulary that indicates class/subclass and whole/part relationships (fossil fuels → coal, oil, gas; marsupial → kangaroo, wombat; kangaroo → short hind legs, long strong back legs, pouch) Simple present tense to express generalizations (*it lives*) Subject-specific vocabulary
Factual or historical recount *The development of Sydney during early white settlement*	Relates a set of facts, gives generalized information about a class of things (focuses on classes of things rather than individuals) Tells what happened by documenting a series of events and sometimes evaluating their significance	1. Orientation (sets context by providing information about who, where, when, etc.) 2. Record of events in chronological order 3. Reorientation (rounds off a sequence of events)	References to time, often at beginning of sentences (*first, after this, in the 1900s, by the early twentieth century*)	Action verbs Past tenses to refer to past time Focus on generalizing about events and actions of individuals and groups of people Reference to specific dates or periods of time

Procedure *Making an electric jug*	Describes "how to" by reporting a sequence of events or steps to follow (directions and instructions)	1. Goal of the activity 2. Materials required 3. Sequence of steps to be followed	Connectives to indicate sequence of steps (*first, second*) OR Steps are numbered	Action verbs as commands/imperatives (*put, place, wind*) Adverbial clauses to give details such as place (where), extent (how much, how long), manner (how something is done) (*heat water until it is boiling; put ten drops of food dye into the 100ml cylinder; construct squares on each of the sides*) Field-specific vocabulary
Procedural recount *A student's recount of an experiment she or he carried out*	Records the steps that have been taken to carry out a particular investigation (particularly important for recording practical learning experiences in science and technology)	1. Aim 2. Record of events, expressed sequentially 3. Results (what happened, statement of results, findings, etc.)	Time connective at beginning of sentences to express sequence of events (*then, later, next, at the same time*) Technical words specific to the field also provide cohesion: especially through synonyms, class/subclass relationships, and part/whole relationships	Action verbs to refer to activities (what happened) Past tenses to refer to past time Relating verbs to introduce concepts (*means, is called*) Expressions of cause and effect (in results stage) Field-related vocabulary
Temporal explanation *How coal is mined*	Relates a general set of steps or events that describe a process OR Gives an explanation through describing a sequence of events	1. General statement to identify the topic 2. Description of events expressed sequentially	Time connectives at beginning of sentences to express sequence of events (*then, later, next, at the same time*) OR Events are numbered	Action verbs to refer to what happens Simple present tense to express generalizations Some use of passive (*the coal is mined*) Field-specific vocabulary

(3) Analytical genres

Genre/Example	Purpose/Description	Typical Organization	Typical Connectives or Conjunctions That Help to Structure the Text (See also Appendix 2)	Typical Language Features
Explanation (causal) *How a circuit breaker works; how a lunar eclipse occurs*	Explains a phenomenon	1. Identification of the phenomenon 2. Cause and effect sequence of events	Causal connectives (*as a result of, for that reason, as a consequence, because of this, therefore*)	General, field-specific, non-human nouns Action verbs to express what happens Nominalizations to turn events into nouns (*this <u>occurrence</u> is called*) Simple present tense to express generalizations Passive voice to talk about the object undergoing the process (*the light from the sun is <u>blocked</u>*)
Exposition/argument *Global warming is a problem created by humans*	Argues why a thesis is proposed, with a sequence of arguments used to support the thesis (indicates one side of a discussion)	1. Presentation of thesis and statement of writer's position (sometimes with preview of arguments) 2. Series of arguments in support of the thesis, with supporting evidence 3. Reaffirmation of writer's position	Connectives to sequence arguments (*first, second, third, finally, in conclusion to summarize, therefore*)	Nominalizations used to name arguments (*the proposal that*) Modality to present arguments or claims as possibilities rather than facts (*it is likely that; it may be that*) Field-specific vocabulary Evaluative vocabulary, indicating writer's personal belief or stance (*it is <u>extremely</u> unlikely*)

Discussion *Should there be an age limit for older drivers?*	Explores an issue from a range of perspectives (indicates more than one side of a discussion)	1. Identification of the issue with relevant information and possibly brief review of arguments 2. Arguments for and against 3. Conclusion that sums up perspectives and suggests recommendations favoring one side	Connectives to sequence arguments (as for argument) and also to present counter-arguments (*however, nevertheless, despite this, on the other hand*).	Nominalizations used to name arguments (*the proposal that*) Modality to present arguments or claims as possibilities rather than facts (*it is likely that; it may be that*) Field-specific vocabulary Evaluative vocabulary, indicating writer's personal belief or stance (*it is clearly a risk if*)
Literary response (interpretation) *In Emma Jane Austin is concerned with appearance versus reality: discuss in relation to Emma's journey of moral awakening* (from de Silva Joyce and Feez 2004)	Summarizes, analyzes, interprets, or responds to a literary text, artwork, or performance	1. Introduction, with context and background information about general themes of the work (e.g., summary of narrative), preview of argument to be presented 2. Expands on (1), argues for a particular interpretation using as evidence discussion of (for example) stylistic features of the text, artwork, or production; uses close reference to text/performance 3. Summarizes writer's judgement, reaffirms interpretation of work	Connectives to sequence ideas (*first, finally, in conclusion, to summarize, therefore, however, nevertheless*)	Reference to specific people and things Negative and positive evaluative vocabulary, indicating writer's personal belief or stance Simple present tense (*Emma gradually realizes*) Quotations to support ideas, especially in (2)

(3) Analytical genres (continued)

Genre/Example	Purpose/Description	Typical Organization	Typical Connectives or Conjunctions That Help to Structure the Text (See also Appendix 2)	Typical Language Features
Historical explanation/ historical argument *In what ways can the ending of World War I explain the origins of World War II?*	Historical explanation explains past events (rather than simply recording the past) by examining causes and consequences and developing an overall argument about the significance of events Historical argument also advocates a particular interpretation of the past through analysis and debate of a range of positions and arguments	1. Identification of the issue with relevant information; possibly brief review of arguments 2. Presentation of causes and consequences of historical events OR An argument for a particular interpretation 3. Conclusion that sums up significance of events	Connectives of cause and effect/consequences (*as a result of, for that reason, as a consequence, because of this, therefore*) May be presented as an argument (*first, finally, in conclusion, to summarize, therefore*)	Action verbs Significance of events presented through evaluative words to express writer's judgment (*this provides clear evidence that*) Nominalization of events (*the horrific massacres of millions of people*)

References

....

Abedi, J. 2005. "Issues and Consequences for English Language Learners." In *Uses and Misuses of Data for Educational Accountability and Improvement: The 104th Yearbook of the National Society for the Study of Education*, Part 2, 175–98. Malden, MA: Blackwell.

August, D., and K. Hakuta. 1997. *Improving Schooling for Language Minority Children*. Washington, DC: National Academy Press.

August, D., K. Hakuta and D. Pompa. 1994. *For All Students: Limited English Proficient Students and Goals 2000*. Washington, DC: National Clearing House for Bilingual Education.

Avi. 1991. *Nothing but the Truth: A Documentary Novel*. New York: William Morrow.

Berman, P., S. Abuto, B. Nelson, C. Minicucci, and G. Burkhart. 2000. *Going Schoolwide: Comprehensive School Reform Inclusive of Limited English Proficiency Students, A Resource Guide*. NCBE Resource Collection Series No. 17. Washington, DC: National Clearinghouse for Bilingual Education.

Brice-Heath, S. 1983. *Ways with Words*. Cambridge: Cambridge University Press.

Brophy, J., and T. Good. 1986. "Teacher Behaviour and Student Achievement." In *Handbook of Research on Teaching*, edited by M. Wittrock, 328–75. New York: Macmillan.

Bruce King, M., and J. Schroeder. 2001. "Authentic Assessment and Student Performance in Inclusive Schools." Publication 5. Research Institute on Secondary Education Reform, University of Wisconsin, Madison.

Calderon, M. 1999. "School Reform and Alignment of Standards." In *Including Culturally and Linguistically Diverse Students in Standards-Based Reform: A Report on McREL's Diversity Roundtable I* (Chapter 3), Mid-continent Research for Education and Learning. Available at www.mcrel.org.

Carrasquillo, A., S. Kucer, and R. Abrams. 2004. *Beyond the Beginnings: Literacy Interventions for Upper Elementary English Language Learners*. Clevedon, UK: Multilingual Matters.

Carrasquillo, A., and C. London. 1993. *Parents and Schools*. New York: Garland.

Carrasquillo, A., and V. Rodríguez. 2002. *Language Minority Children in the Mainstream Classroom*. Clevedon, UK: Multilingual Matters.

Chang, G., and G. Wells. 1988. "The Literate Potential of Collaborative Talk." In *Oracy Matters*, edited by M. Maclure, T. Phillips, and A. Wilkinson. Milton Keynes, UK: Open University Press.

Christie, F. 1990. "The Changing Face of Literacy." In *Literacy for a Changing World*, edited by F. Christie. Hawthorn, Victoria: Australian Council for Educational Research.

Christie, F., and J. Rothery. 1990. "Literacy in the Curriculum: Planning and Assessment." In *Literacy for a Changing World*, edited by F. Christie. Hawthorn, Victoria: Australian Council for Educational Research.

Chomsky, N. 1976. *Reflections on Language*. Fontana, CA: Fontana/Collins.

Collier, V. 1995. *Promoting Academic Success for ESL Students: Understanding Second Language Acquisition for School*. Alexandria, VA: TESOL.

———. 1989. "How Long? A Synthesis of Research in Academic Achievement in a Second Language." *TESOL Quarterly* 23: 509–31.

Collier, V., and W. Thomas. 1997. *School Effectiveness for Language Minority Students*. Washington, DC: National Clearinghouse for Bilingual Education.

Collins, A., J. Seely Brown, and A. Holum. 1991. "Cognitive Apprenticeship: Making Thinking Visible." *American Educator* (Winter). Available at www.21learn.org/arch/articles/brown_seely.php.

Crawford, J. (2004). "No Child Left Behind: Misguided Approach to School Accountability for English Language Learners." Paper presented at Center on Educational Policy's Forum on Ideas to Improve the NCLB Accountability Provisions for Students with Disabilities and English Language Learners. Available from http://www.cep-dc.org/pubs/Forum14September2004/CrawfordPaper.pdf.

Cummins, J. 2007. "What Works? Research into Practice." Research Monograph No. 5. The Literacy and Numeracy Secretariat and the Ontario Association of Deans of Education. Available at www.edu.gov.on.ca.

———. 2000. *Language, Power, and Pedagogy*. Clevedon, UK: Multilingual Matters.

Darling-Hammond, L., and E. Schon. 1996. "Who Teaches and Why: Dilemmas for Building a Profession for Twenty-First Century Schools" In *Handbook of Research on Teacher Education*, edited by J. Sikula, T. Buttery, and E. Guyton, 67–101. New York: McMillan.

Delpit, L. 1998. "The Silenced Dialogue: Power and Pedagogy in Educating Other People's Children." *Harvard Educational Review* 58 (3): 280–98.

Derewianka, B. 2003. "Grammatical Metaphor in the Transition to Adolescence." In *Grammatical Metaphor: Views from Systemic Functional Linguistics*, edited by A. Simon-Vandenbergen, M. Taverniers, and L. Ravelli. Philadelphia: John Benjamins.

———. 2001. "Pedagogical Grammars: Their Role in English Language Teaching." In *Analysing English in a Global Context: A Reader*, edited by A. Burns and C. Coffin. London: Routledge (in association with Macquarie University and The Open University).

———. 1998. *A Grammar Companion for Primary Teachers*. Sydney: Primary English Teaching Association.

———. 1990. *Exploring How Texts Work*. Sydney: Primary English Teaching Association; Portsmouth, NH: Heinemann, 1991.

Des-Fountain, J., and A. Howe. 1992. "Pupils Working Together on Understanding." In *Thinking Voices: The Work of the National Oracy Project*, edited by K. Norman. London: Hodder and Stoughton.

De Silva Joyce, H., and S. Feez. 2004. *Developing Writing Skills for Middle Secondary Students*. Book 2. Sydney: Phoenix Education.

Dillon, J. 1990. *The Practice of Questioning*. London: Routledge.

Droga, L., and S. Humphrey. 2003. *Grammar and Meaning: An Introduction for Primary Teachers*. Berry, NSW: Target Texts. Available from www.targettexts.com.

Dufficy, P. 2005. "'Becoming' in Classroom Talk." *Prospect: An Australian Journal of TESOL* 20 (1) [Special Issue: *Rethinking ESLL Pedagogy: Sociocultural Approaches to Teaching and Learning*]: 59–81.

Echevarria, J., and A. Graves. 1998. *Sheltered Content Instruction: Teaching English Language Learners with Diverse Abilities*. Needham Heights, MA: Allyn and Bacon.

Edwards, D., and N. Mercer. 1987. *Common Knowledge. The Development of Understanding in the Classroom*. London and New York: Routledge.

Farr, N., and R. Roser. 1979. *Teaching a Child to Read*. Sydney: Pearson Education, Australia.

Freebody, P., and A. Luke. 1990. "Literacies Programs: Debates and Demands in Cultural Context." *Prospect: An Australian Journal of TESOL* 5 (3): 7–16.

Freeman, Y., and D. Freeman. 1998. *ESL/EFL Teaching: Principles for Success*. Portsmouth, NH: Heinemann.

Gamoran, A., M. Nystrand, M. Berends, and P. Le Pore. 1995. "An Organizational Analysis of the Effects of Ability Grouping." *American Research Journal* 32 (4): 687–715.

Garmston, R. 2005. "How to Turn Conflict into an Effective Learning Process." *JSD* 26 (3). [National Staff Development Council.]

Gibbons, P. 2008. "'It Was Taught Good and I Learned a Lot': Intellectual Practices and ESL Learners in the Middle Years." *Australian Journal of Language and Literacy* 31 (2): 155–73.

———. 2002. *Scaffolding Language, Scaffolding Learning: Teaching Second Language Learners in the Mainstream Classroom*. Portsmouth, NH: Heinemann.

———. 1993. *Learning to Learn in a Second Language*. Portsmouth, NH: Heinemann.

Goodall, J. n.d. "The Promise: Jane Goodall Reflects on Working Towards Peace." Architects of Peace, The Markkula Center for Applied Ethics, Santa Clara [CA] University.

Goodman, K. 1967. "Reading: A Psycholinguistic Guessing Game." In *Language and Literacy: The Collected Writing of Kenneth S. Goodman*, Vol. 1, *Process, Theory, Research*, edited by F. Golasch. London: Routledge.

Halliday, M. 1975. *Learning How to Mean: Explorations in the Development of Language*. London: Arnold.

Halliday, M., and R. Hasan. 1985. *Language, Context, and Text*. Geelong, Victoria: Deakin University Press.

Hammond, J. 2008. "Intellectual Challenge and ESL Students: Implications of Quality Teaching Initiatives." *Australian Journal of Language and Literacy* 31 (2): 128–54.

Hammond, J., and P. Gibbons. 2005. "Putting Scaffolding to Work: The Contribution of Scaffolding in Articulating ESL Education. *Prospect, An Australian Journal of TESOL* 20 (1).

Harcourt Science. 2006. *Physical Science*. Units E and F. New York: Harcourt School.

Harklau, L., K. Losey, and M. Siegal, eds. 1999. *Generation 1.5 Meets College Composition: Issues in the Teaching of Writing to U.S. Learners of ESL*. Mahwah, NJ: Lawrence Erlbaum.

Hoetker, J., and W. P. Ahlbrand, Jr. 1969. "The Persistence of the Recitation." *American Educational Research Journal* 6 (2): 145–67.

Krashen, S. 1982. *Principles and Practices in Second Language Acquisition.* Oxford: Pergamon.

Kress, G. 1985. *Linguistic Processes in Sociocultural Practice.* London: Routledge and Kegan Paul.

Laidler, G., and A. Sartor. *Science Search.* Book 4. Oxford: Oxford University Press.

Langer, J. 2001. *Guidelines for Teaching Middle and High School Students to Read and Write Well.* Albany, NY: National Research Center on English Learning and Achievement.

———. 1992. "Critical Thinking and English Language Arts Instruction." *National Research Center on Literature Teaching and Learning (Report Series 6.5).* Available at http://cela.albany.edu/reports.critical.index.html.

Langer, J., and A. Applebee. 1988. *Speaking of Knowing: Conceptions of Learning in Academic Subjects.* Final Report to the United States Department of Education, Office of Educational Research and Improvement, Grant Number G008610967.

Lave, J., and E. Wenger. 1991. *Situated Learning: Legitimate Peripheral Participation.* Cambridge: Cambridge University Press.

Macken-Horarik, M. 1996. "Literacy and Learning Across the Curriculum: Towards a Model of Register for Secondary School Teachers." In *Literacy and Society,* edited by R. Hasan and G. Williams. Essex, UK: Addison and Wesley Longman.

Mariani, L. 1997. "Teacher Support and Teacher Challenge in Promoting Learner Autonomy." *Perspectives: A Journal of TESOL Italy* 23 (2).

Martin, J. 1990. "Literacy in Science: Learning to Handle Text as Technology." In *Literacy for a Changing World,* edited by F. Christie, 79–117. Hawthorn, Victoria: Australian Council for Australian Research.

Martin, J. 1984. "Language, Register and Genre." In *Children Writing: Study Guide,* edited by F. Christie. Geelong, Victoria: Deakin University Press.

Martin, J., F. Christie, and J. Rothery. 1987. "Social Processes in Education: A Reply to Sawyer and Watson (and Others)." In *The Place of Genre in Learning: Current Debates,* edited by I. Reid. Geelong, Victoria: Centre for Studies in Literary Education, Deakin University Press.

Martin, J., and D. Rose. 2008. *Genre Relations: Mapping Culture.* London: Equinox.

McConachie, S., M. Hall, L. Resnick, A. Ravie, V. Bill, J. Bintz, and J. Taylor. 2006. "Task, Text, and Talk: Literacy for All Subjects." *Educational Leadership,* October, 8–14.

McGroarty, M. 1993. "Cooperaive Learning and Language Acquisition." In *Cooperative Learning: A Response to Linguistic and Cultural Diversity,* edited by D. Holt. Washington, DC: Center for Applied Linguistics.

McKay, P., A. Davies, B. Devlin, J. Clayton, R. Oliver, and S. Zammit. 1997. *The Bilingual Interface Project Report.* Canberra, AU: Department of Employment, Education, Training, and Youth Affairs.

Mehan, B. 1979. *Learning Lessons.* Cambridge: Harvard University Press.

Mehan, H. 1992. "Understanding Inequality in School: The Contribution of Interpretive Studies." *Sociology of Education* 65: 1–20.

References

Meltzer, J. and T. Hamann. 2005. "Meeting the Literacy Development Needs of Adolescent Language Learners Through Content-Area Learning, Part 2: Focus on Developing Academic Literacy Habits and Skills Across the Content Areas." Northeast and Islands Regional Educational Laboratory, The Education Alliance at Brown University. Available at www.alliance.brown.edu.

Mercer, N. 2000. *Words and Minds: How We Use Language to Think Together*. London and New York: Routledge.

Mohan, B. 1990. "LEP Students and the Integration of Language and Content: Knowledge Structures and Tasks." Paper presented at the First Research Symposium on Limited English Proficient Student Issues, OBEMLA. Available at http://ncbe.gwu.edu/ncbepubs/symposia/first/lep.htm.

Mohan, B., C. Leung, and C. Davison. 2001. *English as a Second Language in the Mainstream*. Harlow, UK: Pearson.

Moulds, P. 2002. "Rich Tasks: Developing Student Learning Around Important Tasks." *Australian Science Teachers' Journal* 48 (4): 6–13.

Newmann, F., and Associates. 1996. *Authentic Achievement: Restructuring Schools for Intellectual Quality*. San Francisco: Jossey-Bass.

Newmann, F., and G. Wehlage. 1995. "Successful School Restructuring: A Report to the Public and Educators." Center on Organization and Restructuring of Schools, Wisconsin Center for Educational Research, University of Wisconsin.

Nystrand, M. and A. Gamoran 1991. "Student Engagement: When Recitation Becomes Conversation." In *Effective Teaching: Current Research*, edited by H. Waxman and H. Walberg. Berkeley: McCutchan.

Oakes, J. 1985. *Keeping Track: How Schools Structure Inequality*. New Haven: Yale University Press.

Queensland School Reform Longitudinal Research Team. 2001. *The Queensland School Reform Longitudinal Study: Final Report*. Brisbane: Education Queensland.

Rose, D., L. Lui-Chivizhe, A. McKnight, and A. Smith. 2004. "Scaffolding Academic Reading and Writing at the Koorii Centre." *Australian Journal of Indigenous Education*, (30th Anniversary Edition): 41–49.

Rosenthal, R., and L. Jacobsen. 1968. *Pygmalion in the Classroom*. New York: Rinehart and Winston.

Sarroub, L., and P. D. Pearson. 1998. "Two Steps Forward, Three Back: The Stormy History of Reading Comprehension." *Clearing House* 72: 97–105.

Schleppegrell, M. 2002. *The Language of Schooling: A Functional Linguistics Perspective*. Manwah, NJ: Lawrence Erlbaum.

Swain, M. 2000. "The Output Hypothesis and Beyond: Mediating Acquisition Through Collaborative Dialogue." In *Sociocultural Theory and Second Language Learning*, edited by J. Lantolf. Oxford: Oxford University Press.

———. 1995. "Three Functions of Output in Second Language Learning." In *Principle and Practice in Applied Linguistics: Studies in Honour of H. G. Widdowson*, edited by G. Cook and B. Seidlehofer. Oxford: Oxford University Press.

Tizard, J., J. Scofield, and J. Hewison. 1982. "Collaboration Between Teachers and Parents in Assisting Children's Reading." *British Journal of Educational Psychology* 52: 1–15.

U.S. Department of Education. 2001. *No Child Left Behind*. Washington, DC: Government Printing Office.

Van Lier, L. 1996. *Interaction in the Language Curriculum: Awareness, Autonomy, and Authenticity*. London: Longman.

Vygotsky, L. 1978. *Mind in Society: The Development of Higher Psychological Processes*. Cambridge: Harvard University Press.

———. 1986. *Thought and Language*. Edited and translated by A. Kozulin. Cambridge: Harvard University Press.

Wajnryb, R. 1990. *Grammar Dictation*. Oxford UK: Oxford University Press.

Wallace, C. 2003. *Critical Reading in Language Education*. New York: Palgrave Macmillan.

———. 1992. *Reading*. Oxford: Oxford University Press.

Walqui, A. 1999. "Assessment of Culturally and Linguistically Diverse Students: Considerations for the 21st Century." In *Including Culturally and Linguistically Diverse Students in Standards-Based Reform: A Report on McREL's Diversity Roundtable I*, 53–84, Mid-continent Research for Education and Learning. Available at www.mcrel.org.

Wells, G. 2007. "Who We Become Depends on the Company We Keep and in What We Say and Do Together." *International Journal of Educational Research* 46: 1–2.

———. 1996. "Using the Tool-kit of Discourse in the Activity of Learning and Teaching." *Mind, Culture and Language* 3(2): 74–101.

———. 1992. "The Centrality of Talk in Education." In *Thinking Voices: The Work of the National Oracy Project*, edited by K. Norman. London: Hodder and Stoughton.

Wiggins, G., and J. McTighe. 2005. *Understanding by Design*. New York: Simon and Schuster.

Zwiers, J. 2005. "The Third Language of Academic English." *Educational Leadership* 62 (4): 60–63.

Index

Abedi, J., "Issues and Consequences for English Language Learners," 9, 164
abstract tasks, situated in authentic contexts, 36–37
academic language, features of, 50–55
academic literacy
  definition of, 4–7
  general principles, 58–63
  integrating language activities with content teaching, 63–78
activities
  after-reading, 100–105
  before-reading, 87–92
  for beginning EL learners, 147–49
  cloze, 103
  communicative, 63
  during-reading, 92–100
  form-focused, 64
  language, as a continuum, 64–78
  summary of teaching and learning, 169–71
  teaching and learning, examples of, 116–21
adjectives, changing into nouns, 52
apprenticeship
  EL learners, 39
  learning in school, 33–37
  learning through, 31–32
appropriating language, 136, 140–41
argument, as a form of writing, 111–13, 120
assessing learning, 164–65
assessing writing using genre framework, 121–127
August, D., and Hakuta, K., *Improving Schooling for Language Minority Children*, 12

August, D., Hakuta, K., and Pompa, D., *For All Students: Limited English Proficient Students and Goals 2000*, 12
Avi, *Nothing but the Truth: A Documentary Novel*, 85

barrier crossword, 71–73, 74–75
beginning EL learners, activities for, 147–49
Berman, P., Abuto, S., Nelson, B., Minicucci, C., and Burkhart, G., *Going Schoolwide: Comprehensive School Reform Inclusive of Limited English Proficiency Students*, 4
bilingual dictionaries, 78
brainstorm, progressive, 64–65
Brice-Heath, S., *Ways with Words*, 86
Bruce King, M., and Schroeder, J., "Authentic Assessment and Student Performance in Inclusive Schools," 19–20
building a bridge to written language, 141–42
building bridges to text
  assembling the jigsaw puzzle, 85–87
  the "best" way to teach reading, 81–85
  introduction, 80–81
  reading-related activities, 87–104
building the field, 115, 116–18
Butt, D., Fahey, R., Feez, S., Spinks, S., and Yallup, C., *Using Functioning Grammar: An Explorer's Guide*, 57

Calderon, M., "School Reform and Alignment of Standards," 12
Carrasquillo, A., and London, C., *Parents and Schools*, 2

Carrasquillo, A., and Rodriguez, V., *Language Minority Children in the Mainstream Classroom*, 2, 4, 9

Carrasquillo, A., Kucer, S., and Abrams, R., *Beyond the Beginnings: Literacy Interventions for Upper Elementary English Language Learners*, 2, 18, 79, 80, 97, 105, 167

cartoon strips, 104

cause-and-effect graphic outlines, 101

challenge zone, learning in the, 165–67

Chang, G., and Wells, G., "The Literate Potential of Collaborative Talk," *Oracy Matters*, 7, 50

Chomsky, N., *Reflections on Language*, Christie, F., "The Changing Face of Literacy," *Literacy for a Changing World*, 63

Christie, F., and Rothery, J., "Literacy in the Curriculum: Planning and Assessment," *Literacy for a Changing World*, 106

classroom talk, traditional, 136–37

classrooms, high-challenge and high-support, 14–17. *See also* planning for a high-challenge, high-support classroom

clauses, changing into nouns, 52

cloze
   activities, 103
   total and vanishing, 75–76
   traditional and specific exercises, 73–74

Collier, V., and Thomas, W., *School Effectiveness for Language Minority Students*, 10

Collier, V., "How Long? A Synthesis of Research in Academic Achievement in a Second Language," *TESOL Quarterly*, 50

Collier, V., *Promoting Academic Success for ESL Students: Understanding Second Language Acquisition for School*, 10

Collins, A., Seely Brown, J., and Holum, A., "Cognitive Apprenticeship: Making Thinking Visible," *American Educator*, 33, 35, 42

communicative activities, 63

compare-and-contrast graphic outlines, 101

complex texts, moving toward, 60

comprehensible input, 133

comprehensible output, 133–34

concept map, 65

conjunctions, changing into nouns, 52

connectives, types of text, 172

content classrooms, EL learners in, 9–12

content, embracing new goals, 154

conversations
   engaging in substantive, 25–27
   planning for substantive, 145–47

Crawford, J., "No Child Left Behind: Misguided Approach to School Accountability for English Language Learners," 4

Cummins, J., Brown, K., and Sayers, D., *Literacy, Technology, and Diversity: Teaching for Success in Changing Times*, xi

Cummins, J., "What Works? Research into Practice," x, xi, 2, 10, 50, 135, 164, 165

curriculum amplified, 156–57

Darling-Hammond, L., and Schon, E., "Who Teaches and Why: Dilemmas for Building a Profession for Twenty-First Century Schools," *Handbook of Research on Teacher Education*, 2

De Silva Joyce, H., *Developing Writing Skills*, 57, 129

De Silva Joyce, H., and Feez, S., *Developing Writing Skills for Middle Secondary Students*, 79, 106, 112, 129, 172, 173–78

Delpit, L., "Silenced Dialogue, The: Power and Pedagogy in Educating Other Peoples Children, *Harvard Educational Review*, 109

Derewianka, B., *Exploring How Texts Work*, 129

Derewianka, B., *A Grammar Companion for Primary Teachers*, 172

Derewianka, B., "Grammatical Metaphor in the Transition to Adolescence," *Grammatical Metaphor*, 52

Derewianka, B., "Pedagogical Grammars: Their Role in English Language Teaching," *Analysing English in a Global Context: A Reader*, 106

Des-Fountain, J., and Howe, A., "Pupils Working Together on Understanding," *Thinking Voices: The Work of the National Oracy Project*, 147

designed scaffolding, 153–58

dictionaries, bilingual, 78

dictogloss, 66–67

Dillon, J., *The Practice of Questioning*, 138

Dong, Yu Ren, "Integrating Language and Content," *Bilingual Education: An Introductory Reader*, 167

Droga, L., and Humphrey, S., *Grammar and Meaning: An Introduction for Primary Teachers*, 50–51, 57, 106, 129

Dufficy, P., "'Becoming' in Classroom Talk," *Prospect: An Australian Journal of TESOL*, 140, 151

Echeverria, J., and Graves, A., *Sheltered Content Instruction: Teaching English Language Learners with Diverse Abilities*, 10, 151

editing sheets, 123

Edwards, D., and Mercer, N., *Common Knowledge: The Development of Understanding in the Classroom*, 154

English and music unit, integrated, 23–24

English learners, defining the issues
in content classrooms, 9–12
current perspectives on "intellectual quality," 12–14
high-challenge and high-support classrooms, 14–17
literacy in the "middle years," 3–8
raising expectations, 1–3
who the EL learners are, 8–9

"expert" ideas, students engaging with, 21

Farr, N., and Roser, R., *Teaching a Child to Read*, 43

field, as topic of text, 47–48, 106

field, building, 115, 116–18

finding the difference, in pictures, 148

focus language, choosing, 159–61

form-focused activities, 64

framework for thinking about language in a subject-based classroom, 161–64

Freebody, P., and Luke, A., "Literacies Programs: Debates and Demands in Cultural Context," *Prospect: An Australian Journal of TESOL*, 85, 92, 98

Freeman, Y., and Freeman, D., *ESL/EFL Teaching: Principles for Success*, 2, 8, 151

functional grammar, 106

Gamoran, A., Nystrand, M., Berends, M., and Le Pore, P., "An Organizational Analysis of the Effects of Ability Grouping," *American Research Journal*, 2

Garmston, R., "How to Turn Conflict into an Effective Learning Process," 68–69

genre, 106, 108–13
implications for teachers, 113–14
introducing and scaffolding, 114–21
modeling, 115, 118

genre framework, to assess writing, 121–27

genres, typical features of some written school-related, 173–78

Gibbons, P., "'It Was Taught Good and I Learned a Lot': Intellectual Practices and ESL Learners in the Middle Years," *Australian Journal of Language and Literacy*, 42

Gibbons, P., *Learning to Learn in a Second Language*, 148, 151

Gibbons, P., *Scaffolding Language, Scaffolding Learning: Teaching Second Language Learners in the Mainstream Classroom*, 15, 47, 79, 138, 142, 148, 151

Gibbons, P., "Steps for Planning an Integrated Program for ESL Learners," *Planning and Teaching Creatively within a Required Curriculum*, 167

Gibbons, P., "Teaching Language Learning," *TESOL Quarterly*, 151

goals, program, 154–55

Goodall, J., "Jane Goodall Reflects on Working Toward Peace," 90–91
Goodman, K., "Reading: A Psycholinguistic Guessing Game," *Language and Literacy*, 82
graphic outlines, 100–102
group work, 155–56

Halliday, M., and Hasan, R., *Language, Context, and Text*, 47
Halliday, M., *Learning How to Mean: Explorations in the Development of Language*, 132
Hammond, J., and Gibbons, P., "Putting Scaffolding to Work: The Contribution of Scaffolding in Articulating ESL Education," *Prospect, An Australian Journal of TESOL*, 153–54
Harklau, L., Losey, K., and Siegal, M., *Generation 1.5 Meets College Composition: Issues in the Teaching of Writing to U.S. Learners of ESL*, 9
high-challenge and high-support classrooms, 14–17. *See also* planning for a high-challenge, high-support classroom
history
    U.S. grade ten, 24–25
    grade seven, 21, 23, 28–29
Hoetker, J., and Ahlbrand, W. P., "The Persistence of the Recitation," *American Educational Research Journal*, 136
Hood, S., Solomon, N., and Burns, A., *Focus on Reading*, 105

independent writing. *See* writing, independent
individual work, 155–56
information
    students taking a critical stance toward, 28–29
    summary, 102
information technology, grade five, 28
initiation, response, feedback/evaluation (IRF)
    definition of, 136–37
    extending the IRF exchange, 137–38
innovating on the text, 104

input, comprehensible, 133
inquiry and elimination, 149
"intellectual quality," current perspectives on, 12–14
integration of content and language, 2, 7, 10–11, 63–78, 114, 121, 154, 160–62
intellectual work in practice
    developing intellectual practices in the classroom, 31–41
    seven intellectual practices, 20–30
    what counts as intellectual quality, 19–20
interactional scaffolding, 153–54, 158

"Janus Curriculum," implementing a, 59–60
jigsaw groups, 146–47
joint construction, 67–68, 115–16, 118–19
jumbled words, 104

knowledge
    links between concrete and abstract theoretical, 23–25
    students taking a critical stance toward, 28–29
Krashen, S., *Principles and Practices in Second Language Acquisition*, 133
Kress, G., *Linguistic Processes in Sociocultural Practice*, 99

Laidler, G., and Sartor, A., *Science Search*, 44, 53
Langer, J., and Applebee, A., *Speaking of Knowing: Conceptions of Learning in Academic Subjects*, 8
Langer, J., "Critical Thinking and English Language Arts Instruction," *National Research Center on Literature Teaching and Learning*, 6
Langer, J., *Guidelines for Teaching Middle and High School Students to Read and Write Well*, 58–59
language
    activities as a continuum, 64–78
    analysis, 99–100
    central to a particular topic, identifying, 159

and content. *See* integration of content and language
embracing new goals, 154
focusing on key, 159–60
framework for thinking about in a subject-based classroom, 161–64
spoken and written, 47–50
"stretched" or "pushed," 134
students making connections between spoken and written, 27–28
last word, the, 68–70
Lave, J., and Wenger, E., *Situated Learning: Legitimate Peripheral Participation*, 32, 42
learning
    assessing, 164–65
    in the challenge zone, 165–67
    language, a collaborative process, 132
    transforming into a new context for a different audience, 22–23
literacy in the curriculum
    developing spoken and written literacy, 45–47
    meaning of being "literate," 43–45
    what makes academic language difficult, 47–55
literate talk, encouraging, 141–42

Macken-Horarik, M., "Literacy and Learning Across the Curriculum: Towards a Model of Register for Secondary School Teachers," *Literacy and Society*, 106, 173–78
Manyak, P. C., "What Did She Say?" *Multicultural Perspectives*, x
margin questions, 94–96
Mariani, L., "Teacher Support and Teacher Challenge in Promoting Learner Autonomy," *Perspectives: A Journal of TESOL Italy*, 2, 15–16, 18
Martin, J., and Rose, D., *Genre Relations: Mapping Culture*, 173–78
Martin, J., Christie, F., and Rothery, J., "Social Processes in Education: A Reply to Sawyer and Watson (and Others)," *The Place of Genre Learning: Current Debates*, 106

Martin, J., "Language, Register and Genre," *Children Writing: Study Guide*, 48
Martin, J., "Literacy in Science: Learning to Handle Text as Technology," *Literacy for a Changing World*, 5, 129
math, grade seven, 27
math, grade five, 28
McConachie, S., Hall, M., Resnick, L., Ravie, A., Bill, V., Bintz, J., and Taylor, J., "Task, Text, and Talk: Literacy for All Subjects," *Educational Leadership*, 24–25, 27, 42, 45–46
McGroarty, M., "Cooperative Learning and Language Acquisition," *Cooperative Learning: A Response to Linguistic and Cultural Diversity*, 39
McKay, P., Davies, A., Devlin, B., Clayton, J., Oliver, R., and Zammit, S., *The Bilingual Interface Project Report*, 10, 50
McKay, P., *Teaching Creatively Within a Required Curriculum for School-Age Learners*, 79
Mehan, B., *Learning Lessons*, 136
Mehan, H., "Understanding Inequality in School: The Contribution of Interpretive Studies," *Sociology of Education*, 2
Meltzer, J., and Hamann, T., "Meeting the Literacy Development Needs of Adolescent Language Learners Through Content-Area Learning," 4, 6–7, 8, 58–59, 79, 87, 152
Meltzer, J., and Hamann, T., "Research-Based Adolescent Literacy Teaching Strategies That Vary by Content Area," 18
Mercer, N., *Words and Minds: How We Use Language to Think Together*, 143–44, 150, 151
message abundancy, 156–57
metalanguage
    developing with students, 62–63
    using in the context of learning, 29–30
mode, 47–48, 106
mode continuum, 49, 50, 155
modeling academic language in interactions with students, 61–62

modeling the genre, 115, 118

models of appropriate language, 135

Mohan, B., "LEP Students and the Integration of Language and Content: Knowledge Structures and Tasks," 1

Mohan, B., Leung, C., and Davison, C, *English as a Second Language in the Mainstream*, 10

mother tongue, a well-developed, 135–36

Moulds, P., "Rich Tasks: Developing Student Learning Around Important Tasks," *Australian Science Teachers' Journal*, 34, 38, 42, 162

music and English unit, integrated, 23–24

narrative, as a part of scaffolding, 109–11

negotiation of meaning, 134–35

Newmann, F., and Associates, *Authentic Achievement: Restructuring Schools for Intellectual Quality*, ix, 1, 12–13, 42

Newmann, F., and Wehlage, G., "Successful School Restructuring: A Report to the Public and Educators," 12

No Child Left Behind Act, x–xi, xii, 4

nominal groups, 54–56

nominalization, 50–54

North Wind and Sun, 109–10

Nothing but the Truth: A Documentary Novel (Avi), 85

nouns, turning various words and groups into, 51–52

Nystrand, M., and Gamoran, A., "Student Engagement: When Recitation Becomes Conversation," *Effective Teaching: Current Research*, 137

Oakes, J., *Keeping Track: How Schools Structure Inequality*, 2

observation, playing a key role, 36

organizational structures, working with a variety of, 155–56

output, comprehensible, 133–34

pair work, 155–56

paired problem solving, 147

paragraph parts, identifying, 98

pausing and predicting, 93–94

personal narratives, 89

picture sequencing and sentence matching, 148–49

planning for a high-challenge, high-support classroom
  assessing learning, 164–65
  designed scaffolding and interactional scaffolding, 153–58
  five steps for planning an integrated program, 159–61
  framework for thinking about language in a subject-based classroom, 161–64
  introduction, 152–53
  learning in the challenge zone, 165–67

planning talk for learning and literacy
  kind of talk that supports second language learning, 130–36
  making talk between learners worthwhile, 144–50
  making teacher-student talk a context for language learning, 136–44

prediction
  from key words, the title or the first sentence, 89
  from a picture, diagram and other visuals, 88–89

previewing the text, 90–92

program, five steps for planning an integrated, 159–61

program goals, shared with students, 154–55

Queensland School Reform Longitudinal Study, 14, 28

questioning the text, 99

reader, as code breaker, text participant, text user, text analyst, 86–87

reader questions, 89

readers theatre, 104

reading
  after-reading activities, 100–105
  before-reading activities, 87–92
  critical and social approaches, 84–85
  during-reading activities, 92–100
  interactive approaches, 83–84

traditional and "bottom up" approaches to teaching, 81–82
whole language and "top down" approaches, 82–83
reading critically, 98–100
Reading First Impact Study, xi
reasoning, making it explicit, 142–43
recasting, 116, 136, 140–41, 143, 158
register, 23, 48, 50

"rich" real-world-like tasks, learners participating in, 33–35
rich tasks, assessing learning through, 37–38
Rose, D., Lui-Chivizhe, L., McKnight, A., and Smith, A., "Scaffolding Academic Reading and Writing at the Koorii Centre," *Australian Journal of Indigenous Education*, 94
Rosenthal, R., and Jacobsen, L., *Pygmalion in the Classroom*, 2

Sarroub, L., and Pearson, P. D., "Two Steps Forward, Three Back: The Stormy History of Reading Comprehension," *Clearing House*, 164
scaffolding
    designed, 154–58
    detailed reading, 94–98
    interactional, 158
    narrative, as a part of, 109–11
    teachers, implications of scaffolding for, 113–14
scaffolding EL learners to be successful writers
    introducing and scaffolding genres in the classroom, 114–21
    introduction, 106–108
    using a genre framework for assessment, 121–28
    what a genre is, 108–14
scanning for information, 93
Schleppegrell, M., *The Language of Schooling: A Functional Linguistics Perspectives*, 6, 43, 129, 173–78
science, grade seven, 26–27
second language learning, factors that facilitate, 133–37

semantic web, 65, 89
sentence
    matching, 77–78
    reconstruction, 103
sentences, changing into nouns, 52
sequencing illustrations, 89
signaling words, 172
skeleton text, 90–91
SLA. *See* second language learning, factors that facilitate
social studies, grade eight, 29–30
social studies, grade five, 22
social studies, grade six, 22
split dictation, 71–72
"stretched" language, 134
student language
    borrowing and reformulating, 140–41
    strengths and needs, noting, 159
student voices, 39–41
subject literacy, implications for teaching, 7–8
summarizing the text, 102–103
summary of teaching and learning activities, 169–71
Swain, M., "The Output Hypothesis and Beyond: Mediating Acquisition Through Collaborative Dialogue," *Sociocultural Theory and Second Language Learning*, 25, 39, 133–34, 144
Swain, M., "Three Functions of Output in Second Language Learning," *Principle and Practice in Applied Linguistics*, 133–34

talk
    about language, planned opportunities for, 158
    form-focused and meaning-focused, 130–32
    teacher, features of supportive, 143–44
tasks
    criteria for well-designed, 149
    sequenced as "building blocks," 155
    for talk, designing, 145–47
teacher-directed whole-class work, 155–56
teacher talk, features of supportive, 143–44

teachers, implications of scaffolding for, 113–14

teaching about talk, 150

teaching and learning
activities, examples of, 116–21
cycle, the, 115–16, 123–28

tenor, 47–48, 106

text, building bridges to. *See* building bridges to text

text types, 106, 108

thinking, made visible, 35–36

thinking sheets, 26–27, 70–71, 145–46

time to think, giving students, 138–40

timelines, 100–101

true/false statements, 100

unit of work, evaluating, 161

Van Lier, L., *Interaction in the Language Curriculum: Awareness, Autonomy, and Authenticity*, 136, 158

verbs, changing into nouns, 51–52

Vygotsky, L., *Mind in Society: The Development of Higher Psychological Processes*, 14–17

Vygotsky, L., *Thought and Language*, 14–17

Wajnryb, R., *Grammar Dictation*, 66–67

Wallace, C., *Critical Reading in Language Education*, 92, 94, 99

Wallace, C., *Reading*, 105

wallpapering, 65

Walqui, A., "Assessment of Culturally and Linguistically Diverse Students: Considerations for the 21st Century," 12

Walqui, A., "Scaffolding Instruction for English Language Learners: A Conceptual Framework," *Bilingual Education: An Introductory Reader*, 18

Wells, G., "The Centrality of Talk in Education," *Thinking Voices: The Work of the National Oracy Project*, 130

Wells, G., "Using the Tool-kit of Discourse in the Activity of Learning and Teaching," *Mind, Culture and Language*, 158

Wells, G., "Who We Become Depends on the Company We Keep and in What We Say and Do Together," *International Journal of Educational Research*, 15, 167

Wiggins, G., and McTighe, J., *Understanding by Design*, 38, 42, 162

word-picture matching, 149

word walls, 76

writing, independent, 116, 119–21

written language, building a bridge to, 141–42

written school-related genres, typical features of some, 173–78

written text, talk occurring around, 157

Zwiers, J., "The Third Language of Academic English," *Educational Leadership*, 46

191032

LINCOLN CHRISTIAN UNIVERSITY

571

127032

ALSO AVAILABLE BY PAULINE GIBBONS

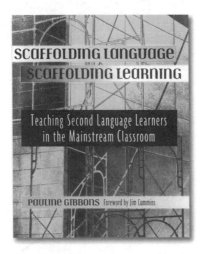

Scaffolding Language, Scaffolding Learning

Teaching Second Language Learners in the Mainstream Classroom

Pauline Gibbons

Foreword by **Jim Cummins**

How do mainstream elementary teachers with little ESL training teach linguistically diverse students? Pauline Gibbons shows how, with ways to integrate the teaching of English with the content areas to ensure that ELLs become full members of the school community and get the language and content skills they need.

978-0-325-00366-5 / 2002 / 176pp / $22.00

Learning to Learn in a Second Language

Pauline Gibbons

Learning to Learn in a Second Language is for all teachers of English learners. Through practical strategies and suggestions, it shows how curriculum can be a major resource for language development, and illustrates how to help children learn a new language and learn to learn in it as well.

978-0-435-08785-2 / 1993 / 128pp / $21.00

Sample Chapters available online at **www.heinemann.com**

DEDICATED TO TEACHERS

To place an order, call **800.225.5800**, fax **877.231.6980**, or visit **www.heinemann.com**

3 4711 00217 5836